DARK MOUNTAIN

Issue 11 · Spring 2017

The Dark Mountain Project

Published by the Dark Mountain Project 2017
www.dark-mountain.net

ISBN 978-0-9955402-1-7

Editors
Cate Chapman
Nick Hunt
Steve Wheeler

Art Editor
Mat Osmond

Proofreader
Mark Watson

Editorial Assistant
Ava Osbiston

Assistant Reader
Harriet Pierce

Production
Charlotte Du Cann

Founders
Dougald Hine
Paul Kingsnorth

Associate Publishers
Charles McDougal
Phillip Lombard

Typesetting
Christian Brett, Bracketpress

Printed and bound by the
TJ International Ltd.,
Padstow, PL28 8RW

Cover Art
Pink Figure, Blue World
by Will Gill

Photograph
Svalbard, Norway

From the series *No Man's Land* made during an artist residency in Svalbard, Norway in 2014. Twenty-eight artists from around the world sailed aboard a three-masted barquentine to one of the most forbidding environments on the planet [for full story see Plates B].

® **Mixed Sources**
Product group from well-managed
forests, controlled sources and
recycled wood or fiber
FSC   www.fsc.org Cert no. TT-COC-002303
© 1996 Forest Stewardship Council

ISSUE 11 · SPRING 2017

Contents

Endings

CONTENTS

Home

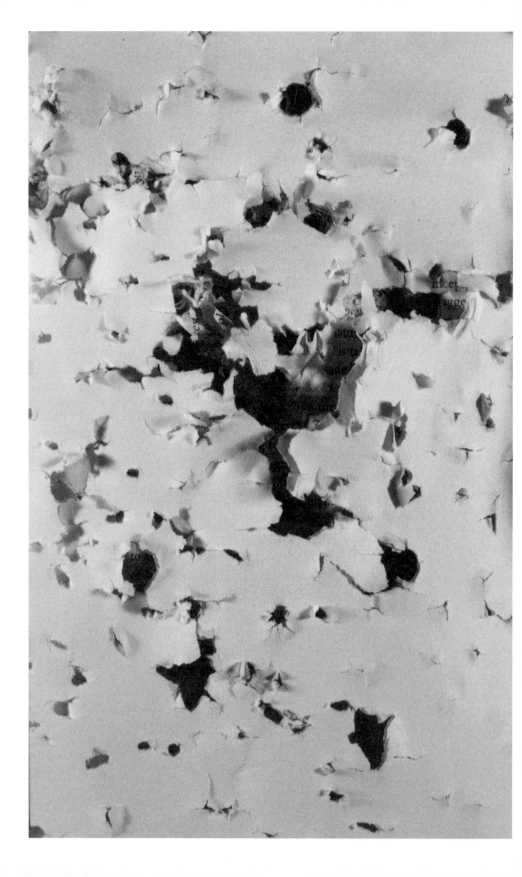

Beyond Straight Lines

When things get messy, people reach for straight lines. In times of confusion, the impulse to take refuge in simplicity – simple choices, simple forms of identity, simple stories – can be deeply reassuring; borders keep entities intact, not just apart. Liminal spaces and in-between zones are things to be feared and avoided. Constructing barriers, real or imagined, is part of an ancient cultural drive to divide the black from the white, and push troublesome grey areas back into the nacreous realms of the subconscious where they belong.

History, especially Western history, provides much evidence of the urge to micro-manage reality's mess. With the simplicity of hindsight the Enlightenment is viewed as a time in which the shadowed superstitions of the past were exposed and swept away, ushering in a rational age of quantification, measurement and ordered progress. Carl Linnaeus, the Swedish botanist and zoologist dubbed the 'father of taxonomy', classified plants and animals into formal hierarchies of kingdoms, classes, orders, genera and species, sorting the seeming chaos of life into a bestial simulacrum of the European class system. In the age of empire – itself an exercise in standardisation as well as military might – much of this systematising drive came from the British Isles; Luke Howard classified the clouds according to Linnaean principles, Francis Beaufort numbered the winds, and the world was divided into time-zones bisecting the globe as neatly as the segments of an orange. Geologists split time itself into eons and eras, epochs and ages that gave the impression of orderly transfer – the Devonian giving way to the Cretaceous like a peaceful handover of power – anchoring our species against the horror of deep time.

But the lines separating these things remained – and remain – illusory. Such borders, powerful though they seem, are only one way of seeing the world; like so many human inventions, they are better understood not as facts, but stories.

This book is published at just such an illusory border. Following the

Brexit vote that shook the EU, and the election of Donald Trump that rocked the US, voices from across the political spectrum loudly called time on liberalism, the post-1945 international consensus and even globalisation; its death throes soundtracked, apparently, by national anthems from the right rather than the protest chants of the anti-capitalist left. Pundits labelled 2016 as the year in which liberal democracy died and something not yet named (Illiberalism? Populism? Nativism? Post-globalisation?) neatly took its place. Suddenly the inter-nationalist era – an age of corporate levelling, ever-increasing connected-ness and political apathy that accompanied the supposed triumph of free-market capitalism – felt as outdated as the one that preceded it. Now, it seems, viewing the world in grand sweeps is back in fashion. End times are in vogue again. As a French nationalist politician tweeted after the US election: 'Their world is collapsing. Ours is being built.'

All very dramatic (and great for news soundbites) until we step back a bit to take a longer view. Is this the dawn of a new era, or rather a tired rehashing of all-too-familiar narratives – national pride, purity, redemp-tion after decline and corruption – just another strand of the time-worn myth of progress? At a time when we need alternative stories more than ever, the 20th century seems caught in a loop: industrial capitalism occasionally spiked by nationalism, occasionally screened by liberalism, but the cogs of the machine keep whirling much the same. Beyond the political-cultural babble the coal plants are still being built, the mountains are still being levelled for mines, the bottom-of-the-barrel scrabble to prop up fossil fuel economies continues with tar sands and fracking, the sale of SUVs booms, and – despite feel-good nativist postur-ing to the contrary – extractive globalisation proceeds apace, driven by the seemingly unstoppable logic of consumption. As a corollary of this, the oceans continue acidifying, Indonesian forest fires raze millions of hectares of trees, another Antarctic ice shelf calves, and non-human species blink out of existence everywhere on Earth.

Still we grasp at solid lines. We border ourselves with a global temperature rise of 1.5°C – a number picked as much for its neatness, and political practicability, as what it actually represents in terms of dangerous climate change – raising the target above our heads like a roof in stormy weather. We bemoan passing the symbolic threshold of 400 parts per million of CO_2 in the atmosphere – a level last seen in the Pliocene, four million years ago – as if everything was 'normal' back at 399. Perhaps most reductively, we tell ourselves that the Holocene has given way to the Anthropocene, an epoch that signifies total human dominance of the planet. But such divisions are seldom so tidy. Even the convenient border drawn between humans and animals – the ultimate 'us and them' – degrades with the uncomfortable fact that our bodies comprise at least as many bacteria cells as 'human' cells; it makes more sense to think of ourselves as colonies of organisms rather than individuals. Once we break free from straight-line thinking, the truth is much more *messy.*

That messiness is, in part, what this book tries to articulate. *Dark Mountain: Issue 11* takes as its premise the notion of endings – cultural, social, ecological, political, existential – but recognises that things seldom end, or begin, in well-mannered ways. The uncivilised writing and artwork you will find within these pages explores the liminal territory between simplistic poles; an untidy realm in which some worlds appear to be ending completely, some partially, some not at all, and in which entirely new beginnings emerge from the cracks in between. Tim Fox suggests that the apocalypse, that hackneyed staple of environmental doom-scenarios, is not some future fantasy but, in ecological terms, an event already underway; but also that mass extinctions lead to mass diversifications. From a Hebridean pilgrimage, Alastair McIntosh reminds us that *apokalyptein* originally meant not the end of all things, but the revelation of something hidden; Charlotte McGuinn Freeman, meanwhile, takes us on a personal journey through family tragedy and explores what happens next, after the world stops. Essays by John Rember, Daniel Nakanishi-Chalwin and others take a long, hard look at the common end that awaits us all, while a striking image from Tanja Leonardt suggests that life, of a sort, continues in the war-ravaged ruins of a Bosnian factory.

Much of the content is rooted in home: Sarah Thomas sends dispatches from a flooded Cumbrian fell, Francesca Schmidt from a village in the former East Germany, and Garry Williams cuts a temporary home from a raft of ice on a frozen Norwegian lake. Darren Allen coins new terms for a world in dramatic – and often humorous – flux, while the Confraternity of Neoflagellants brings us a kind of 'high-tech uncivilised' writing we've never seen before. Elsewhere Matt Miles views human migration as the canary in the coal mine of ecological disruption, Caroline Ross sources art materials from a world that ended a thousand years ago, and Jane Lovell's poetry sifts through the paleological rubble of cosmic upheaval.

As old certainties unravel ever more suddenly, and with consequences that grow increasingly unpredictable, our 11th publication reflects these turbulent times as they are: uncivilised, seldom straight and defiantly unsimple. We hope you enjoy the diversity of beginnings and endings inside, and join us in navigating new stories among the remains of the old.

The Editors,
Spring 2017

Dark Mountain would not exist without the support and generosity of its readers. There are many ways to get involved with the project, but the simplest and most direct form of support you can offer is to become a subscriber. For more information, visit: dark-mountain.net/subscribe

CHRISTOS GALANIS
[p.8 and opposite] The Time I Shot the *Iliad* (2 of 5) [detail]
New Mexico, USA

The Time I Shot the Iliad is part of a series of 'shot books' I created in the deserts of New Mexico that began as both an interrogation of US gun culture, and the role of books in the development and dominance of civilisation. These dusty discarded books – mined from charity shops – eventually became sites for re-inscribing contemporary narratives of contraction and loss. Their desecrated pages are perhaps the visceral embodiment of a more faithful articulation of the arc of time we are living through. For full story see page 121.

BOOK ONE

Sing, goddess, the anger of Peleus' son Achilleus
and its devastation, which put pains thousandfold upon the
Achaians,
hurled in their multitudes to the house of Hades strong souls
of heroes, but gave their bodies to be the delicate feasting
of dogs, of all birds, and the will of Zeus was accomplished
since that time when first there stood in division of conflict
Atreus' son the lord of men and brilliant Achilleus.

What god was it then set them together in bitter collision?
Zeus' son and Leto's, Apollo, who in anger at the king drove
the foul pestilence along the host, and the people perished,
since Atreus' son had dishonoured Chryses, priest of Apollo,
when he came beside the fast ships of the Achaians to ransom
back his daughter, carrying gifts beyond count and holding
in his hands wound on a staff of gold the ribbons of Apollo
who strikes from afar, and supplicated all the Achaians,
but above all Atreus' two sons, the marshals of the people:
'Sons of Atreus and you other strong-greaved Achaians,
to you may the gods grant who have their homes on Olympos
Priam's city to be plundered and a fair homecoming thereafter,
but may you give me back my own dear daughter and take the ransom,
giving honour to Zeus' son who strikes from afar, Apollo.'
Then all the rest of the Achaians cried out in favour
that the priest be respected and the shining ransom be taken;
yet this pleased not the heart of Atreus' son Agamemnon,

MATT MILES
Indicator Species

The migration of the Mexican poor is the largest human movement
across a border on the planet. It was triggered by the destruction of
peasant agriculture at the hands of the North American Free Trade
Agreement, by the corruption of the Mexican state, by the growing
violence in Mexico, and exacerbated by the millions of Mexicans
working illegally in the US who send money home to finance their
families' trips north. It should be seen as a natural shift of a
species. We need ecologists on the border; the politicians have
become pointless.

– Charles Bowden

The Anthropocene – a neologism advanced by some for the new geologic
age the planet has now entered, owing to the wild success the human
species has enjoyed up until the present, and at the expense of most other
species – is synonymous with the Sixth Great Extinction. The impetus
of either phrase suggests the dominance of humanity to the detriment of
non-human lifeforms, and this is certainly true.

Less spoken of is the fact that the drivers of the Sixth Great Extinction
– science, technology, mass culture and mass communications, consumerism, natural resource depletion, economic globalisation, overpopulation
– are also contributing to declines within the anthropic milieu. Humanity
is encountering an intra-species cultural extinction – an extinction in
human cultural diversity on an equally alarming scale as that of non-
human species. We are also experiencing a concomitant decrease in
diversity in the so-called domesticated plants and animals that previous
generations grew up relying on primarily for food.

While many living in the affluent cultures of the Global North have
the luxury to fret over the decline of heritage pig breeds or the threat
that GMO monocultures pose to heirloom vegetables and grains, billions
of less fortunate human beings struggle just to have something to eat
every day. As their physical, economic, and cultural habitats have been

destroyed by the rapacious hunger of our consumerist society for ever more goods at ever cheaper prices, they have been forced by circumstance to assimilate with this alien culture, choosing physical survival over the loss of their own cultural identity. This choice usually entails the abandonment of the rural, the tribal, the local, or the ancestral landscape for jobs hundreds or thousands of miles away in the big cities.

In biological terms, the migration of species is nothing new. The ability to migrate for any species may be the greatest tool in the toolkit of evolutionary adaptation. Just as our hominid ancestors left Africa's Great Rift Valley fleeing an evolutionary bottleneck for greener pastures elsewhere, humanity has always harboured the myth of the 'Promised Land'. This myth for most of human history has held true: no less so for the first Native Americans who crossed the land bridge of the Bering Strait from Siberia into North America than for my own ancestors who more recently fled the famine in Ireland in the mid-19th Century for a new life here in the US.

But the myth of the Promised Land is predicated on the existence of a relatively unpopulated, resource-rich, and abundant territory in which to expand and prosper. With a population of 7.4 billion and growing, the world is now a crowded place, and abundance is relative as we enter a period of increasing global resource scarcity.

*

In ecology, there is the notion of the 'indicator species', a canary in the coal mine of sorts, the animal or vegetable most sensitive to change which, when present, indicates a healthy ecosystem. Conversely, when this species becomes suddenly absent, it's often an early indicator of a declining or failing ecosystem.

Species that are capable of travelling any considerable distance from their habitat usually will when their habitat begins to fail. Migratory birds in particular are increasingly viewed by scientists as indicators of the relative health of an ecosystem. They preferentially seek habitat with the requisite resources to sustain them. Human beings, other land mammals, and various forms of aquatic life – among others – all possess the ability to travel in order to seek out better habitat.

On the other hand, most human societies are very resilient and are the opposite of sensitive, as far as being any kind of early-warning system. Beginning in Neolithic times with the birth of agriculture and the domestication of animals, many formerly nomadic or tribal groups began to settle down and found cities and civilisations that were characteristically rooted in place. Humans generally adapt to the circumstances of their habitat until it is no longer feasible to do so, and the survival instinct takes hold, and then they migrate. Humanity is not in any strict sense an indicator species, but please bear with the analogy for the moment.

Take for example, the Joad family in Steinbeck's *The Grapes of Wrath*, or virtually any dustbowl family from the agricultural American southwest of the 1930s. When the dual catastrophes of economic depression and climatic disruption set in, a mass exodus from the affected areas of Oklahoma, Texas and surrounding areas to the then relatively less populous and prospectively more prosperous state of California occurred, but only after these families endured years of hardship and uncertainty on their farms. For most it was a matter of survival when they finally made the tough decision to hit the road.

*

Human beings also like to understand things, to recognise patterns, to infer the outcome potential latent in any given course of events. It's one of the things that is also responsible for our survival in the context of evolutionary history, and we've become pretty good at it. We look for signs, portents, omens, indicators. We try to establish the nature of cause and effect. We theorise and postulate, reckon and predict; we create stories and narratives to explain things. It's the instinct at the root of both science and religion, and it may be the defining hallmark of humanity in relation to other species.

Since at least the time of Thomas Malthus but probably even much further back in history, there has been an endeavour to apply this human urge to understand and predict to the issue of populations and resources. In other words, to figure out the carrying capacity of the human ecosystem before population overshoot occurs and the ecosystem collapses. In the last 50 years, scientists such as Garret Hardin, Paul Ehrlich, and the *Limits to Growth* working group headed by Dennis and Donella Meadows, among others, have warned that systemic collapse is approaching, as the exponential curve of population growth crosses the line representing the finite resources available to sustain that growth.

Even the scientist Norman Borlaug, widely hailed as the father of the so-called green revolution in agriculture, has warned of the limits of technological intervention to stave off the effects of our numbers here. But thresholds have already been crossed, emergent systems too complicated to extrapolate or model outcomes from are faltering. The problems we have created continue to outstrip our ability to solve them before it is too late.

Economists, petroleum geologists, and financiers have likewise warned of the phenomenon of Hubbert's peak in relation to cheap and readily available oil, and more importantly, all of its ramifications for our advanced civilisation. While global peak oil has likely already occurred, it is unlikely that an equivalent green revolution breakthrough in energy will occur to save humanity from an impending crash. It won't matter how much food can be grown (food heavily dependent on petroleum-based fertiliser inputs) if it can't be efficiently harvested and brought to market. Fracking and deep-water drilling are temporary stop-gaps, fingers in a dike that is failing.

On the contrary, as we've seen over the past decade, increasingly complex and interconnected systems fail in strange and unpredictable ways. For example, as a result of NAFTA in particular and economic globalisation in general, the support price for corn (the staple food in the Mexican diet) moves in relation to the price of oil, as that corn may now be turned into ethanol when oil prices cross a certain threshold, as they did in 2007. Americans will keep on driving and Mexicans will starve.

The increasingly dire predictions of scientists regarding rates of species extinction, climate change, population overshoot, and resource limits can continue to go mostly unheeded by the populations of the Global North because these things are, for now, an abstraction to the well-insulated societies we have built up for ourselves. We can just turn up the air conditioning and pay a little more for food and fuel.

But it is impossible to ignore the massed evidence, standing at our national doorsteps, of fellow human beings who have had to flee their homelands at great personal risk, to seek a better life – the only life now possible for them. Under the best of circumstances, all they can hope for is to live as strangers in a strange land.

In 2017 the unthinkable has already become reality, amidst a referendum for the United Kingdom's exit from the European Union, a Trump presidency in the US, and massacres perpetrated by Islamic extremists occurring with increasing regularity in continental Europe, provoking predictable political reactions.

The immigrants of the Global South, the cultures we've turned our backs on even as we profit from their labour, are the indicator species of our own societal collapse. The most sensitive and susceptible elements of our own species – the ones from whom everything has already been taken, the ones who have no recourse to technological mediation, whose subsistence economies have already been wrecked by globalisation, whose land succumbs to the rising seas, whose societies have been destroyed by imperial land grabs and resource wars – they are here now, knocking on our front doors, because they have nowhere else to go. On a planet dominated by the movements of human beings, we are our own indicator species.

*

The unprecedented numbers of Syrian, Iraqi, and North African immigrants that have flowed across Europe's borders in recent years are for the most part casualties of the resource war that the US, Great Britain, and 'the coalition of the willing' brought to the Fertile Crescent and Libya. Though really this war has been fought in the name of progress – for anyone anywhere who drives a car, uses a computer, and enjoys the comforts that easy access to fossil fuel resources afford. Currently, that includes most of Europe and North America and much of Asia – the Global North. We are all complicit in this, and we'll take whatever our populations believe we must to sustain it, under whatever pretence.

As much as we like to think about it as a culture war, a conflict of one cultural or religious identity over another, it really just boils down, at the end of the day, to who eats and who doesn't. The Arab Spring, for all its much-touted utilisation of social media for political organisation, democratic principles, et cetera, was precipitated by the self-immolation of one Tunisian street vendor, Mohamed Bouazizij. Bouazizij's livelihood was selling food on the street, and this was taken from him one day by municipal officials in the city where he lived. So he set himself on fire in protest.

*

In the US, immigration from Latin America has been a major political issue for my entire life. I don't remember a time when Mexican and Central American Latinos were not present in my community, though. Some of their children were my classmates in grade school, we grew up speaking English and attending school and Mass together, and they are as American as I am.

In the run-up to the 1980 US general election, immigration from Latin America was an issue then as it is today. In video footage from a debate during preliminary campaigning for the Republican nomination that year, both Ronald Reagan and George H.W. Bush, the man who was to become Reagan's vice president, sounded – there is no other word – compassionate. It was something to see, each one trying to outdo the other in demonstrating his sensitivity to the plight of those just then seeking to join in the so-called great American melting pot.

This is in stark contrast to the language Donald Trump has used recently to characterise Mexican immigrants in the United States. He has publicly suggested on numerous occasions that they represent the worst elements of Mexican society and that they are responsible for an increase in crime in the US. This is in addition to reinforcing the long-standing prejudice held by many Trump supporters that Latino immigrants are too lazy to work, but nonetheless somehow taking American jobs. I have to question the intelligence of those who make this inherently oxymoronic claim, which seems to be perennially applied to immigrants anywhere. An Austrian friend of mine recently posted a tongue-in-cheek infographic to his Facebook page, explaining the paradox as 'Schrödinger's Immigrant'.

*

Charles Bowden wrote, 'A Mexican dictator once noted that nothing ever happens in Mexico. Until it happens.' Bowden was an American writer and journalist who spent a lot of time in Mexico, especially in the border city of Juarez, 30 feet across the Rio Grande from El Paso, Texas. The city he described in much of his writings over the last two decades is a hell on earth, a rapidly growing community already populated by well over a million souls, most of them living in squalor.

Many are forced here by the poverty of the rural outlands, but all are trapped between the hammer of the failing Mexican state and the anvil of an exploitative and indifferent United States, to whom most are denied legal entry. Juarez has recently been called 'the most dangerous place in the world', but this would already have been apparent to anyone in 1996 who read Bowden's unique book, *Juarez: The Laboratory of our Future*.

The book is uncommon in many interesting ways, but foremost in that it is a collaboration between Bowden and the Mexican street photographers who risked their lives to document the cruelty, terror, and degradation that is everyday life for many in Juarez. In photographing the victims of the police, the gangs, and the drug cartels responsible for most of the violence, the photographers risked the same fate as that of their subjects. Many of the photos in this book are of cadavers, some of them showing signs of having been viciously tortured before being killed and left in the dumping grounds of the adjacent desert.

The photos as much as the writing bear witness to the plight of those who will inhabit the world we are now bringing into being everywhere. The rural poor, whose agricultural livelihood has been destroyed by the economics of globalisation or the general anarchy of living in a failed state or the vicissitudes of an increasingly unpredictable climate, wind up in Juarez.

Or they end up in cities just like it, the world over, working for slave wages in the usually foreign-owned sweatshops. In the case of Juarez, these are called *maquiladoras*, and many are situated just across the physical border with the United States. Here the cheap and easy conveniences of global trade are churned out by the truckload. This work never pays well enough to sustain the workers, so many turn to crime – prostitution, drug trafficking, gangs – just to survive.

Or they try to cross the border into the US. In a later work, *Some of the Dead Are Still Breathing: Living in the Future* (2007), Bowden writes:

> They are sleeping on the street or under the trees down by the river, and they tell me of their journey north, tell of the men who tried to kill them or rape them or rob them and they are rolling over Jordan as soon as night comes down but they are so very hungry and I start handing over money, ten dollars, twenty dollars, forty dollars, and they stream towards stands selling tacos in the street, and there are many words for them and their fate, studies of migrations, failed economies, declining resources, words that clatter on the floor of a bar like small change, and I turn to leave and get into my car and they claw at the windows like animals and follow me as I plow down the rutted street and flee from what is everywhere but now is hot breath on my neck.

Juarez could be anywhere, and soon it will be almost everywhere. In the words of Joe Strummer: *It could be anywhere / Most likely could be any frontier any hemisphere / In no-man's-land / There ain't no asylum here / King Solomon, he never lived 'round here.*

Juarez, Caracas, the Gaza Strip, Baghdad, Karachi, Manila, Cape Town, New Orleans, Aleppo—

Go straight to hell, boys...

*

Charles Bowden through his writings, and his photographer-collaborators in their images, show us a world of consequences – none of them happy – for the societal choices we've made in this life, knowingly or otherwise. The laboratory of our collective future is a hellish place: It looks a lot more like the favelas of São Paulo than the pipe dreams of Palo Alto. And *the future is already here, it's just not evenly distributed.*

What can we do besides turn away in despair? Bowden has summarised the question more succinctly: 'How can a person live a moral life in a culture of death?' This is the question of our times. It has been since at least the Second World War, when our philosophers and writers, artists and cultural leaders – the better among them anyway – seriously began asking it.

Still the question remains, growing in urgency as the circle of death spreads outward, consuming ever more. The alarms are all sounding, the indicators, either through their absence or presence, are piling up daily. Will we ever have the courage to seriously ask ourselves such questions? If so, will we have the courage to answer honestly? I hope so.

DANIEL MARRONE

Junkyard

god was an ugly woman but she was nice to talk to. she came down to earth on august 13th, 2016. i was on the second floor of the ol Junkyard and i had just put my lighter under my spoon and flicked the striker wheel with my bad thumb (the one with the blisters on it from my Pipe. sam always told me i held it too close to the bowl. what are you doing you idiot do you wanna burn yer goddamn thumb off??? he was just a goddamn pillhead what the hell did he know. hes dead and im not and ill hold my Pipe any fuckin way i want to.) and the blisters popped and blood and pus oozed out and it hurt and i dropped my lighter. thats when i heard the knock on the door downstairs. mike and sharon were passed out on a ripped up mattress and a few other people thought it might be the cops so they ran and hid. cops dont knock though.

i went downstairs and opened the door and an ugly woman was standing in the doorway soaking wet from the Rain. her hair was buzzed off and she looked about 30. i said hello and she said hello may i come in and i said yes. we dont normally let people into the Junkyard. but she was shivering and cold and even though she was ugly i still wanted to touch her. her skin had a golden glow and i rubbed my eyes but the glow was still there. i let her into the Junkyard and i brought her up the stairs and i watched her climb the stairs and she was staring at the ripped up wallpaper and the spiderwebs and the dust and plaster all over the floor. she looked like a part of the Junkyard.

i took her to the second floor and dragged my mattress over to her and we both sat on opposite ends of the mattress facing each other. she looked sad. i said welcome to the Junkyard. she didnt say anything so i said its not an actual junkyard we just call it the Junkyard because of all the. i was gonna say because of all the Junk but i didnt want to share it. my flannel shirt stuck to the bloody marks on my arm. entrance and exit wounds from the needle. it stung. i did share a few sips of my water bottle and a few bites of a halfeaten sandwich i found in the dumpster behind kevins deli. but i dont share Junk unless i love someone more than i love myself.

she looked into my eyes and said i have something i must confide in you. i said what is it and thats when she told me that she was god and that she came down to earth for a short time. i said that i never even knew there was a god and that i always thought if there was it would be a giant old man with a beard. she smiled a little but it wasnt a pretty smile. her teeth were all crooked and cracked and yellow just like sharons. i looked over at sharon and she and mike were still passed out on the mattress a few feet from us. there were a couple other empty mattresses but the room was empty except for the four of us. it used to be full of machines and weary sweaty empty workers wondering what and why. blood at the fingertips. dad worked here but the factory closed down when i was a kid and now i live here. the factory made metal but dads coffin was made of wood. the look on his face in the coffin was the same expression he wore when he came home from work every night. everyone trapped either in a planet or a factory or a home or a love or a brain im trapped and nobody can free me please help.

i apologised to god and told her that i was an atheist all my life. then i got scared about going to hell. i looked out of one of the openings in the wall where a window used to be and i stared into the blackness of night surrounding the building and i thought of all the lonely people around the city in freezing apartments trembling and frightened and the walls are closing in tighter and tighter thinking of their mothers and fathers and dead dreams and tv. and it made me wonder if i already died and went to hell. i asked god am i in hell and it looked like my words hurt her and she said hell doesnt exist there is only this one life and theres no heaven either. so this is it? yes. trapped again.

i was glad that god was sitting there with me on the mattress because i dont like being around people except for sharon and mike theyre both okay. they have good heads on their shoulders especially when we run out of money or Junk and have to find ways to get more. all i can think to do is take some fuckers wallet hit him in the back of the head with a bat and just take his money. i hate seeing people with rich clothes and three or four kids all dressed nice going out to fancy dinners money falling out of their pockets only sparing a penny for the hopeless it makes me want to take that bat and crack their skulls and do it over and over and over again. but we dont do that because sharon and mike know where to find copper and stuff to sell. theyre good to have around. people arent. there is We and there is people. We know exactly where We are in the universe and know that when theres something broken you fix it and when theres a pain you heal it and when theres horror you walk away.

We walked away years ago. We have love for our Bodies and our Brains and Air and Dirt and Bones and Trees and Junk and Blood and Shit and Cum and all that is Real. people are comfortable in misery and think the solution is more tv channels or a promotion or a sports car or sex or art. im stuck in the Junkyard but were all stuck in the earth and in the end We and people are buried at the same depth (6 ft.) in the same earth. they should be buried in big tvs thrown into an ocean of money bags and cars and love and suits and books and set it all on fire and turn it to Ash. nothing exists until its destroyed.

she was watching me and my thoughts and she looked like she wanted to say something and there were Tears in her eyes. she spoke: i created all of this the galaxies the planets light and dark you and every living creature it is all my fault. i created you all out of loneliness and selfishness i am just as trapped as you i created you all in my image and if i could take it all back i would if i could turn it all to a crushing weight i must carry on my back alone i would for that weight now weighs upon my heart and the heart of humanity what have i done. god wept into her hands and Tears dripped between the cracks in her fingers.

there was something familiar in the way she wept. the vibrations from her aura. i asked her why did you come down to earth and she only answered by sobbing convulsively but i knew the answer. when my son had Leukemia and i would spend all my nights at the hospital holding onto his pale hand i wept the same way god wept on the mattress in front of me. all you want is for there to be a combination of words to lift the curse of guilt. im sorry. no. thats nothing. pathetic. im sorry. NO. SHUT UP. Pain coursed through my sons body doubled over Tears and scream-ing shivering daddy make it stop it hurts and before he was put in that tortured body he was a spirit floating free in blackness and my Bloody hands ripped him out of that pool of Infinity and put him into a skeleton covered in skin that would snare him and poison him and his screams told me it was all my fault. he didnt blame me but theres nothing i wanted more than for him to just shout at me DAMN YOU FATHER GOD-DAMN YOU TO THE PITS OF HELL BURN FIRE SCREAM BEG LOOK WHAT YOUVE DONE TO ME but instead he pleads for my help. i created suffering out of nothing. i am god.

i wrapped my scarred arms around god and she buried her face in my shoulder and wept until her eyes ran out of Tears. i kissed her ears that held the cries of humanity. i kissed her head that held a tortured mind. i kissed the lips that begged for forgiveness. i took off her clothes and kissed the breasts that nurtured us and the Cunt that created us. i climbed on top of her put myself inside of god and our Sweat and our Tears and Skin rubbing Skin holding on and push myself inside warm and wet and yes oh please bury me in you and i kiss god and she grabs my back we are Skin twitching friction Sweat soft i am Meat no soul BURY please BURY ME IN YOU i want kissing and your Cunt is a bullet in my head and clutching Dirt returns to Dirt of the earth i am a wilted flower in gods stomach and. BURY. HIDE. IN YOU. waves of warmth roll over my body our body BURY ME IN YOU.

i lay naked next to god and i held her in my arms but it was still cold and raining outside and the Wind didnt care and the Rain landed on the Dirt and fed Plants and Trees and i held god and didnt want to move. i didnt move for a while but picked up my Spoon and Lighter after a few minutes and asked god if she wanted to stay here on earth with me and she cried curled like a foetus on the mattress and i handed her my syringe and thought of my son. We.

ELEANOR HOOKER

Singing Ice

Across the rigid icescape they heave
and haul colossal cables to the shadows
on the opposite shore. We shudder at the echoing
crack and coil of tensile steel on the cold lid of winter.

Back and forth the spectres murmur.
We hear them hum the hymns of the dead;
ceremonial chants that rise and fall for hours,
that, gathering volume, resonate like breathless

air across empty glass. We venture out a foot or so.
beneath us air-sharks drop and dive through
slivers of thickening water, then rise to slam
the frozen under-surface. They tear long rips

that roar along the night, tracking us and splitting
the marbled floor at our feet. The percussions
petrify the living and the dead sing on.

STEVE WHEELER

Water Shoots

If we were to tell you the story of how human beings were born long ago, we would say that a gourd fell down from heaven, broke open, and two persons came out of it. The man and the woman from the gourd became husband and wife, and their children multiplied.

    – Formosan legend

We live in a kind of dark age, craftily lit with synthetic light, so that no one can tell how dark it has really gotten. But our exiled spirits can tell. Deep in our bones resides an ancient, singing couple who just won't give up making their beautiful, wild noise. The world won't end if we can find them.

    – Martín Prechtel

In the beginning were the dark waters of chaos. From them rose a form. Something simple – something spherical. Perhaps an egg, or a turtle shell, or a round fruit. 'Self-willed, Atum appeared amidst the waters of Nu,' said the Egyptians. 'Needing somewhere to stand, he created a hill – the first land; upon which this city was built.'

As children, we grasp for something solid, something stable, upon which to build the towers of our self. We must fix, hold, control, the flowing experience of being alive in order to begin laying down the layers of our nascent personality.

And with the creation of the first form, the contrast with what went before can be apprehended. 'There is This', we say, 'and therefore there is also That'. From two comes three – the comparison of This and That. From three comes … the rest of it.

We must do this, of course, because those around us, upon whom we rely for our food and shelter – towards whom our instinct for love and emulation is bent – demand it of us. And who are we to say they were

19

wrong so to do? This is not about 'Culture' versus 'Civilisation': the myths of double-edged awakening to the knowledge of This and That predate the hierarchies and written histories of grain-cultivating city states. Every culture has its Totem and Taboo, its Cooked and Raw. Language itself is a system of binary differentiations, at first a primordial matrix of immanent categories, subdividing with time into the abstractions of unrooted thought.

No, the creation of a stable form, and the possibilities of further development by building upon it, are merely recapitulated in the human mind. They were written in the fabric of life from the start: the first protein complex to have the bright idea of developing a cell wall around it; the first multicellular organism to differentiate organs within it; the first organism that deputised a set of cells to build a lignin wall around the whole, the better to protect against outside attack and to keep in water and life.

And, of course, once you have a human mind capable of holding fast to the mast of stable thought, you can create form at larger scales as well – like a city, or a nation, or an empire.

Or a book.

*

One hundred years ago, an irascible former schoolteacher began to saw up one of his last remaining items of furniture in an attempt to heat the small Munich flat in which he lived. He then returned to the task that had occupied him for the past six years, since world events had first convinced him that cataclysm and geopolitical upheaval lay ahead in both the near and the far future. The pan-European conflagration that had broken out in 1914 had seemed to confirm his thesis and, as the Kaiser's forces eked out their last days on the front – a front he had desperately wanted to serve at, but which had been denied to him by his poor health – he sat by candlelight, untying bundles of small cards filled with his tiny, crabbed handwriting. These cards contained the notes for the book he was completing – an epic, meandering, non-linear machine of a text, painstakingly tracing his philosophy of art, politics and civilisation, and ranging over the historical and cultural landscape of the past 6,000 years through interlinked chapters, sections and charts.

The man's name was Oswald Spengler, and the book – which, launched into the fractured, disoriented, pessimistic atmosphere of post-war

Germany the following year, made him wealthy, famous and a deeply contentious intellectual figure for the remaining two decades of his life – was called *Der Untergang des Abendlandes*; or, in the English translation a few years later, *The Decline of the West*.

Everything about Spengler was a paradox. He was dismissed by the academic establishment as a dilettante, while simultaneously feted as a great thinker. He was a reactionary political thinker (and responsible in part, some assert, for enabling the rise of Fascism) who, at heart, had always wanted to be an artist. The work itself was ostensibly a hard-headed, nationalist response to the politics of his time, but its vision of human history sang the praises of Chinese painting, Indian philosophy and Arabic architecture, and lingered on the religious atmosphere of Hellenic cults and Egyptian funeral rites; and, throughout, the strange, Modernist, machinic proto-hypertext of the book was informed by the organic poetics and mysticism of Goethe.

*

In 1790, Johann Wolfgang von Goethe published a brief treatise entitled *An Attempt to Interpret the Metamorphosis of Plants*. In 123 short paragraphs, he described the dynamic archetype underlying all vegetal organisms – the *Urpflanze* – and outlined his vision of a new science of 'morphology' that would explain the forms of different species as variations on this ideal form. Rather than focusing on the mechanisms and components of plants, the more usual concern of botany at the time, he saw the whole of the plant; and rather than focusing on the measurable differences between disparate organs or species, he saw the underlying unity of form from which they sprang.

This vision, which had a pivotal influence on the burgeoning biological sciences, and much of which would later be confirmed by genetic analysis, was the fruit of Goethe's years of study of the natural world. But key to his insights, he insisted, was the unique approach and form of perception he had employed: 'My thinking is not separate from objects; the elements of the object, the perceptions of the object, flow into my thinking and are fully permeated by it; my perception itself is a thinking, and my thinking a perception.'

Goethe would cultivate this 'exact sensorial imagination' by sitting in quiet community with a plant, feeling into its being with mind, heart and body. To him, this was not merely an alternative tactic of empiricism, but a moral and poetic imperative: 'We may force no explanation' from nature, he would write, 'wrest no gift from her, if she does not give it freely... Nature becomes mute under torture.'

*

From Goethe's work on the inner form of plants, Spengler drew the idea of a 'morphology' of cultures; each carrying an inner style and feel, each distorted to greater or lesser degrees by the impacts and exigencies of manifestation into the material world:

> Cultures are organisms, and world history is their collective biography... A Culture is born in the moment when a great soul awakens out of the proto-spirituality of ever-childish humanity, and detaches itself, a form from the formless, a bounded and mortal thing from the boundless and enduring. It blooms on the soil of an exactly-definable landscape, to which plant-wise it remains bound. It dies when this soul has actualised the full sum of its possibilities in the shape of peoples, languages, dogmas, arts, sciences, and reverts into the proto-soul.

Just as there was an *Urpflanze* for Goethe, so for Spengler there was a common pattern to cultural development. And, from this, he believed it was possible to trace the youth, adulthood and old age of each culture as it passed through the same cycle; and so too was it possible to anticipate the imminent forms of our present culture's arc:

> The aim once attained, the Culture suddenly hardens, it mortifies, its blood congeals, its force breaks down, and it becomes *Civilisation*... As such, they may, like a worn-out giant of the primeval forest, thrust their decaying branches into the sky for hundreds or thousands of years, as we see in China, in India, in The Islamic world... This is the purport of all historical 'declines,' amongst them that decline of the Classical which we know so well and fully, and another decline, comparable to it in course and duration, which will occupy the first centuries of the coming millennium but is heralded already and sensible in and around us today – the decline of the West.

Spengler was not the first to perceive a cyclical form to human history – the Arabic philosopher Ibn Khaldun and Giambattista Vico had preceded him – nor the last – Alfred Toynbee and Pitrim Sorokin would venture their own models in the decades that followed. But it was this vision of the culture-as-plant that lay at the heart of those who would dismiss Spengler as merely an imaginative crank. For the most critical, he was a throwback to the vitalist philosophers of previous centuries, with their irrational belief in a mysterious 'life-force' animating the mechanisms of the physical world. Even sympathetic analysts, like H. Stuart Hughes, tended to agree that 'Spengler's whole "morphological method"… is simply an elaborate metaphor drawn from biology.'

*

A seed is a single node, replete with potentiality. As it grows, that potentiality unfolds into diverse and divergent elements: tissues, organs, structures and appendages that have their own demands and requirements, that monopolise an increasing share of the physiological throughput of the organism. In some cases, such as with the hollowing of an old oak or the expansion of a mangrove network, the original centre is sacrificed to the needs of continual outward expansion.

Each new layer of growth adds a greater volume of biomass – in this sense, a tree's growth accelerates with age, so long as its roots can proportionally increase their intake of water and nutrients. Eventually, though, the sheer size creates physical problems: the distance across which the sap must circulate, the reduced flexibility, the increased force of gravity on the structure as a whole. As the bark becomes more brittle, the cambium – the outer ring of living material that retains the potential for further growth – is more often exposed to harm. Eventually, the tree dies.

Although the growth and life are usually concentrated on the periphery of the structure, when a tree suffers outside attack, it will sometimes throw up a 'water shoot' from its very centre – a perfectly straight, vertical pole that produces neither flower nor fruit.

*

The phenomena of convergence, centring, and anastomosis are not peculiar to flower and fruit alone.

– Goethe, #*118*

There is a strange duality in Spengler's thought. Whenever he compares the life of the mind with that of deeds, it is in favour of the bold and decisive act. He implores the youth of his time to abandon poetry and take up engineering; he mocks the ideologues and philosophers for their belief that their writing and thinking might change the course of a politics ultimately ruled by will and life-force, and asserts that the people of a civilisation must remain loyal to the demands of their dying culture, no matter how onerous or inhumane. And yet, whenever he writes of the monks, the thinkers, the mystics and the poets, of their loneliness, austerity and alienation from the people of their time, it is impossible not to believe that he is writing of himself.

In the days when a civilisation hardens into fixed form, Spengler observes, the inner life reawakens into 'Second Religiousness' – 'only with the end of grand history does holy, still Being reappear'. In the mid-1940s, just as America acceded to the position of globally pre-eminent military and technological power, *The Decline of the West* was passed around a group of friends at Columbia University in New York. These individuals would later become known as the core figures of the 'Beat Movement'; and in the word-magic of Burroughs, the fellaheen cry of Kerouac and the rabbinical entreaties of Ginsberg, echoes of Spengler can be found. But, while they may have agreed with his diagnosis of the historical era they found themselves in, the Beats drew exactly the opposite conclusions regarding the appropriate response.

For them, the coming era of decline represented liberation from the suffocating carcass of civilisation; Second Religiousness promised the transcendent, psychedelic 'Beatitude' from which they took their name; while Spengler's observation that late civilisations are routinely enthralled by foreign, exotic spiritualities, like Buddhism in China or the Roman Isis- and Mithras-cults, helped trigger their exploration of Zen, Daoism and Vedanta – thought-currents that they played a major role in popularising in the West. 'If the deluge is coming,' they appeared to surmise, 'dutifully manning your post is the height of insanity – better, surely, to throw off the shackles of civilisation and retreat to the mountains, seeking a simpler life of poetry, nature and spirit.'

*

Lao Tzu, we are told, at the beginning of another cycle's transition into materialist civilisation, left his post as Keeper of the Royal Library and headed up into the mountains of the west. Along the way, a border guard begged him to leave a record of his philosophy, and Lao Tzu duly penned the 81 verses of the *Dao De Jing*.

Daoists have often been pilloried by practically-minded 'men of the world' for their alleged quietism and resignation in the face of social and political problems. Yet this criticism ignores what, to the mystic, is the hidden reality. In the Daoist cosmology, everything that exists in the material world has its root in the immaterial – in the 26th chapter of the *Dao De Jing* is written: 'The permanent is the root of the transient; serenity lies at the heart of movement.'

Thus, every culture that arises, from the Daoist perspective, has its origin in the spiritual, and any society that loses touch with its source will trend towards entropy no matter what measures, policies or technologies it employs:

> When the people rely on rules,
> There arises a great hypocrisy,
> Family values fall apart,
> And we are amazed at 'dutiful children',
> Political corruption is rife,
> And we marvel at 'moral politicians'.

In Daoist cosmology, the first step in the creation of the material world from the source of the Dao is a division into two – *yin* and *yang*. It is the multiplication and proliferation of this primordial split that creates the architecture of reality, of acquired mind, and of the human systems built upon it. And the way to return to the source is precisely to mend this cosmic split – to merge yin with yang at deeper and deeper levels, to let go of the unnecessary complexity of society and personality, to live simply, the better to pursue a life harmonious with the natural order of things.

*

Those who stand too tall,
Have no root.
Those who stride too far,
Never reach their goal.
   – Lao Tzu, #24

The outer bark is unsuited to yield anything further; in the long-
lived tree it is too separate and too hardened on the outside, just as
the wood becomes too hard on the inside ... the wood is rendered
inactive by its solidity; it is durable but too dead to produce life.
   – Goethe, #*111*

In 1957, Amaury de Riencourt, a Sorbonne-educated Frenchman living in
America, published a book titled *The Coming Caesars*, which, despite
borrowing Spengler's terms and intellectual framework, ungenerously
limited reference to him to a single footnote.

One of the key ideas that Spengler derived from his morphological
model was that the long-held ideal of a 3000-year-old 'Western Civilisation', incorporating the Greeks, the Romans and the modern nation
states of Europe and America, was an illusion. The Classical culture had
had its own arc of birth, growth and decay, the Roman imperium forming
its civilisation stage; its lack of organic continuity with later European
culture had been disguised by the historical accident of shared Christianity, and the half-millennium gap between its demise and the beginning of
the next cycle furtively dismissed as the inconsequential interlude of 'the
Dark Ages'.

This understanding formed the basis of Spengler's favourite game:
matching patterns in our own incipient age of civilisation – which he
called, after Goethe, the 'Faustian' – with that of the Roman world.
Among the parallels he drew were the development of massive, centrally-
planned cities; rampant hedonism; an obsession with the material over
the ideal; the boastful gigantism of structures and institutions; the
extended reach of a technologically-empowered military; exoticism in art
and religion; the rise to power of the structures of finance and their
continual debasement of the currency; an increasing shallowness of
public thought and philosophy; colonialism, followed by imperial
overstretch; a painful domination of the intuition and the body by an
overweening intellectualism; declining birthrates; and a generalised
feeling of loss and purposelessness.

In essence, de Riencourt's book was an extended riff on this comparison, with specific reference to Spengler's notion of Caesarism – the idea that, when the inner structure of a civilisation has been flattened by democracy, and that democracy corrupted by the unfettered influence of high finance and the media, the power network of the civilisation suddenly reverts to a single, central node. Wrote de Riencourt:

> Caesarism is not dictatorship, not the result of one man's overriding ambition, not a brutal seizure of power through revolution. It is not based on a specific doctrine or philosophy. It is essentially pragmatic and untheoretical. It is a slow, often century-old, unconscious development that ends in a voluntary surrender of a free people escaping from freedom to one autocratic master.

Unlike Spengler, de Riencourt believed there was still a possibility that this fate might be avoided. For years, he gave lecture tours across America, attempting to revive the aristocratic spirit of the Republic that he felt was the only bulwark against the erosion of its ideals. 'Maintaining a civilisation takes a continuous input of matter, energy and morale,' notes William Ophuls in *Immoderate Greatness: Why Civilisations Fail*. 'In theory, moral restoration should be possible at any point along the way, thus forestalling the descent or even restoring the original élan. But it rarely happens in practice …'

*

> Becoming has no number. We can count, measure, dissect only the lifeless and so much of the living as can be disassociated from livingness. Pure becoming, pure life, is in this sense incapable of being bounded. It lies beyond the domain of cause and effect, law and measure.
>
> – Spengler

The first piece of work a young student called Ludwig von Bertalanffy ever got published was a review of *The Decline of the West* for a Viennese newspaper in 1924. Von Bertalanffy would later become known as 'the father of General Systems Theory', an all-encompassing model of the functioning of complex systems which would have a profound influence on the fields of biology, cybernetics, anthropology and mathematics, and which laid the groundwork for new fields such as emergence theory and complexity theory.

Central to General Systems Theory is the recognition that complex, dynamic systems exhibit capacities and characteristics that cannot be explained through a reductive account of their component mechanisms; that to understand such systems requires a holistic, non-linear perspective that considers the dynamic interaction of the whole. In a universe of increasing entropy, von Bertalanffy pointed out, the existence of 'open systems' that are capable of absorbing energy flows from larger entropic contexts, and thereby of creating islands of self-organising 'negative entropy', is a surprising phenomenon. Clearly, in addition to the known material mechanisms of reality, a unique and vital role is played by a non-material principle of *information* or *organisation*.

This approach also enables the boundaries between disciplines and objects of analysis to be dissolved – with the addition of the concept of organisation, the separation of physics, chemistry, biology and sociology can be replaced with a single, all-encompassing view of the thermodynamics of emergence: as the sun pours its energy onto the earth, it organises itself into increasingly complex molecules and proteins; with the ongoing input of sunlight, they bound themselves into biological cells; which then join in common cause as plants; animals absorb the energy stored in the tissues of the plants; while predators take the same energy directly from other animals. In the same way, as humans learnt to appropriate the energy flows of animals and crops, to dig deeper into the stored sunshine of forests and fossil fuels, and to gather in the fertility, resources and labour of distant lands and people, higher and higher pyramids of mental architecture and social organisation were enabled by the increased energetic throughput.

Apprehending the world from this perspective, 'isomorphisms' can be perceived where the same patterns of energy flow and organisation recur in different areas and at different scales. In von Bertalanffy's words:

> System isomorphisms also appear in problems which are recalcitrant to quantitative analysis but are nevertheless of great intrinsic interest. There are, for example, isomorphies between biological systems and 'epiorganisms' like animal communities and human societies.

Many have suggested causal mechanisms by which civilisational decline might take place – ecological overshoot, the ascendancy of a repressive minority, or the sclerotic 'institutionalisation' of old habits and structures, for example. Even those who have attempted a holistic view of civilisations as complex non-linear systems, as in Tainter's model of 'declining returns on complexity', have still had a tendency to emphasise the material aspect of the civilisation over the psychological – as if they have feared that acknowledging a 'moral' or 'spiritual' dimension would leave them open to accusations of insufficient scientific rigour.

But a true application of General Systems Theory to the phenomenon of a civilisation – something akin to Goethe's 'exact sensorial imagination', perhaps – would draw no distinction between the material and mental aspects of the system. Just as the energy is drawn up from the surrounding lands to create the grand structures of a civilisation's sprawling cosmopolis, so the energy extorted from the 'proletariat' is drawn up into taller and taller social hierarchies of wealth and power; and, in the same way, energy is drawn up within each member of the civilisation, to greater or lesser degree, to fuel the vertiginous intellectual constructs required by civilisational life. To focus on the exhaustion of the soil's fertility, or the exploitation of the human labour fed by it, or the harm done to the body by keeping the mind continuously attentive and employed, is merely a matter of emphasis; it is the same sunlight flowing up the pyramid at every stage.

It seems, however, that in every civilisation the trajectory of the mental and the material diverge – while technical power and material comfort increase (for those at the core, at least), the spirit that first animated the culture is already declining. At first this seems like a loss of religious piety; later it is only the concern of artists and poets, who sense the pulse of creative force diminishing; but increasingly, as the civilisation begins to founder on the rocks of material exhaustion and complexity, the feeling begins to spread amongst the whole of the populace.

Unlike previous civilisations, our own has had an additional factor affecting it – the input of supplementary 'energy slaves' from fossil fuels has increased the material rewards of membership, forestalling the voice of 'spiritual' complaints a while longer, while simultaneously both extending the footprint of the empire and increasing the speed with which it exhausts its resources.

*

When we are born we are soft and supple,
When we die we are stiff and hard.
Plants and trees are soft and flexible in life,
They are dry and rigid in death.
So: to be soft and flexible is the way of life,
To be rigid and stiff is the way of death.
The inflexible fighter will be defeated,
The solid tree will be felled,
Thus the mighty will fall whilst the soft will rise.
  – Lao Tzu, #76

In 1970, at the age of 20, Martín Prechtel fled his life on an impoverished New Mexico reservation and found himself, after years of wandering, part of an intact tribal community in Mayan Guatemala. He married, had children and, over the course of a decade, was trained by a local shaman to take on his role in preserving the spiritual heart of their culture.

But the reach of empire is long, and the encroaching predations of evangelism, money and military technology forced him to flee back to America with the sacred medicine bundle of the 'Village Heart', while his fellow villagers were slaughtered, raped and tortured. 'Never in my entire life did I think I could be convinced to write any kind of book whatsoever,' he writes at the start of his *Secrets of the Talking Jaguar*:

> much less a chronicle in English that would include my most treasured and grief-burdened memories... Among the pre-European Guatemalan Maya, writing was a ritual activity and never done in a casual way. Writing was not done to communicate or express ideas in the strictest sense, but rather to create a visible 'word of roads' between the ancestral beings at the beginning of life and the eternal now of our world.

*

Only when the natural state divides,
Does existence come into being.
  – Lao Tzu, #24

But these attempts at division also produce many adverse effects
when carried to an extreme. To be sure, what is alive can be
dissected into its component parts, but from these parts it will
be impossible to restore it and bring it to life again.
  – Goethe

In 1703, the priest and philosopher Gottfried Leibniz published his
*Explanation of the binary arithmetic, which uses only the characters
1 and 0, with some remarks on its usefulness, and on the light it throws
on the ancient Chinese figures of Fu Xi.*

The work was his first public demonstration of his differential calcu-
lus, a new mathematical tool with which the analogue organicity of the
world could be represented through multiple strata of binary division.
Far from wishing to reduce the world to dry mathematics, however, to
Leibniz the 1 and the 0 were emblems of the primordial split between the
Godhead and the material world, and the fact that the world could be
understood through the mind a confirmation of their underlying unity.
('Goethe was,' according to Spengler, 'without knowing it, a disciple of
Leibniz in his whole thought.')

The binary calculus formed part of Leibniz's lifelong project to create
a new symbolic language that could incorporate the whole of human
experience, just as the teeming multiplicity of the visual space around
him could be subordinated by the power of numbers; Spengler cannot
have been insensate to the parallel with his own cloistered, conflicted
ambitions in the long hours spent constructing the symbolic system of
The Decline, creating a network of gathered knowledge and texts, the
thoughts and images of distant centuries and far-flung lands.

The Faustian soul, Spengler believed, as expressed in Gothic architecture, Beethoven, frictionless capitalism and technological hyper-ambition,
had as its archetype the lonely ego at the centre of a web of dynamic
forces, stretching out with weightless yearning towards the infinite in all
directions:

The intoxicated soul wills to fly above Space and Time. An ineffable
longing tempts him to indefinable horizons. Man would free

himself from the earth, rise into the infinite, leave the bonds of the body, and circle in the universe of space amongst the stars... Hence the fantastic traffic that crosses the continents in a few days, that puts itself across oceans in floating cities, that bores through mountains, rushes about in subterranean labyrinths, uses the steam-engine till its last possibilities have been exhausted, and then passes on to the gas-engine, and finally raises itself above the roads and railways and flies in the air; hence it is that the spoken word is sent in one moment over all the oceans; hence comes the ambition to break all records and beat all dimensions, to build giant halls for giant machines, vast ships and bridge-spans, buildings that deliri-ously scrape the clouds, fabulous forces pressed together to obey the hand of a child, stamping and quivering and droning works of steel and glass in which tiny man moves as unlimited monarch and, at the last, feels nature as beneath him.

The binary calculus, of course, would also come to form the basis for computational programming languages, and the extension of the Faustian will-to-infinite into new electronic realms of telecommunica-tions, technological power and artificial intelligence. All this too, Spengler seemed to anticipate:

And these machines become in their forms ever less human, more ascetic, mystic, esoteric. They weave the earth over with an infinite web of subtle forces, currents, and tensions. Their bodies become ever more and more immaterial, ever less noisy. The wheels, rollers and levers are vocal no more. All that matters withdraws into the interior.

*

It is a curious phenomenon of imperial ages that the power centre of the civilisation always shifts away from its origination point towards what had been the periphery of its territory. In China, following the Warring States period, it was the far-western state of Qin that finally dominated the older eastern principalities; in the Near East, the Arabian civilisation found its new centre in the Ottoman Empire; while the Greek city states begrudgingly gave way to their less-refined counterpart on the Italian peninsula. Perhaps it is that, as with a hollowing oak, the last remnants of living tissue are found on the periphery, while the old core is suffocated by the legacy of its prior positioning.

There is little doubt that, in the past centuries of our own civilisation, the centre of power has shifted from continental Europe, first to London, and then across the Atlantic. But America is a strange, virtualised imperium. Partly because of its geographical distance from its parent countries, partly because of its historical birth through rebellion against distant and centralised power, it (and the rest of the Western world) has difficulty accepting the reality of its imperial role. Its mythos demands it still see itself as horizontalist, libertarian, exceptional, independent; newspapers yet warn us of the dreadful consequences of 'American isolationism'.

And yet its armies still linger in every corner of the world, its agencies still manipulate the politics of far continents, and the petrodollars still recycle global tribute back to the imperial capital through invisible, binary lines of influence and coercion. And the contradictions of being a 'deniable empire', the dual necessities of keeping the illusion in place and the energy flowing in, demand an ever-greater concentration of power. De Riencourt warned in 1957: 'Americans will accept immense, almost autocratic power over them so long as they don't have to see in it a transcendent authority, and they will always attempt to "humanise" such authority with the help of humour or incongruity…Through the gap thus opened between appearance and reality, the coming Caesars will march in if left free to do so.'

There can be little doubt that the gap between appearance and reality has grown wide of late. As the shared dream of civilisation breaks down, the spirit that animated it seeks final, desperate lines of escape: into futurism, technophilia and fantasies of electronic transcendence; into renewed conquest, domination and aggression; into archness, irony and the endless narcissistic mirror-worlds of modernity.

The bark, it seems, is becoming brittle.

*

At the beginning of Han times (c. AD 200) the troops of the Shen had ceased to be 'moral representations' and become kindly beings. The wind-, cloud-, thunder-, and rain-gods came back. Crowds of cults which purported to drive out the evil spirits by the aid of the gods acquired a footing. It was in that time that there arose ... the myth of Pan-ku, the prime principle from which the series of emperors descended.

 – Spengler

The 'Fu Xi' of Leibniz's title was the mythical Emperor of China, to whom is attributed the invention of the divinatory and cosmological system of the I Ching. The stories say that he saw the patterns of broken and unbroken lines, representing yin and yang forces, written on the back of a 'water dragon' as it emerged from the Yellow River. In 1701, a Jesuit priest stationed in China sent Leibniz a woodcut detailing the I Ching; having already been toying with ideas of binary notation for years, this proved the inspiration that led to Leibniz's publication of his work.

Another story tells that, in the beginning, there was an egg of chaos, Hun Tun. From out of this egg broke the cosmic giant Pangu, who divided the Sky and the Earth; his body, in death, then transformed into the rivers, mountains, plants and animals. Among these was an entity called Hua Hsu, who gave birth, in turn, to Fu Xi and his wife, Nu Wa, the 'original humans'. Fu Xi and Nu Wa then created humanity from the clay of the mountain on which they lived, and gave to them the culture and language which sustained their lives on earth.

*

The people of the world accumulate, the sage sheds.
 – Lao Tzu, #20

There is no physiological reason why a tree could not live forever. Their demise is almost always the result either of violent attack from outside, or of inner dysfunction from having grown too large, for too long. Trees that are continually cut back or coppiced exhibit lifespans far in excess of their unhindered brethren.

So too do indigenous cultures endure far beyond the lifespans of civilisation, by developing patterns of habit and perception that continually block the pathways of continual growth, that break down the incipient power hierarchies of their societies, and that keep their energy and attention centred in the heartwood of their being. If you sit down in quiet community with indigenous people, you may learn that what seems to the eye of empire as wasteful inefficiency is in fact a deliberate cultivation of longevity, a lifeway rooted in the primacy of the 'other world', where material well-being is sacrificed in remembrance, recognition and repayment of the source of all things.

The penultimate verse of the *Dao De Jing* advises:

> Remain in a small place with few people,
> Though they may use tools to benefit them,
> They have no interest in great gain.
> Let the people place importance upon the process of death
>   and not move far away.
> They may have boats and carriages,
> But they do not care to use them.
> They may have weaponry,
> But they do not care for conflict.
> The people should live simply,
> Not care for fine food or clothes.
> The people should enjoy the current moment.
> Communities should care for each other,
> Let the sound of dogs and roosters float in the air,
> The people may die of old age without ever having left their community.

Metaphor is a kind of community. It is a way of holding two seemingly disparate things next to each other, and intuiting a hidden commonality between them, an underlying pattern that unites what appeared to be divided. For those who are capable of employing an 'exact sensorial imagination', metaphor itself begins to appear ubiquitous: 'analogy' seems indistinguishable from 'systemic isomorphism'; the pattern-matching capacity of the mind not separate from the organisational principles of material reality.

Western botanists once saw plants as strictly-bounded entities – our own civilised concern for the hard borders of individuality projected onto a biological reality far more gregarious and generous in its ways. Plants routinely merge, graft, split, and rejoin with one another; genetic material recombines and mutates; forest communities share food and information through underground networks of roots and mycelia. If a tree is split in two, both halves may continue to live side by side, and perhaps even rejoin again in time. If a tree topples, so long as there are any roots left in the earth, it may yet sprout new shoots, reaching up towards the sun from its flank.

At the end of the book he thought he would never write, Martín Prechtel says:

> Shamans say the Village Heart can grow a brand new World House if it is well-dressed in the layered clothing of each indigenous soul's magic sound, ancestral songs, and indigenous ingenuity. The wrecked landscape of our World House could sprout a renewed world, but a new language has to be found. We can't make the old world come alive again, but from its old seeds, the next layer could sprout.

SOPHIE MCKEAND

Rebel Sun

(i)

Your alarm rings beetles. Opening curtain-heavy eyes you waterfall out of
bed. Regrouping in the bathroom you notice manes of dune horses patterning
through the window onto new tiles that march like soldiers. Slicing knife-edged
blinds across golden plumes, you frown and stand on scales that burp toads –
you still haven't lost ten pounds. You try to shower flabby thoughts away but
the seal blubber in your mind holds fast and John Lewis doesn't sell the correct
excavation knife.

Your car is a tortoise and you grovel to work together. Outside your office the
daily protest march has begun. Thousands of bricks defend workers from the
insurgent army of brilliant light demonstrating across courtyards. You shield
poached eyes from the insurrection and scurry indoors to where striplights and
air-con salve jittery skin. Someone has opened a window near your desk so that
you are forced, again, to confront the agitators outside. A swarm of birds
occupy plastic trees chanting *comrade! comrade!* to the Rebel Sun.

You decide to take a stand and, lassoing your desk that floats down-office in
the flood, type a strongly-worded e-complaint.

You try to sign off with your name but cannot remember. The letters are ants
marching determinedly in circles. You brush this diversion aside and type *yours
sincerely desk 391.* They will know who you are. At break time you eat the
lunch you brought then buy more food from the sandwich van parked in tar
sands at the back of the building. You are a caterpillar deliberately gnawing
through another day. You consider taking up smoking again to curb your
appetite.

Some workers are cavorting with birds in the sunlight. They won't last. You've
seen it before. Socialising with agitators burns skin to ash. Soon concentration

will slosh around the office like over-watered concrete and you will have to dismiss those who are not already blown away by the afternoon hurricane.

You finish work late. There is no traffic. The tortoise is now a hare. Black skies are punctured by bright laser eyes as you surge home exhausted. You are a plague of locusts devouring the contents of the fridge. Blood red wine flows as you settle alone with friends whose scripted conversations intertwine like ivy with social media feeds across the lounge floor. A river of wine finally engulfs the tiny boat in which you are trying to ascend.

(ii)

Saturday screams by in a murder of crows that claw you into Sunday. You intend to spend the day working. The white screen lights a fishbowl around your face as you yank seaweed across the window and submerge. It is cool in the semi-darkness and you breathe into aqua-blue. You could have finished this work on Friday, probably by Thursday; if you're honest, Wednesday, but that's no example to set staff who will loiter like seals at any given opportunity.

The email you are typing refuses to conform, continuing instead to shape the names of places you only know through five-star-all-inclusive-package-holiday-deals. You wonder for a moment about the wider country outside these resorts, maybe next time you'll be more adventurous. You close that screen, cast your net wide, plunge for the depths and begin writing. This is an important document. You know because it arrives as a pulsating, red jellyfish. You have written these reports a hundred times but it is becoming increasingly difficult to square thoughts. Coming up for air you realise the Rebel Sun has made a tactical manoeuvre across the nihilist sky and is streaming into your eyes.

You have no time for distractions and climb onto a chair to block out the mutinous light but the chair is a cockroach and you scream in disgust. Lunging backwards you shatter like a crystal vase across the black slate mountain of the dining room floor.

It is dark. Your eyes are open but filling with thick, black oil. In the corner of the room a white glow beckons. You want to move towards the light but your limbs are shards sunk into coal. Someone will come for you.

It is bright. You are still alone. A mass-lobby of gulls squawks outside in support of the Rebel Sun who parades across your body like a brass band. You try to move away but you are still in pieces. Your laptop is chiming butterflies; your phone rings hedgehogs. It is impossible to reach either. You would sob but that is for feeble people and you are not weak.

(iii)

You lie prostrate before an oppressive sun. The hospital have pieced you together to the best of their ability but insist on rest and recuperation. In sunlight. Your body is a shipwreck. At first you scream every time they weasel you outside but your actions are perceived as a sign of a volatile and unstable character so you acquiesce.

You watch your skin slowly break into dirt and feel your mind crumble. Day after day as the Rebel Sun graffities propaganda across fractured limbs you hold fast to what you know: the sun's malice has caused this depression; you were born to work – to be productive, to give everything to the job, to climb, to improve, to be the best, to be unique, irreplaceable. You hold fast to these thoughts and glare at the sun in the hope he will cower in the face of your defiance but instead you melt into nothingness: you are not special; your employer has already replaced you.

Dissident sparrows squat amongst the shards of your hips and thighs so that you cannot see where you end and they begin. You are pained by their chirrups bouncing around the seashell of your skull and mentally compose their eviction notice.

As the days sloth by a beehive takes shape in your heart. This is totally unacceptable but your complaints go unheard. Time and stillness have gifted you the perception of a hawk and you become engrossed with the actions of certain 'innovator' bees.

At first these tiny entrepreneurs are a mirror in which you vainly admire your own productivity and problem-solving capabilities but, as another afternoon whales past, you realise they are allowing other bees to copy their actions – for free. Not only that but the 'mimic' bees return to the hive to teach other bees the new technique. Each time this happens the hive, and your heart, strengthen and expand but you are aware that the innovator bees hold no leverage, no advantage, and are quickly relegated to being *exactly the same as all the other bees*. You eye them with disgust and begin plotting their removal while surveying the broken remains of your body:

The Rebel Sun has bronzed your skin to dust. Your bones have taken root and are now a hedgerow for sparrows' nests. Your heart is a socialist beehive. Your head is a seashell echoing birdsong. Everything is seasoning by organically. You are no longer needed, or in control. Perhaps this is hell, you muse.

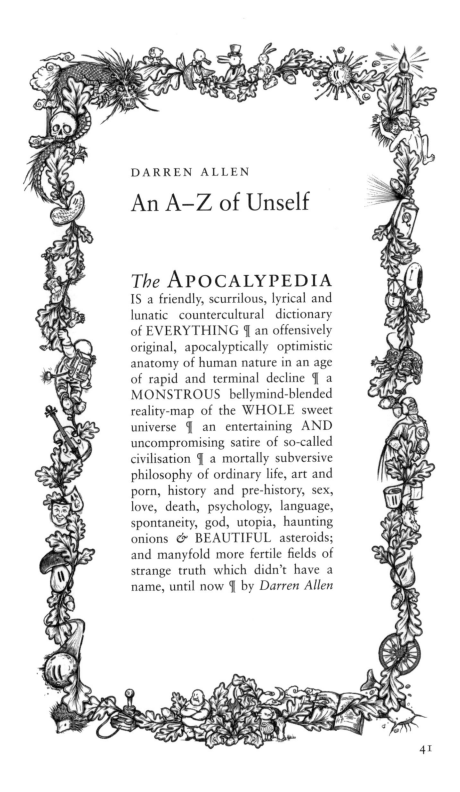

DARREN ALLEN

An A–Z of Unself

The APOCALYPEDIA

IS a friendly, scurrilous, lyrical and lunatic countercultural dictionary of EVERYTHING ¶ an offensively original, apocalyptically optimistic anatomy of human nature in an age of rapid and terminal decline ¶ a MONSTROUS bellymind-blended reality-map of the WHOLE sweet universe ¶ an entertaining AND uncompromising satire of so-called civilisation ¶ a mortally subversive philosophy of ordinary life, art and porn, history and pre-history, sex, love, death, psychology, language, spontaneity, god, utopia, haunting onions *&* BEAUTIFUL asteroids; and manyfold more fertile fields of strange truth which didn't have a name, until now ¶ by *Darren Allen*

abreact [abrɪakt]
vb 1 to avoid a subtle point by restlessly or emotionally 'skidding' over the message, blunting (or DIGITISING) its nuance, thereby creating a crude meaning to be of-fended by, or an excuse to stop paying attention 2 to focus exclusively on the technical meaning of an utterance, in order to avoid its VIBE

——— BOREDOM ———

To BE BORED is to come up with inadequate reasons not to talk to shop assistants with lungs full of helium, play recordings of ecstatic laughter on the tube, SEE sparrows, bring up death in unlikely places, smear yourself over the walls of your house moaning in gratitude, foxtrot through no entry signs, interview your friends, perform daily actions as if holy rituals, visit a prison, leave root vegetables on steps, wrestle with your friends, make bread, trombone up your girlfriend's arse, picnic in a cemetery, learn mycology, lie about your job to taxi drivers, organise a treasure hunt in your house for your lover ending with you, naked, hiding in the cupboard, do the poxy washing-up, make love in a hedge, give everything away, master impro, master joinery, build an organic shed-cathedral in the garden then impersonate the pope for your neighbours, organise situationist theatrical protests in corporate coffee shops, fast for five days, turn up for work dressed as spiderman, heavy metal drum roll as your arse hits cold toilet porcelain, grow fins, learn to crack necks expertly, sniff the smell of now, live alone in a shack, feign elk, or strobe blue, cry '*I am the expressive egg!*', shoot up into a little white ball, and fly out the window

canerated [kanəreɪtɪd]
adj 1 to be prematurely aged through a dissolute life 2 to look like you are wearing a latex suit of your former self

deruet [deruːət]
vb & n 1 to mistake the noise in one's head for oneself 2 to mistake a magpie for a miniature flying killer whale

ecoshism [iːkəʊʃizəm]

n a SEMI-MYSTISHIST CULT that privileges community, 'conversation', ecology, relativism and relationship over the experience of consciousness, the absolute present, UNCONDITIONAL LOVE, the whum-whumming void and radical critiques of institutional sources of funding

· the ECOSHIST almost never expresses views that might jeopardise a spot on Radio 4, an occasional commission with *The Guardian* or a nice TEDX talk; all of which he undertakes with uncritical pride

friend [frɛnd]

n either 1 one's other heart or 2 a VIRTUAL PRODUCT to be MANAGED, accumulated or CONSUMED (or a loved-one, reduced by CAPITALIST specialism, to someone with whom one does nothing but offload on or have FUN with)

· often unconsciously sought to nourish fears, addictions and slave-master subroutines; when these branches are cut off, or wither away, the friend who fed them will continue to keep the old self alive, until he or she adapts, or is also cut off

A BRIEF HISTORY OF GOD

1. PRIMITIVE GOD
The SELFLESS self is a welcome guest in a mysterious, friendly, TRANSDIMENSIONAL universe (an organism called 'God') comprised of immediate, living qualities (understood as MYTHIC 'gods')

2. SUPERNATURAL GOD
The integrated self is an ally, or a hanger-on, in a universe of capricious 'good and evil' forces and divine personalities which must be honoured or superstitiously appeased

3. RELIGIOUS GOD
The individual self is a tenant / employee in a universe-corporation run by an absolute manager (with a beard), who wrote down a series of rules which must be SUBMITTED to

4. MODERN GOD
The isolated self is the proprietor of a mechanical universe comprised of separate interrelated parts, or people, which must be grasped and controlled

5. POST-MODERN GOD
The sole self *is* the universe

These five stages blend into and overlap each other, with two, three, four or all five potentially coexisting in one person's beliefs

PRE-HISTORY

PROTO-HISTORY

ANCIENT HISTORY

HISTORY

POST-HISTORY

holiday [hɒlɪdeɪ]
n stressful time-filling man-aged gawk used by those so scared of free time they must fill it up with FUN
· tends to create impatience, guilt, PHOTOS, status anxi-ety and (like VR) stories that nobody wants to hear

interview [ɪntəvjuː]
n humiliating performance of ambition, interest, happiness and confidence designed to test enthusiasm for EMO-TIONAL LABOUR

jaywalk [dʒeɪwɔːk]
n & vb curtailment, by law, motorway and stereotype, of the freedom to roam by spontaneous inspiration

kinertia [kɪnəːʃə]
n 1 feeling that you never have enough time while, at the same time, that nothing is really happening 2 to be simultaneously paralysed by and overwhelmed with agitated inner movement 3 constant movement at the service of nothing changing
· a.k.a. NON-STOP INERTIA

leg [lɛg]
n manifestation of the love between foot and hip

munge [mʌndʒ]
vb to ruin a lovely unspoken little ritual by mentioning it

news (media) [njuːz]
n 1 a boring dream told by a nutcase in a prison 2 rich people paying middle-class people to blame, distract or SENTIMENTALISE the poor 3 visual and textual frag-ments of contextless events used to create, in its consum-ers, a fragmented virtual image of remote problems so that they can forget about their nearby sadness 4 tittle-tattle and bitching for *serious* men 5 a convenient means of enjoying a little murder, WAR, fear, SEX and violence with one's breakfast 6 the PROPA-GANDA voice of ego, state and the corporate-profes-sional market system
· the [unconscious] purpose of the news is: A) to make the clear-cut 'debatable' B) to make the god-awful trivial C) to accustom consumers to events with no cause and no context D) to promote WORK, POST-MODERNISM, SCIENTISM, GROUPTHINK and RELIGION E) to make dis-sent seem bitter, ridiculous or completely incomprehen-sible

orboing [ɔːbɔɪŋ]
  n **1** being forced, by a long, shallow staircase, to take a series of lorby loping mega-steps or dainty mini-steps; thereby temporarily inhabiting a strange and awkward otherself **2** dignity-thieving little run forced upon you by a closing lift door

———— A GÜELL OF PHILIAS ————

AVEVAPHILIA · love of uncertainty, discomfort, mortality, nevermind, oh-well and sod-it STREPIPHILIA · love of distant blue, long grass, ice-cold, fast water, apples, silent hills, solitary oaks, forgotten shacks, shy yellow shards and distant woodpecking sorts of thing KONTOPEPHILIA · love of waddling around, hips akimbo, going *'pahkeek, pahkeek'* NARIBUPHILIA · love of squidbeaks, cats' ELBOW-THUMBS, cock-crests, friendly storks, galaxy-emulating spiders and secret jaguar go-kart tracks

INFINIPHILIA · love of ant's nests softly viewed as a whole organism, woodworm routes, dewy spider's webs, roosting starlings, queen sago spines, blizzards by moonlight, huge chestnut trees booming in the wind, milk slow-mo detune in tea and cloud shadows slipping over distant hills QUIRINDIPHILIA · love of the flaws that make for flawlessness; such as endearing fears, font-bleed, beauty-enhancing facial quirk and the 0.5% piss flavour of prawns AMAPHILIA · godlove (sense 1)

❧

qwoth [kwɒθ]
  n **1** lightning strike of divine rapture that rattles the spine and makes the teeth glow **2** an overwhelmingly powerful inner sensation of galaxy-wide waves of ecstasy; plus astonishment that you can bear so much pleasure · can be shared

repandrous [rɪpandrəs]
  adj descriptive of A) glowing exaltation of affection B) a face hot with absorbed BEAUTY C) joy that can be seen wafting from delighted skin in heaty ripples and D) a gratitudegasm of freedom upon re-realising you *never have to do that again*

stagversion [stagvə:ʃən]
n 1 FUTILE protests
(marches, petitions, votes,
strikes) or attempts to reform
the world through participating in it 2 hating the world
or moaning about it, blaming
it for your vices or directing
all your rebellious energy,
first of all, at 'them' instead
of at the 'I' that is angry (*see*
FALSOLIS) 3 cynically knowing that the WORLD is a lie,
or that its WORK is a prison,
while wearily, sardonically,
ironically participating in it
4 HUXLEYAN journalism and
academia; promoting
MYSTISHISM, ECOSHISM,
FEMINISHISM and SOCIAL-
ISHISM while working for a
TOTALITARIAN, corp-funded
UNIVERSITY or NEWSMEDIA
CULT
5 anarcho-punk groupthink
rebellion-consumption
· stagversion is not just
  effortlessly subsumed by the
  world, the world actually
  requires stagversion to
  effectively operate; without
  the eco, female, 'radical',
  artistic and philanthropic
  veneer created by
  PROFESSIONAL stagversives
  (esp. journalists) the entire
  system would lie exposed
  and threatened
· antonym of SUBVERSION

twilt [twɪlt]
vb & n to imperceptibly wilt
when blocked by a literal
response to one's playfulness,
when forced to play a
professional part or when
confronted by ludicrously
shaved genitals
unhappy [ʌnhapi]
adj happy, unhappy, happy,
unhappy, happy, *unhappy*...
verigag [vɛrɪgag]
n an unconscious truth or
desire manifesting as a weak
joke; normally of a sexually
suggestive nature
woo, court[ship] [wuː, kɔːt]
vb & n **either** 1 an unpredictable, dramatic, tender
or vivid romantic encounter
followed by unpredictable,
leisurely and organic
FOREPLAY **or** 2 a planned,
abstract, market-exchange
of VR profiles, followed by a
short, predictable exchange
of likes, followed by rapid
fucking – depriving woman
of her spontaneous instincts,
and of the time required to
see if a man's DATE-FACE will
melt away (after orgasm or
after his genetic-robot fuck-
self feels that she is probably
impregnated), depriving
man of the sublime opportunity to overcome himself;
and depriving them both of
the delightful unfolding of
the genuinely new together
· 1. must never end

PLANET X

WHEN RELATIONSHIPS END, ex-lovers all fly off to live together on a beautiful planet with all your lost biros, peanuts, pieces of paper with important information, beloved shirts, misplaced umbrellas and scarves left in restaurants. All the perfect fruit you've ever eaten, that made your eyes pop open – the complex, fragrant lemons, the watermelons that were sweet right down to the rind, the buttery mangoes that dribbled jungle gold – it all grows there, on that planet. The vague, freakish, sweet, wrenching flashes of youth and winter sunshine, and the fizz of long-ago thunderstorms, and the voices of long-dead friends – everything good that is lost forever to you lives there still, on a beautiful planet, far away, which, not long ago, collided with a huge asteroid and exploded. Gone *forever*. Okay?

yinyin [jɪnjɪn]
n 1 mysterious muse at the heart of the VOID, silently beating in the bellymind of all absolutely present, beautiful and terrible women 2 the ineffable source of all inspiration, all joy, all pain, all soft, spectacular creation and all the death-or-glory triumphs of true love 3 the hips of the world
· does not need to create art, because she *is* that which poets write of

zeng [zɛŋg]
n sickening realisation that
1 life does not treat you the way your mother did
or 2 after graduating from nineteen years of schooling, you know and can do next to nothing (i.e. are FUNCTIONALLY ILLITERATE)
· those who are passed from the care of institutionalised parents to the care of institutions do not get the opportunity of feeling this instructive PAIN

CHARLOTTE MCGUINN FREEMAN

Clothesline at the End of the World

On the first warmish March day, I'll be outside hanging my wash on the line even if my boots are crunching on snow. If the sun is shining, if there's even a hint of warmth on the breeze I'll be bringing my wash outside, freeing it from the clotheslines in the basement. I am a tiny bit fanatical about my clotheslines. The outdoor line is attached to my side yard fence and, like all people who engage in a repetitive physical task, I have a specific method for hanging the clothes. Pants, dresses, bathrobes – long items get hung on the back line against the fence. Then shirts, which must be hung upside down, connected at the corners to save on clothespins. (If you hang them right side up by the shoulders, you get weird bumps dried into your shirts that make you look like you're continually shrugging.) Smalls get hung on the end furthest from the street, between the dresses and the shirts. No need to embarrass the neighbours. Then last are the socks – matched together, hung in pairs. A load of wash takes me maybe ten minutes to hang. I work at home so it makes for a nice break in the day, and I love my washline. I love the way things look hanging there in the breeze.

But I don't hang clothes just because I like the way they look. I am a true believer in the power of the clothesline. For one thing, the clothes dryer is second in American homes only to the refrigerator for electricity consumption, and while I know that eliminating my use of the dryer individually isn't going to slow the onslaught of climate change, it's something concrete I can do. Also, as a freelancer, I'm broke, so anything to bring down the electric bill. But I hang laundry for a less concrete reason, because hanging the laundry is about taking care, it's about a version of domesticity that is not oppression, but which models the sort of caretaking we're all going to have to learn to value in order to make a hotter, drier, more crowded world habitable.

I live in a small town in Montana, a town that until about 20 years ago was solidly working class. It was the headquarters for the Northern Pacific Railway, and it's a town of small railroaders' houses with tiny

48

yards, nearly every one of which has a sturdy clothesline out back. Because we're one of the windiest towns in America and these are serious clotheslines – usually built from six-inch plumbing pipe, sunk into three or four feet of concrete.

And yet, I'm one of the few people I know who actually dries my clothes on the line. As the cost of appliances dropped and dryers became ubiquitous, clotheslines came to be seen as 'trashy', a symbol of poverty and sloth. Even as the new people moving to town buy hybrid vehicles and put solar panels on their roofs, even as greenhouses and chicken coops spring up in backyards, those sturdy old plumbing-pipe clotheslines, painted silver, are always empty.

I moved here from California in 2002 for a number of reasons, but chief among them I was anxious about climate change. It made me nervous, California. It had been good to me career-wise, twice. First when I moved there to do my master's degree at UC Davis; then when I left Salt Lake City after my PhD and went back out to live with my brother and find a job. Desperate to pay off my student loans, I got work in a tech company, editing user and administration guides. I liked it. I liked the people I worked with and the intellectual challenge of figuring out how to present information to people in the most useful format possible. But California was giving me the willies. It was so crowded, and the Bay Area is such an enclosed space, bounded by the Pacific on the one side and the coast hills and Sacramento-San Joaquin River Delta on the other. Three years into my tech job, I'd seen field after field on my evening commute disappear under the onslaught of ugly housing developments, just as I'd watched the last few migrant workers hoeing a zucchini field that was doomed to become another Cisco campus. I wish I'd had a camera that day. I was stopped in traffic, and across from me were several guys with computer cases standing at a bus stop, while behind them four or five Mexican guys hoed zucchini rows, and behind them another three-storey Cisco building, identical to all the others, was going up.

I could feel the big change coming – whatever we want to call it, climate change, global warming, the Anthropocene, the great acceleration – I don't know what it is, but having been raised by unreliable parents you develop antennae for impending doom. You can tell by the energy level, the degree of frantic vibration, that something bad is about to happen. And that's how I felt in California. I couldn't put a finger on it exactly, but I knew something wasn't right and I wanted to get out of the way.

I knew about Livingston from having run writers' workshops while I was in graduate school. The nature and western writers were a friendly lot, most knew one another, and talk across the patio tables at Squaw Valley often turned to places where a person could live cheap. Livingston was one of them. Like a lot of beautiful places left empty when an industry implodes, Livingston has attracted writers and painters and fading movie stars for decades now, along with a vibrant population of hunting and fishing guides, building contractors and former cult members. It's a creative bunch and, with the exception of the rich summer people who build trophy homes in the valleys that radiate out from town, it's a place where no-one has ever had much money. Most of us live in one- and two-storey houses on small lots in town. Old railroaders' houses like the one I bought. Mine was built in 1903, and hadn't had anything much done to it since they put the indoor plumbing in sometime in the forties. It's a small house on a town lot that I bought for a number of reasons, chief among them the five-foot clawfoot tub, and the well-used vegetable plot that took up half the back yard.

I was lucky enough to get to hang around Gary Snyder when I was at UC Davis, and Snyder's advice to us wasn't about poetry, well, not directly. Gary told us that if we wanted a creative life, we should find someplace cheap to live, where a person could afford to buy and pay off a house. Cheap housing attracts artists, he said, so chances are you'd wind up with interesting neighbours, and if you had a place to live you wouldn't have to go teach in places you didn't want to be. You'd have your freedom.

And that's what I was aiming for when I moved here. I'd been living with my brother for four years, a roommate arrangement that had worked out so well we thought we'd better break up before we wound up like one those pairs of spinster siblings you used to see sometimes out in the country near our grandmother's farm. The ones in the white farm-house they'd been raised in, still sleeping in their childhood bedrooms. In the four years we'd lived together we'd both found better jobs and had repaired some of the anxiety we had about domestic life. We'd been raised in a world of unstable alcoholics, the kind who pick a fight whenever they're feeling existentially itchy. By teaming up, we'd figured we could practise domestic life on one another, see if we could figure out how to live in a house with another person you love without screaming fights or tears of recrimination. That we'd done it and had righted our little ships, both financially and emotionally, was a major accomplishment. But it was time to move on. Time to take those skills and go find real partners. And so when my manager agreed to let me telecommute, I went looking for a house I could afford, and since I wasn't tied to the Bay Area anymore, a house I could afford back in the Rocky Mountains I loved.

Pretty quickly, things fell into place and I found myself in possession of a mortgage and the keys to a small bungalow in Montana. I packed the cat and computer and boxes of books into my Honda, and arrived three days ahead of the moving van. That I'd been able to not only buy a house, but could afford a moving van felt miraculous to me. We'd moved every 18 months or so growing up, renting U-Hauls or borrowing horse trailers. Despite having managed to get a mortgage, purchase a house and arrange for a moving van, I still felt that first night, setting up the inflatable mattress in my empty house, that I'd broken in, that any moment someone was going to burst through the door and shout at me to leave.

The first year went pretty well. Patrick, my brother, wound up moving here after me, having been laid off from his job just as I was leaving California. I got a dog, and built raised beds in the existing vegetable patch, and made friends. Patrick found a cheap apartment on the other side of town, took up with his first girlfriend in ages, and set about building himself a niche running events and helping with wedding planners, work he'd done since his teens. We were settling in. At his birthday party in early September he made a sentimental speech to our new friends, thanking them for taking us into their lives, saying he'd never had such a happy year.

On 28 September that first year I lived here, on a beautiful, blue-sky, golden sunshine autumn day, I was in the hammock strung between my apple trees when the Assistant Coroner of Park County Montana walked through my front gate. I got up to see what the dogs were barking about only to meet this big man, taking off his feed cap as he saw me, who put one enormous hand on my shoulder and said, 'Ma'am. There's no good way to say this. There was a car accident last night. Your brother is dead.'

Time stopped.

The world as I knew it ended that day, and while a new life has taken root, it is not at all the same. It is a replacement world.

Patrick dying was the one thing I had feared above all others. It was like being simultaneously orphaned and widowed. Our divorced parents are unreliable at best, our youngest brother had died as a toddler, and we had survived it all together. We were less than two years apart, and in every photo I have of us, from earliest childhood until the end, one of us has an arm around the other. I'd gone from the oldest of three, to being the big sister, to being an only child. In losing Patrick, I lost the one person on this earth who loved me absolutely, whose faith in me was unshakeable. Without Patrick, it took me a very long time to piece together some kind of identity, and even now, 13 years later, it feels false, because he hasn't been here to see it.

It was terrible, and I survived it in large part due to the tender ministrations of the town of Livingston. 'If you're going to have a disaster,' I tell people when the story comes up, 'you want to have it here. Everyone came, and they stayed.' My house filled up that first night as word got out. They got me through a funeral, and saw that I was never left out. I had people to go to Happy Hour and dinner with on Fridays, and they took me in for holidays, and some, like my friend Jennifer, occasionally walked in my front door that first year or so and said, 'No really, how are you?' My best friend had twins (after a terrifying pregnancy), so for a couple of years there was always a screaming baby to tend, and her two big girls needed an auntie as much as I needed kids to take care of. I was taken in by a tribe of people, people who became my new family, people who I love with all my heart. And yet.

When I say the world stopped, I mean that I have a very strange relationship to time now. There was my life until 2003, a life that hummed along and things changed and I moved from place to place and attended schools and published a novel and got a job and eventually moved to Montana. My story kept unfolding. And then Patrick died, and it feels in some weird way like my story ended. However, I'm still here.

To compare my personal loss to the avalanche of loss that is heading our way as a planet would be unbelievably callow, and yet there are things you learn when you lose the person you thought you could not live without that seem germane. For one thing, the surprise at still being alive. You have to figure out how to live in this diminished world. You have to figure out how to go on after the fourth, or seventh, or 15th time you pick up the phone to call the person who is no longer here. Those first months after Patrick died, I remember thinking, 'Forty years? Fifty years? I have to live like this for *how* long?'

The literature of climate change is mostly of the apocalyptic variety. There will be a disaster and then it will ALL END. But if there's anything I have learned in these intervening years, it's that it doesn't end. You're still here. The sun comes up. The apple trees bloom in the spring, and the garden needs planting, and the children you love will keep growing and even, eventually, you might be lucky enough to meet someone who loves you and who doesn't mind when you spend the first three or four years telling him stories about your dead brother, and who you love back even though you find it inconceivable that you're spending your life with someone who didn't know Patrick, and who Patrick will never know.

Apocalyptic stories are sexy in their drama. The end of the world as we know it will be big and dramatic and everything will change, and we will be living in some mythical landscape where we'll be freed from all the boring conventional aspects of our daily lives. My instinct, however, is that this is not how things are going to unfold. More likely it'll entail the slow chipping away of things we're accustomed to, changes like our fruit trees dying. We had a frost three years ago, a freak freeze in October that killed every cherry tree in town. We didn't find out until spring, when they didn't come back. Here in Montana we get much of our fruit in the summer from Utah. Orchardists will drive up and set up roadside stands where they sell raspberries and plums and currants and peaches. Beautiful peaches. They were late this year, and my first thought was, 'Is this it? Is this the year they don't come? Is this the year we'll look back on and say, "Remember when there were peaches?"'

One reason I'm such a fanatic about the clothesline is that, like clearing the table after dinner and doing the dishes in the sink with soap and hot water, hanging your wash on the line keeps you in actual physical contact with the world. You have to touch each piece and in doing so you can see which t-shirts are wearing thin, which socks have holes in the heels, which trousers are getting worn in the knees. It is this physical contact, this clearing up of messes that I think is at the root of the peculiar hostility toward clotheslines that has taken root in those neighbourhoods where clotheslines have been forbidden and even outlawed.

For two or three generations now we've been told by the culture that success is measured by the distance we can put between ourselves and the physical acts of both making and cleaning up. I know perfectly competent grown people who cannot cook themselves dinner, who rely on restaurants or make a sandwich, who have no idea how to do something as simple as roast a chicken. People rely on clothes dryers and dishwashers. We hire cleaners for our houses. We hire gardeners to mow our lawns. We sometimes have to hire people to raise our babies so we can continue to work at jobs we might love, or just need in order to bring in the money we require to keep the machinery of consumption humming along. We rent storage units where we put the stuff we worked all those hours to buy but that no longer fits in our houses.

That my household chores are largely physical in nature – hanging out wash, cooking dinner and then cleaning the dishes, mucking out a chicken coop, tidying the garden to get ready for winter – marks me as old-fashioned and an outlier. I don't live in a city, or even a particularly large town. I cook all my own meals, in part because our town is so small that there aren't cheap takeout places. I work at home so I don't have a commute anymore. I'm already a throwback, to the extent that when I visit folks 'out there' I do find the noise and pace and sheer amount of disposable trash of modern life a little disorienting.

What I learned when my brother died and left me here alone is this: it is in taking care that we can save ourselves and others. Nina's twins, with all their mess and screaming those first few years (and they were screamers, those two), that's what saved me. Having something useful to do. Something immediate. The baby cannot sleep without being held, and there are two of them. So days we spent, on Nina's big white sofa, watching Barefoot Contessa reruns and trying to get those girls to sleep. What I learned is that the garden can save you, because it doesn't give a shit if you're having a freaked out, weeping kind of a day. It's spring and things need planting, or it's the end of the season and snow is coming and if you don't get the tomatoes in and taken care of the whole summer will have been a waste. And so you do it. You find a rhythm in the physical world that carries you through, because the bottom line is that you are not dead. You are still living on this earth, and there are days of stupendous beauty, even in the midst of unbearable sorrow.

And so, because I love the world, even in its diminished state, I hang the laundry outside. I hang laundry and refuse to use my clothes dryer. I bought a tiny, efficient little car. I grow food in my backyard and put it up in jars for the winter and I've pretty much stopped flying on airplanes. I know that these actions, taken as an individual, are not going to slow down the changes we see happening. The freak frost that killed the cherry trees. The fish parasite that bloomed in the Yellowstone River this summer, when the river was at its lowest-ever recorded flow, when the water was hotter than it had ever been and so a parasite bloomed and thousands upon thousands of fish died. So clear was the danger that the state banned our sacred sport, fly fishing, for a month. Which was unprecedented. For the 14 years I've lived here I've watched that rusty brown creep across the mountains as the pine beetle kills off the trees and, more years than not, there are no chanterelles or boletes in the fall, not even up high in the mountains, because the late summer rains didn't come.

But I hang my wash on the line, and grow vegetables in the backyard, and love the girls I'm helping to raise even when they turn into terrible teenagers who are acting out in the most ridiculous ways possible. Because I'm still here.

Apocalyptic stories about of the end of the world are sexy, in part because they allow us, in much the same way as fantasies of past lives do, to cast ourselves as important players in grand historical dramas. They strip us of boring domestic chores. They set us free from our stuff and give us a blank slate with which to start over. However, I think our job is going to be more complicated than that. My hunch is that we're not going to get a big, sexy, end-of-the-world do-over. What we'll be faced with is more ordinary. A series of diminishments. The loss of one thing we thought we could not live without, and then another, and then another yet.

Every so often, when someone mentions that something happened years ago, in say, 2011, I'll find myself startled at how far in the temporal past 2003 has slipped. For me, it's still right here. The day the world stopped. The day that Mike Fitzpatrick, that big kind man who is himself dead now, walked into my side yard bearing the worst of all possible news. It's right there with me as I hang wash in that same side yard, dresses and pants and shirts waving in our stiff winds, as the cottage roses and cosmos and hollyhocks wave back. We might all be living in the end times, living in the aftermath, but we are still living.

CAROLINE ROSS

Made and Unmade

A pre-1066 drawing kit

Two years ago I bought a copy of Paul Kingsnorth's *The Wake*, set during Saxon resistance to the Norman Conquest. The book spurred me to research materials from that era, often entirely natural things that I could source locally. In pre-Norman times women's crafts were mostly fibre-based – weaving, dying, stitching – and rarely would have outlived the woman herself. Most art was made within the monastic environment, for an ecclesiastical or noble audience. In subverting this, and in creating my 'shadow-making basket', I find a path through experiments to leave traces on vellum and paper. As I learn how to make everything I need, I find nothing is wasted: by-products become raw materials, mistakes become solutions.

Most importantly, my 'new ancient' materials do not pollute the planet. Originally all tools and materials came from the earth, returning to it when no longer needed. Handled well, wood, gesso, oils, egg and simple pigments have lasted over 500 years; ochres on cave walls have lasted 50,000. Such longevity contrasts starkly with art created from modern plastics or video screens; the materials may never biodegrade, but the art they constitute breaks down very quickly.

For rich blacks I boil up Welsh oak galls with rusty nails to make ink for use with goose-feather quills. For coloured paints I crack an egg, whip the whites and wait for the liquid to settle underneath; mixed in a mussel shell with the ground earths it makes glair, a wonderful paint, famously used in illuminated manuscripts.

Making drawings for a new edition of *The Wake* I'll be using green earths from the Lake District, yellow sinopia from Oxfordshire, red ochre from the Forest of Dean. This is not an elaborate re-enactment. There is a way to make my marks in the context of a beloved and beleaguered Earth, which I do not wish to harm further.

CAROLINE ROSS Made and Unmade
Natural colours, tools, containers and works in progress

TANJA LEONARDT Angel of the Old Factory
Former textiles factory, Kulen Vakuf, Bosnia

Twenty-five years after the last Bosnian war, the BEBI Art and Community Centre at Kulen Vakuf invited the artist Tanja Leonhardt to document the state of a former textile factory called 'Bebi Tricot'. The rooms had been abandoned in a mad rush in the face of approaching troops, and in the subsequent years were plundered and left to ruin. In 2014, the history of these events was still both palpable and unreconciled. This was a place which spoke, a storehouse bearing the harrowing testimony of a humanity which, in an endless circle of hope and violence, had reached rock bottom. Yet at the same time the whisper of nature, with her eternal offer of healing and renewal, could still be discerned.

KATIE CRANEY Feedback Loop
Silver leaf on hand-cut scrap metal

What are the consequences of surface colour and reflectivity? This question has loomed over my research, process, material choices, and how I live on the land. I spend hours at a small table under a north-facing window where two trees frame the left view. Below them, the land drops to a small inlet fed by a glacially carved fjord, connecting my view to the Pacific Ocean, ultimately lessening the isolation of where I sit. Surrounded by this landscape, I contemplate the dialogue between forest and ice, darkness and light, and how their albedo directly affects the survival of each.

MAIREAD DUNNE
The Last Fall
Photographic print and charcoal on paper

A Chinese philosopher once described the camera obscura as a 'locked treasure room'. A locked room perhaps points to the existence of other unexplored chambers and passages – a portal to another world. In order to gain the rite of passage, we must first enter the darkness of the antechamber. The passage from Darkness to Light. For Nietzsche, the key to the chamber conceals what should never be brought to light. And 'it would be dangerous to want to look through the keyhole – dangerous and impertinent.'

HAL NIEDZVIECKI

This Sad Little House

On mourning in America

It is better to go to the house of mourning, than to go to the house
of feasting: for that is the end of all men; and the living will lay it
to his heart.

– Ecclesiastes 7:2

We're in the midst of an unprecedented outpouring of public grief.
The 2016 US election unleashed a flood of despair. For those in the heart-
land who have been stuck in grief-stricken rage for at least the previous
decade, the despair is as familiar as apple pie: gay marriage, pot legalisa-
tion, socialised medicine, legal flag burnings, jobs to China – an indefinite
glooming of mourning in America culminating in their new president
publicly keening over a USA of 'rusted out factories scattered like
tombstones across the landscape'. Trump's victory marked the rise of a
new mainstream consensus – America disintegrating, despairing, divided.
Not surprising, then, that his inauguration, under a drizzle in front of
a desultory crowd, was more wake than awakening. His win did not
produce delight, but instead deepened the gloom and gave the previously
optimistic ranks of the bicoastals a focal point for their own emerging
narrative of grieving. Enter the Googlites, Manhattanites, and various
other incarnations of the pseudo-left techno-intelligentsia who once
believed in progress, and now believe in survival bunkers and info-
bubbles. And so here we are, an entire country sitting perpetual shiva,
their pre-ripped ties swaying gently as they croon kaddish for the antedi-
luvian good old days.

Though America remains a land of plenty and more than plenty, its
extraordinary expression of public misery is no accident. The grief has
been there all along, just waiting for some galvanising moment. Trump,
primal rambler through the age of disruption, displacement and so-called
innovation, was the catalyst for an uncovering and channelling. And

57

though the principle mourners seem to have little or no connection to each other, living as they do in different regions, tax brackets and realities, it's possible that they share more than it seems. Disparate, legitimate grievances and grieving processes connect to a larger whole. To paraphrase Descartes, we grieve because we are. Whether the different sectors, sects and affiliations can consciously articulate it or not, in some fundamental way they are all mourning for the same thing.

We mourn for our lost sense of community and civility, blown apart by the faceless state of cyberspace. We mourn for economic and social stability, displaced by technocratic, neoliberal adoption of the notion of disruptive 'advancement' at whatever the cost. We mourn for the ideal of progress, the increasingly hard-to-believe conception that we are moving forward and towards some great golden age of techno-enabled infinite possibility. And we mourn, most of all, for the collapse of the natural world, a lament which most of us, desperate not to implicate ourselves, channel into anger against corporations, governments, minorities, the poor or the rich, but which, ultimately, must be placed at the alligator-shod boots of humanity itself.

This inability to fully articulate our (interconnected) pain is at the heart of a deeper conflict. We struggle to articulate, let alone resolve, our grief because it is our collective failure to reign in our greed, to curb our inexhaustible hunger, that underpins it. Whether we are the Dakota Sioux standing up to another pointless pipeline, a Michigan hunter stalking absent moose in a landscape dotted with clearcuts, a California hiker kicking up the powdery silt of dried-up rivers, we mourn the land itself, though many don't or won't say it, largely because admitting what we are, or what we have been, is not something we have ever been much good at. Think Manifest Destiny. Think an exhausted, plague-ridden Europe outfitting cocky Columbus with three boats and a promised cut of the untold riches of the New World. Think roaming bands crossing the Bering Strait in pursuit of the big game that was hunted, over a short thousand years, into nothing but folk legends and museum curiosities.

The election and its ongoing narrative of public mourning shows that people are not just disappointed. They are bereaved. But they are also confused. Where do these feelings come from? What are they about? A tiny portal opened, and out poured a torrent. Can I, should I, talk about a grief that I've always been told was a set of disconnected *feelings* I would do best to repress? This matters more than it seems. If we can't grieve, if we feel like we aren't *allowed* to grieve, we end up at best depressed and bitter, at worst filled with rage, anxiety and the need to make that pain manifest in the world. But how to talk about something we've lost that we either can't bring ourselves to say, or can't quite will ourselves to know?

In the fifties, my grandparents and their counterparts, the Jews of North America, turned their backs on grieving. They turned away from memorials and memoirs. They sought to bury their own shame and guilt by declaiming that no-one wanted to talk about what happened, least of all the survivors of it. Why talk about it? What could be gained from going on about the six million, lambs to the slaughter? The result was the next generation, my parents and their peers. They did more than alright. They overcame the lingering anti-Semitism of the old order to take their place in the legacy of hardworking immigrants who came to places like New York and Montreal with less than nothing and departed the mortal coil with their names on diplomas, business empires, book covers, hospital wards and street signs.

And yet next-generation overachievement did not dispel grief. The Jews of the New World paid a price for channelling their grief into the material trappings of success. They have been besieged ever since by depression, anxiety, anger – much of it emerging from the unspoken demands of immigrant parents and grandparents demanding that their humiliation, hunger and poverty be redeemed. You can only suppress so much, push things so far under the surface. Though in my house it was never discussed, the Holocaust that claimed the lives of my grandparents' parents, brothers, sisters, cousins, teachers and rabbis lived like a brooding boarder in the corner room of our placid suburban manse. Today, it continues to shape our lives. Every member of my immediate and extended family has struggled with anxiety, depression, addiction. Tragedy resists truth-telling almost as much as it demands it.

The tragedy was too big to successfully repress. Eventually the Jews, and indeed the world, began to mourn. We mourned at first reluctantly and oddly through stilted sixties pop culture spectacles like *Fiddler on the Roof*, the musical, and *Anne Frank*, the movie, and then profoundly. We discovered and began to allow the universality of works like Frank's *Diary*, Victor Frankl's *Man's Search for Meaning* and Elie Weisel's *Night* (works that were at first ignored and are now considered some of the most important documents of the 20th century). We discovered ways to express our sorrow, collectively and personally. The cycle of intergenerational trauma, the passing on of repression, rage, guilt and shame, has only now started to be broken.

Collective trauma and collective mourning are not easy things to grapple with on a societal level. The trauma must be identified, recognised, and turned into a comprehensible narrative for a culture, or even a world, to mourn. The process is slow, and often doesn't happen at all. In Canada, where I live, the last ten years have seen attention turned to the hundred-year legacy of the white rulers of the dominion plucking native children from their families and sending them to what were then euphemistically called 'residential schools'. These were re-education prisons run by Catholic priests where the children were beaten for speaking their native languages, poorly fed, systematically sexually abused and so ill-tended that thousands of them died of disease. An apology by the prime minister, testimonials by survivors now in their sixties and seventies, lawsuits, documentaries, songs and comic books have created that collective space for mourning. The initial outpouring included not only the victims and their families, but also those who taught in the schools, and those who lived near native communities and stood as mute witness to the tragedy. This is collective grieving, and it brings people together in a way that nothing else does.

Is the Trump election going to bring disparate groups who never speak to each other – and, indeed, often claim to be anathema to each other – together? Will we link arms and put aside our differences, attend spiritually wholesome non-denominational wakes, shivas and new-wave decomposition ceremonies? Probably not. But that doesn't mean that we aren't closer to each other than we know. We have entered an extremely uncertain future in which all groups and demographics are motivated by a sense of mourning. On the surface, some mourn a past which never existed. Others mourn the death of a future of technological progress that was never more than a fantasy. Still others mourn the present in which we bury our noses in touch screens, focusing on a series of refracted branded selves that are as much of an existential threat to humanity as climate change and nuclear war.

But below that, there is the shared intensity of feeling, apolitical and shockingly deep. Formerly, there were few if any outlets for this shared feeling. Our society only allowed public displays of loss if they were harnessed to better days ahead courtesy of the emergence of stronger, more relatable, more marketable personal narratives. In other words: get over it, channel it, sell what you can sell and bury the rest in a spot you move on from as fast as you can. Alas, in today's world, it's harder and harder to move on. Though we might not all be willing to admit it, we can feel our backs pressing against the proverbial wall. Now, in the aftermath of an unprecedented election that uncovered long hidden truths, there is, at least temporarily, a new way to speak about where and who we are. Stop telling us to move on, goes the shared cry. We have nowhere else to go.

When we think of the modern world, we tend to think of technological advancement. We pick the arrival of a particular technology and argue that here was the moment when we entered the present, with its experts and comforts and strategies. The wheel, what turns the wheel, what the wheel turns. The steam engine, the combustion engine, the electric engine. The telegraph. The telephone. Computers, dirigibles, factories and their churning assembly lines; guns, planes, and more than anything else, our beloved automobiles. But a human-centric history tells a different story of the arrival of the modern world. It tells the story of the distance each new technology creates between individuals, between communities. It tells the story of a yearning for meaning that increases with each supposedly connective technology. Before wheels could bring us back to each other, they took us away from each other. The great 19th-century era of industrialisation, the throbbing heart of the supposed advancement of civilisation, also prefigured and oversaw the collapse of agrarian society and the large-scale, heretofore-unthinkable scattering of innumerable communities and families.

Each technological 'advance' allowed for and eventually demanded greater and greater separation. For the first time, we lived apart. For the first time, we worked not with but against each other. Modernity turned creature comforts mundane by ushering in an era of compulsive, consumptive technologies we cannot imagine living without today. Generally, we are not consciously aware of how separate we are from everyone else, not least because of all the stuff that surrounds us, filling those empty spaces before we have a chance to contemplate them. Today, the space between selves is something we have to struggle to notice, though it is a wider space than ever before in human history.

As we've often heard, nature abhors its vacuums. Since Freud gave name to it, psychological trauma has been understood as a condition that

Illustration for *The Little House,*
Virginia Lee Burton, 1942

takes advantage of void, however momentary. It is, if nothing else, an extremely opportunistic affliction. Something happens that makes it very difficult or perhaps impossible to stay attached, to remain in a stable orbit around what we know. For a moment, sometimes an extremely prolonged moment, there is a rupture, a sudden void of detachment. Into that void comes an inability to recognise ourselves as people in mourning and grief. The result is mental trauma, a cycle of suppression and fragmentation.

Our world is small. It is made up of those in our orbit, of the people who know us and the people we know. It is made up, centrally, of the people we are attached to, by blood, or community and shared conviction; the people we are supposed to love, and the people who are supposed to love us back. From this community of people, we develop our sense of purpose and meaning. If we are suddenly ripped from this community, or if, as in some cases, we are not born into or placed into such a community, we face the ongoing, very stark awareness of our aloneness. We face the awareness of gaps and cracks, the stuff of separateness, the stuff of the looming vacuum. Then comes trauma, in which we begin to doubt that there were or could ever be people who cared for us. The trauma comes because we cannot truly grieve. And so the void is filled – anxiety and then panic, terror, rage and ultimately nothingness; finally lassitude and distance, a shutdown of emotions, an inability to care anymore.

There's a picture book my five-year-old daughter dug up the other day, from where I have no idea, I'd never seen it before. But she told me that mommy had read it to her and that it was very very very beautiful and that she wanted me to read it to her also. And so I did. The book was called *The Little House* and it was written by Virginia Lee Burton and published in the early 1940s. In the book a house is happy in the country, watching the stars and the moon, anticipating the rise of the sun, the fluctuations of nature, the way things can change without ever actually changing. But then roads are built, dwellings arrive in adjacent lots and gradually the house discovers that it is now in the middle of the city. It is flanked by skyscrapers, fronted by train tracks, abandoned and forgotten. The house is miserable and misses what it has lost: fresh air, starry skies, changes of the seasons, children playing in a front lawn stretching into field and forest. It is a sad little house.

As you might imagine, the sad little house has a happy ending that looks increasingly unlikely to be replicated in our sad little world. Back then, unlike today, we could still imagine reverting to a time or place before inevitable 'progress'. All the same, even in early 1942, before the US had fully joined the Second World War, before the full brutality of industrial civilisation in the form of the Holocaust and Hiroshima had been put on display, the book clearly struck a chord. It was widely read at the time and remains in circulation today as one of the best picture books of any era. The story evokes emotions we could not and still cannot easily express. It suggests that since at least, and probably well before, the 1940s, we were already in mourning for something that had irrevocably been lost to us. Call it nature, or community, or the pre-industrial rhythm that evoked not the endless anxiety-ridden quest for progress but the calming, pre-literate belief in continuity; the sun comes up, day in and day out, people die and are born, day in and day out, the salmon run, the birds fly south then north, the snow comes, then melts, then comes again. Even then we mourned as a collective for the collapse of what the Spanish thinker Daniel Innerarity calls 'social certainty': the cultural knowledge that things would be the same the next day and the day after, the same as they were and are. Having been stripped of that, we are all sailing aimlessly downstream, without purpose, clinging to a diminished sense of place and purpose, deprived, even, of the most basic connection with the natural world.

Scientists are calling our age 'the sixth extinction'. Philosophers are dubbing our times 'the Anthropocene'. These are attempts to rationally assess and label the undeniable decline of the state of the planet during our lifetime. Buttressed as we are in the Global North by high-speed internet, 4G TV and all you can eat, it's hard to see that as the planet goes, so we go. But there are times when rifts appear in the cheery façade of positive marketing environments. Our grief streams through. The events around the Trump election have opened a fleeting moment of mainstream public mourning. Buffered, as always, by the awkward mawkishness of popular culture, the temptation is to look away from the mourners. Or better yet, tell them: move on, you got what you wanted; move on, you lost, deal with it.

But for once, let's not look away. Let's do as the Bible tells us: enter the house of mourning and linger there for a while. Let's take this opportunity to locate the paved-over streams of our own grief.

If we were to follow those streams, we'd find that they all flow from the same source. Perhaps we are not quite ready to put our great underground ocean of loss into words. Perhaps we will never be ready. Perhaps it doesn't matter, not if we can acknowledge the shared grief inside all of us. This isn't just to help us mourn. It's to help us beat back the tidal wave of trauma by expressing – to each other, to our children – a heretofore all-but-inexpressible sentiment. Let's take this rare opportunity to stare unstintingly over the wreckage and into each other's eyes. We might see each other as we are, vulnerable and sad, displaced, disrupted, yet guiltily clinging to the human routine in our little house shadowed by Trump's towers. What if we find a way to come together? Let us gather on the trampled grass of our tiny backyards. Let us turn our muted howls into a new litany sung under the smoke and smog and spotlights of the night sky.

DAMIAN VAN DENBURGH

What's Real and What Truly Matters

Peace. Or something like it.

Lydia was in her kitchen drinking tea, the world outside at bay for the moment. Cyrus' door was closed, his light off, the TV too. His meds were laid out, the coffeemaker set. The same routine, going on three years now. Lydia had moved past resenting the task, how it always fell to her even though Cyrus was Tommy's father. Because once Tommy left, who else was there to do it? Who was there to even notice?

She'd had to switch to a farmer's schedule when he moved in with them just to get a wedge of time to herself in the morning, and she'd kept that schedule, clung to it really, the only time in any given day where she didn't feel the tug of somebody else's need. At this hour, she could be nothing to no-one.

Free. Or something like it.

Lydia put her mug down and looked over at her fuzzy, ageing mutt, Emma, who stood panting and smiling. Emma shambled over and Lydia pulled her in.

'Okay, babygirl,' she said. 'Let's get going.'

Lydia stood and downed the rest of her tea. She swung her jacket over her shoulders like a toreador, snatched up her keys and her pamphlets and pushed through the front door.

There was work to be done.

'You sure you need to be here?'

It was Deputy Morris again, the one who'd arrested Lydia six months earlier for, of all things, solicitation. It took serious work for her not to stare at his Dudley Do-Right hat, so she focused instead on the strap wedged into his chin.

'If they're still putting those wells in, then yes. If you need me to move over a little I'll be happy to.' Lydia took a half step back from the entrance to the parking lot.

'No, you're fine. I just... It's over.'

'Not yet,' Lydia said.

Tad Gurlick's pickup pulled in and slowed to a stop behind the deputy.

'Tell me you're arresting that dumb bitch,' he said.

'Fat chance, cowboy,' Lydia yelled over the deputy's shoulder.

'Mr. Gurlick, please,' Deputy Morris said. Tad gunned it into the lot, his tires squealing, an invisible banner of hate snapping in the air behind him.

The deputy turned back to Lydia and said, 'I cannot stay here all day. And I cannot protect you.'

'I'm not asking to be arrested again, if that's what you mean by protection.'

Deputy Morris blinked. 'Have it your way.' And he started to go.

'This isn't *my* way,' Lydia said, pivoting and tracking him. 'This isn't about me. This is for the people of this community who can't be bothered to stop and think long-term and really consider...'

But he was in his car and pulling away.

Lydia leaned down to Emma and stroked her bony head. Emma had been out here with her every Saturday for the last year and Lydia knew she couldn't have survived it without her. The angry men – always and only men – shouting threats from their car windows, framed like satanic puppets. The take-out trash they threw at her. The spit. Emma would bark at them and Lydia would stare the cowards down, Emma's leash wrapped tight around her fist.

Did she really think she could change anyone's mind? In her heart, yes. But the point she wanted to make was to remind people that they *could* say 'No'. That they didn't have to give in every time some smiling bullshit rolled into town with a new plan and a big chequebook. The Pinetop Mall with its half-empty, oceanic parking lot that Lydia stood at the entrance of every Saturday was the perfect cautionary tale. It radiated misery from its site in the middle of the Pine Brush Preserve. Half-a-million square feet of retail space, sold on the idea that it would create jobs, which it did – low-wage, service industry gigs with no growth or future, but yeah, jobs. The ugly thing was just an air-conditioned, dead-end mill for high school kids who needed money for cigarettes, gas, beer, and their shattered, smudgy phones. But building the mall required cutting down and clearing acres of preserve land. And once that had been accomplished, once that door was opened, every sniffing developer wanted in. A year after construction on the mall started, the mayor unbelievably approved the town moving its dump into the preserve. Right after that came a new housing development. By the time enough people started wondering if there was something at stake in giving up the land so easily, another housing project was already under construction.

Finally there were some protests. Two or three, even. And then they stopped.

Lydia got it. People had jobs, responsibilities, kids. People had hangovers. People didn't give a fuck. She knew because she had a job and responsibilities, too. She had a son, Alex, though he was gone these days. She had Cyrus, Tommy's father, who lived with her because Tommy couldn't bear to put him in a home after Tommy's mother died. So Lydia was dealing with all kinds of stuff, too. It was just that, as she saw it, if somebody didn't say *we won't stand for this*, they were signing away their rights to everything.

When the fracking plans were announced, she knew she wouldn't be able to stop the wells from going in, especially when so many people had already been approached and promised crazy money for selling off their property. But she knew she'd have to try.

Did they really need to drill so close to the tributary *and* the dam? Wasn't there supposed to be a safe-distance barrier in case something went wrong, the way something always did? And if she knew this, other people did too, right? Didn't that mean anything?

But jobs. Money. Security. Lydia got it. So okay. It wasn't her planet. She just lived on it.

Cyrus was smoking in the backyard when Lydia got home. She watched Emma lope out to him and nudge at his leg where he stood staring at the wall of trees along the property line. Cyrus pulled his leg back and turned away. Emma, unfazed by his rudeness, looked around once, sniffed the ground quickly and came back inside.

'I know, babygirl,' Lydia said, stroking Emma's ribcage and ruffling her fur. 'He's an old fart, isn't he? And you're a good girl.'

The backdoor slammed and Cyrus walked through the kitchen. 'Barely enough food in the fridge to make a goddamned sandwich.' He continued to his bedroom and closed the door.

Lydia checked the refrigerator. Bread, provolone, some smoked turkey just picked up yesterday, condiments. Everything Cyrus said he liked. There was juice. Milk for coffee. There were leftovers from other meals, all perfectly edible.

She closed the door.

Did he eat and just forget?

No, he needed to complain. To trail his powdery misery everywhere. Never mind that Lydia had *not* dropped his scowling self in a nursing home despite having ample temptation to do so, especially once his own son had left him in the dust. Never mind that even with Cyrus' social security checks coming in – which Lydia never touched – she provided food, clothing, and shelter. She took him for all his check-ups. She waited in the car for him during all his AA meetings while he no doubt complained about what a walking, talking 24/7 trigger she was to a room full of anxious people. Never mind all of that. Cyrus was a wretch, plain and simple. Nothing would be good enough, ever. And as long as she was willing to look after him, she had to accept everything that came with her decision, including the daily urge to accidentally hip-bump him down the cellar stairs.

Because she knew what the dreary truth was like in some nursing homes, where you sat, alienated, tolerated and terminally alone while the colour and flavour and soul drained out of you. Even a wretch like Cyrus didn't deserve that kind of treatment. At least not today.

Lydia walked into the living room and sank onto the couch.

She wasn't 'allowed' to call in to the women's shelter on the weekends to check in. The director had had to explain to her that some of the newer employees felt that their competence was being questioned when she did that.

'They're qualified health professionals, Lydia, just like you. You have to let them do their job and trust that they can handle it.'

'I know,' Lydia said, 'but if someone has a question—'

'Then they'll figure it out. You did once. They can too.'

So what was it this afternoon, this moment exactly, that was troubling her? Garden-variety loneliness? That seemed unlikely because she had Emma and her job – and even Cyrus when she got right down to it – to take up any slack. And even if she drove her co-workers a little nuts, Lydia felt accepted and valued by them. Maybe it was an accumulation of sadness and hurt and anger that had fused into a kind of ghost? That actually sounded plausible, if also ridiculous.

It wasn't like she was looking for a new relationship. Her plan from day one of Tommy's departure was to keep busy, keep moving. Try to get back some of the time she'd lost down the sinkhole of her marriage.

So probably it was Alex. She wasn't even sure where he was. Still in

Guatemala? He'd check in once his money got low, she hoped. Last she'd heard he didn't have a job or any sort of income. But that had been months ago. He was supposedly staying with friends. And he'd said in his last email that his phone was gone, lost or stolen in his travels, vanished into the big *whatever*.

It terrified her to think of him on his own somewhere and beyond her reach. She still hadn't made peace with that. Each day she felt worse and burdened with a growing sense of guilt. Because anything could go wrong. And, though she hated herself for it, he seemed a little dumb to her sometimes. Naïve. Whatever it was, she felt like she hadn't equipped him properly. Had she driven him away?

Lydia surrendered and lay down. She rolled on her side and picked up the latest issue of *Natural World* magazine from the coffee table, only because it was there. Tommy had bought a subscription about two years earlier and its annoyingly reliable monthly appearance in the mailbox seemed to be nearly menstrual in nature. She leafed through it, distracted.

Until she saw Tommy's face smiling out from a full-page ad.

Let experienced travellers Tommy and Piper take you to the beating heart of the countries and sites you need to see. We'll help you fully experience what's real and what truly matters. And we'll steer you clear of the clutter and consumerism – and all the earth-damaging waste – that come with package tours. If you're tired of toxic swimming pools, lethal golf courses, and overly air-conditioned rooms, come talk with us. We'll take you on a trip to the real world.

Lydia sat up. Well, god damn. He really did it.

He'd been talking this thing up for ages before the divorce, though of course he'd never said a word about Piper all that time. But why would he? What he *had* gone on and on about – when they were still talking, that is – was his *realisation* that rich people would be the only ones who could save the planet, and that if anyone really wanted to figure out a way to protect what was still alive and viable, they had to find a way to *reach the rich* and talk to them *on their level*. This load of bilge from a guy, Lydia fumed to herself, who in the early years of their life together had said that money wasn't as important to him as making a difference in the lives of people who needed help. And, chump that she was, she'd believed him.

Unable to stop herself, Lydia looked closer at Piper – her toned yoga body vacuum-sealed into her neon hiking gear, her credulous green eyes, her brunette hair pulled into a tight pony tail under a hot pink baseball hat. All told, about a decade younger then she had any right to be, and just beaming next to Tommy, the two of them glinting with sweat and shouldering what looked like weighty backpacks while standing on a boulder near the edge of a carbonated, white-water river.

They looked happy. She had to admit it.

She got up from the couch, gathered all the issues of *Natural World* that she could find in the house and plunged them into the recycling bin in the garage. Then she called her next door neighbour, Bonnie, the one other person who used to protest with her before she simply got tired of trying, and invited herself over for coffee.

On the way out the door, Emma slipped past Lydia and began padding across the lawn. Emma liked to wander and had been doing it for years without a complaint from anyone. A ravine divided the neighbourhood they lived in and Emma and a few of the other dogs from around the way tended to confine themselves to it. Lydia wasn't worried about what she'd get up to. Watching her trot away, she even felt a pang of envy. 'Have fun, babygirl,' she said quietly.

It was dark by the time she got home. Lydia hated daylight saving time for the feeling of loss it kicked up in her.

She could hear the television through Cyrus' closed door as she knocked.

'Can I come in?'

The volume dropped and she opened the door.

'You need a ride to your meeting tonight?'

'Not going,' he said to the television.

'You feeling okay?'

Cyrus didn't move.

'Are you hungry?'

'No.'

Something was off. She walked closer and looked down at him. He returned her look, his face pale, his eyes wide behind his glasses. Lydia saw that his hands were trembling in his lap.

'Is everything all right?'

He swallowed. 'I'm scared.'

'What's wrong, Cy?'

'I don't feel right. Something is different.'

She felt his forehead. No fever. She knelt down and looked in his face. He'd been a handsome man when he was younger, which had been passed on to Tommy. The good looks were still there, but battered, lost to hurt and diminished expectations.

'Can I get you anything?'

'Tommy's not coming back, is he?'

She wondered if he'd seen the magazine. 'No, I don't think so.'

Cyrus clutched her hand with surprising strength. 'Will you watch TV with me?'

Lydia sighed. 'Of course, sweetie.'

She'd never called him that before. Ever.

She came around and sat next to him on the couch.

When it came time for dinner Cyrus said he just wanted to sleep. Lydia left him and went to the kitchen to make a sandwich. And that was when she realised that Emma hadn't come home. Grabbing her hoodie, she set out walking through the neighbourhood.

The night air was crisp with wood smoke. Nobody was out and half the homes she passed were dark. She called Emma's name, trying not to wake anyone up. But, as she continued walking and not getting any response, she stopped caring and began to yell.

To her left, a light splashed on and a door opened.

'What's going on?'

'Hey, I'm sorry,' Lydia said. 'I'm looking for my dog.'

A silhouetted woman came down her slate path and stopped at the edge of her lawn.

'It's a little late.' She took a drag off her cigarette and blew smoke to the side. Lydia caught a look at her. It was a face she recognised from the neighbourhood, but nobody she knew.

'Sorry. She's usually in by now.'

The woman was staring at Lydia, not giving anything away until something broke across her features, a kind of loosening that settled into judgment.

'You're from the mall.'

Based on the appraising look she received, Lydia was made to understand that this woman in her pyjamas with her nicotine-haunted breath was not a friend.

'So I guess you haven't seen her?'

'Why do you keep going out there and doing that?' the woman asked.

'Those wells are built. I got a couple friends who made a killing on that.' She took a drag on her cigarette and exhaled through clenched teeth in a shivery way that sounded like a laugh.

'Well, that's great for them, I'm sure,' Lydia said. 'I'm just trying to find my dog.'

The woman stared at Lydia and said nothing.

'However,' Lydia said, 'if you want to talk about the killing that's *really* happening, you can always come out and join me next Saturday. I'll be there all day.'

'Yeah,' the woman said. 'Look, I haven't seen your fucking dog so why don't you take it somewhere else before I call the cops on your ass.'

Lydia walked off, feeling the woman staring at her back. She took the long way home, hoping that Emma would come jaunting up to her out of the dark, her tongue lolling from her shiny black lips, her coat freckled with the lacy remnants of crushed leaves and smelling like the woods and the earth and the night.

Come back to me, little girl, Lydia whispered to herself all the way home.

Lydia upholstered her neighbourhood with flyers, tacking them up inside shops and grocery stores, stapling them onto telephone poles, taping them to electrical transformers, bus stop shelters, library bulletin boards. After some wheedling, she even managed to post one where she worked despite the fact that the board there was reserved for information about vocational and housing services available to women in crisis.

Nobody responded.

Each night after making dinner for Cyrus and making sure that he was okay, she went out in her car and trolled the neighbourhood, making ever wider circles and sweeps but still coming up with nothing.

Four days after Emma went missing, Lydia got a call.

A dog had been found in a field. Buckshot was embedded in her chest and side, and she had a hole in her skull from what was probably a .22. The chip traced Emma back to Lydia. Did she want to come and get her?

Lydia said she'd be right over.

They didn't tell her over the phone that Emma had also been beaten. That she'd been broken down to a heap, her muzzle scored with a deep gouge.

Lydia gently lifted Emma's ruined body from the gurney and carried her out to the trunk of her car. She took her home. Cyrus helped bury her in the backyard.

That night after Cyrus had gone to bed, Lydia bought herself a pint of scotch and a pack of cigarettes, and stood out in her backyard and tried to get drunk. The few long slugs she took made her gag and left her weak and sweaty and shivering. Twenty minutes was all she could take.

She walked to the edge of her property, gently dropped the flask and the cigarettes over her neighbour's fence, then stumbled inside her house and collapsed on her bed. She called in sick to work the next day, a first.

That Saturday, she stood outside the mall parking lot with a sign that read:

WHICH ONE OF YOU
COWARDS
KILLED MY DOG?

Nobody stopped. Nobody looked at her or said a word, including the sheriff, even though she stood there all day until it got dark.

'Hey, Mom.'

It was Alex. Finally. Lydia sprang out of bed and stood in the cool air of her bedroom, shadowboxing with her twisty bathrobe sleeves.

'Sweetie, where are you?'

'I'm in Lee.'

'What's that?'

'Lee. In Massachusetts.'

Her mind was still playing catch-up, the gears still slipping. 'Oh. Right. Okay. Well, how are you? Last I heard you were in Guatemala.'

'Yeah, I know. Sorry.' It was clear from his tone that he wasn't. 'I'm here with Dad.'

Lydia chose to ignore that information for the moment.

'Is everything all right?'

Alex laughed. 'Yeah, everything's chill. I'm living here now. I just got back a day or two ago.' There was a pause and then Alex asked, 'Are you okay?'

'Everything's fine, sweetie. It's just so nice to hear your voice again. But wait, back up a sec. You're living with your father?'

Alex laughed again. 'No. I'm just crashing here until I get a place. But I am working with him.'

Lydia experienced a mild psychic tremor and exhaled.

'You want to tell me about that?'

And that was when she heard how Alex had been *hired* by Tommy to ferret out any cool, off-the-beaten-path spots that could be slotted into the ever-growing TeePee portfolio. Tommy, as it turned out, had been funnelling money to Alex for months, courtesy of Piper and the trust fund that had come to her when she hit 35. Last year. So the plan now was for the three of them to make a new family, one structured around work, with Alex the location scout, Piper (how Lydia hated that name) the money behind the franchise, and Tommy the front man, the friendly face, leading the mega-wealthy into the raw, untouched piece of paradise they could grab for themselves before it was too late.

'Gee Alex,' she said, 'that sounds great.'

'I'm so stoked, Mom,' was her son's depressing answer.

While they talked, Lydia paced and turned. The more awake she became, the more she wanted to smash something, to scream loud enough to turn her son back into a decent person. The more she wanted to just fall into a hole in the ground and curl up there and die.

And then she had to get ready for work. Or so she said. But really, she just needed to sit down and not be somebody's caretaker for half a second.

In the silent and sudden wake of hanging up, it occurred to Lydia that she was tired of being a mother. Tired of the tearing at her spirit. Tired of being hurt and being the one to dish out the hurt by *having to* care. Tired of sending love out of her heart – when it wasn't being sucked out or siphoned off or shunted – and having it land nowhere and never make a difference.

She was only 47 years old. She had no business being tired like this. But she was exhausted.

Lydia went to her bathroom to take a shower. She took off her robe and looked at her naked self in the mirror.

She'd let too much time go by since she'd done anything like this. Too long since she'd seen a forgiving face looking back at her. So yes, she'd been thin once. So what? The thin young woman she'd been then was full of ideas, many of them wrong. And so what to that? She'd had to let go of it all. You have to let go of everything, Lydia thought. Your family, whatever ideas of control you might have that make you feel secure, your routines, the things you love. The planet. You don't own any of it and none of it needs you. You float along on the surface of things all your life and then disappear. And anyone who remembers you now, who might think about you once in a while, won't last much longer than you will, and they'll take the last scraps of you with them. So, what matters, really?

Go ahead and pick something. Anything. One's as good as another.

She looked at herself again.

Leave me alone, she said.

On the other side of the wall, she heard Cyrus' door open. She heard him shuffle into the kitchen, heard the coffee pot get lifted and then replaced on the warmer. Heard the soft bark of a chair leg as it scraped against the kitchen floor.

At the sound of it, Lydia thought of Emma and felt pain gouge through the centre of her.

She couldn't do this anymore. She had to leave. Everything. Everyone. Staying there was killing her but without the oblivion of dying.

She turned on the hot water and let it run while a cloud of steam enveloped her.

The night shift was fine with her.

It was unpredictable – some nights quiet, relatively speaking, some nights chaos. She'd come to recognise, if not really know, many of the folks who cycled through. The 'chronic inebriates' as they were called, picked up from the season's increasingly cold streets where they were usually found passed out between parked cars, curled up in the doorways of closed shops, or in ramshackle tents tacked up in the woods, just yards from a shopping plaza with a liquor store; filthy, wheezing and, more often than not, insistent that they were not drunk, that they were fine, that they didn't need anything or anyone. Until they got in somewhere warm, where there was food and a bed for them to pass out in. Then, come morning and breakfast, they were released back to the streets to do it all over again. Because nobody could stop them, only hope to catch them each time they fell until they decided to either change their lives or die, done in by their drug of choice, the unforgiving cold of winter, or both.

The homeless population, made up in the majority by native Alaskans, was huge. And it wasn't uncommon when she was working with a client that Lydia would get hit with a look that seemed to say, 'Why the fuck is another white person getting in my face on our land and telling me what to do?'

But if you saved one person out of fifty – and those were the odds on a good day – it was worth it.

As for Anchorage, well, she was still trying to figure it out. The few people she worked with who bothered to ask her anything about herself dismissively pronounced her moving there a *geographic cure*. And they were quick to add they'd seen too many people like her roll into town and then just as quickly slink out with their tails between their legs. Every day some new, clueless Christopher McCandless popped up, itching to go off the grid and get back to a more authentic, pioneer-type of existence; to become, in many ways, and despite their best intentions, a cliché. Lydia had seen that the streets of her new home held scores of white men driving pickups and brandishing Maori-style tats and grizzly beards, dressed in their blocky cold weather gear and clearly digging the manly figure they cut. But she didn't mention this observation to anyone.

In fact, Lydia had already picked up on that last-ditch element in the atmosphere of Anchorage. She was aware that, statistically speaking, it wasn't a safe place for women. But where *that* mythical place might actually be, she still didn't know. Eventually she'd need to get a dog – for protection and companionship – but she wasn't up to it yet.

What she had discovered in her time here – what comforted her – was that wherever she went, nobody wanted to know about her, particularly since she was new in town. She was a permanent outsider, identifiable at a glance. And being a middle-aged woman from out east who was divorced and working in a homeless shelter on the night shift made her as good as invisible, a state of post-being that required no effort to maintain.

If she looked at her situation in a particular way, she came to the conclusion that she was here to drive her own back against a wall so that she'd have no choice but to take another step. To find a way out and into somewhere else.

But beneath all the practical, boot-strapping propaganda she fed herself just to get out of bed most mornings, she felt shattered in a way she'd never felt before.

In the meantime, she worked and kept her head down. Made her weekly calls to Cyrus, to check in. Physical distance had opened something between them, some channel of fondness that it seemed had run between them all along beneath the patterns they'd locked into when they lived together.

'You don't need to call every week, Lyd,' he'd say. 'I'm fine.'

'I'm calling because I want to, Cyrus.' And it was true.

He'd agreed to go into a home, much to her relief. And Tommy, or rather, Piper, had agreed to cover the expenses. Anything to avoid contact.

Lydia could still hear what Cyrus had said when she told him she was moving to Alaska.

'Good. Get out of this place. And don't look back.'

Who knew he'd felt that way? And why had this variety of kindness emerged between them only at the end, once it couldn't be sustained in real time?

Questions were Lydia's enemies these days, and she did what she could to avoid them. But sometimes they got through anyway.

She wasn't supposed to but Lydia checked her personal email one night at work and saw that Alex had sent her something with the subject line, 'Home'. She opened it and saw a link to a video and immediately closed it. She'd have to look at it later. But knowing it was there haunted her for the remainder of her shift. What did *home* mean at this point, with her and Tommy on opposite coasts and Alex off roving again?

She got home as the sun was cresting the horizon. She ran inside and made herself a cup of tea to warm up. Then she went to her computer.

There was a new email from Alex, with a subject saying READ THIS FIRST!!

And that was where Lydia found out that the dam had burst back home near the fracking wells. The dam flooded the nearby tributary and sent the two sources crashing into town. She read that there was a concern that waste water had mixed in, that the streets were filled with hazardous waste water, and there was worry about the safety of the drinking water. Low-level tremors had been picked up but not really reported on during the drilling of the wells, and the article suggested that the dam had burst from being weakened by those tremors. Countering these statements, a spokesperson for the fracking concern said that while what had happened was indeed unfortunate, there was no link between the drilling of the wells and the subsequent disaster. Safeguards against such things were a standard consideration and a built-in part of the procedure.

Lydia stopped reading and clicked on the link in the other email.

The video opened in mid-air, shot from a hovering camera like in a helicopter but without sound or a plummy voice-over to describe the flooded town below, the wide brown ribbons that lay flat and smooth over the streets. Lydia thought she was looking at a photograph it was so still until she noticed that the surface of the water reflecting the off-screen sun was rippling as it rolled and flowed around cars and street signs.

The visual moved somehow, a quick tilting upward that took in more of the horizon while it remained stationary, as if it were shot from the back of a dragonfly. Then the image lowered itself, sinking smoothly like an elevator, coming to a gentle stop about a foot above the water's surface, and began to move forward, slowing and circling curiously as it approached the odd abandoned car in the middle of the street – this one with a trunk left open as if someone had grabbed something crucial and run off in a panic, that one almost completely submerged, not much more than a beige hood looking like an exposed kneecap – before continuing.

The movement was the meaning of it. The searching was the story. It was a serene vision that sought disaster – the hoped-for corpse floating over the intersection, the child trapped and screaming through the fogged windows in the waterlogged car – and that took its serenity from know-ing it would not be responsible for anything it found. It could see and record and share and then float away. Free. And it was compelling in a way that sickened Lydia but that also demanded she continue watching.

She had no idea what was doing the looking. But if felt alive to her whatever it was, felt like some kind of floating consciousness.

Then she realised. It was a drone.

The drone moved forward now, picking up speed, but as it moved it pivoted, following the invisible contours of some kind of seeking logic, heading first west then pivoting again and veering south only to turn east again, defining a broad curving arc without a destination point, occasion-ally floating up to a higher altitude then back down to near the surface of the water.

It felt to Lydia like a ghost. A spirit looking for something it couldn't remember.

When the video ended, back at the water's edge where it shallowed out at the sneakered and rubber-booted feet of a cluster of people, one of whom was operating the drone, Lydia froze the frame, and tried to see if there was anyone there she recognised. But there wasn't.

Then she watched it again. And again.

There was no vindication in what she felt, no *I told you you'd be sorry* attitude. If anything she felt crushed by the flood, the damage it brought, the waste. Any lingering thoughts of that place still being a kind of home for her, even just as a memory, the flood had swept all of that away.

There was nowhere to go back to. And it wasn't until the option was gone that Lydia realised she'd been holding on to it as a remote possibility. The final last-ditch place.

The feeling started coming back to her as she sat at her kitchen table watching the sun light up the windows. It was a feeling of despair, of hopelessness. Of accumulated loss – Emma, Cyrus, Alex, and even Tommy. Her former life. All of it gone. And her current life a flimsy replacement until something real could grow in its place.

She'd come this far in her life and she had nothing.

She sat with that for a minute or two. And then she felt it pass, leaving nothing in its wake.

She looked at her computer, at the video still there, frozen on an image of a place that wasn't a town anymore but a piece of the earth, a patch on a much larger planet. As she stared at it, the patch of earth changed to a thing that was really just taking care of itself. That was, as far as she could see, in the process of healing itself. Removing that which had disturbed it. Doing away with trouble.

The planet is going take care of all of us, Lydia thought. It'll take us back in when it's ready. Swallow us up. Strip us clean of our little troubles and worries and plans. Our greed. It will mulch us and replenish itself and start over.

Which, she realised with relief, meant that she *did* belong there. That she actually was needed after all. She served a purpose.

To disintegrate, to discorporate.

To become matter.

To matter.

GRAM JOEL DAVIES
Another Door Closes

GRAM JOEL DAVIES

Closure

We duck the Securicor lens and cast a sly light onto flakegreen radiators.
Embered beams cross a hall touched with arson. If this is how the world goes,
like a hospital built to the plan of an evening star, we arrived too young.

In its derelict heart we find a chapel filled with splintered pews. Now, here is
a room of framed beds and ringed curtains, ragged with echoes, a flower vase
tipped.

Through wired glass lies a blitz of battleship cabinets, a fly's flicker on patient
records. We wash the pastel bricks with our torches. Pads unfold, crayoned for
somebody's grandpa or niece.

Elsewhere, in cliques vested with power, there must be a man who dismantles
this institution ghost by ghost. Not us. If the State leaves corridors to despair,
we thrill for it.

Along the radials between clinics, let us paint that we were here, stepping out
over glass dust to a line of rusted wheelchairs, our names across the ward doors,
hyphenated by their swing.

TINA CARLSON

Fin Feather Bark and Skin

Truth be told, we live in the depths of an ocean of air.
Bottom suck the muck of our lives, rely on those with
bark to breathe. Palola worms are luminous at the surface
of waters. Wind roots for the girl who is storm-whirled
above the earth on the back of her horse, drops back down
still snug in the saddle. Herds of cows fly like geese in a
mackerel sky. Listen to the trees breeze about fall and you
too will rise up.

Come out, o you attic trunks and fire-tips! You saddle girls
and fog fish, potted plants, you sly worms making light!
We are drowning in our air ocean. Simmered to a boil,
punching holes in our sky, waging war with our kin.
What sleeve of snow can save us now?

BRENDAN BYRNE

Outside

A blur of grey and blue: late-'80s fabric, the kind that stands to your touch, sticks to the pads of your fingers. A collection of human legs, with scrunched panty-hose and billowing slacks, perpetually rearranging themselves like the slow, fluid bars of light which slipped through the window. Out there a wide, white, flat sky. It gnawed at the passengers' auras, consuming the personas they realised on their faces, leaving only a greasy residue. The unpeeling of cellophane wrappers, the crunch of baby carrots between kiddie molars, the hissing of freed CO_2, the indecipherable conversation of adults, couched in lingo, lazy diction, and impenetrable jokes. The noise washed over me like murky, milky sea foam, then settled down to soak in. Cigarette burns dotted the arms of the seats; discolourations bloomed between plastic windowpanes. Air vents spluttered and giggled, and the AC barely functioned. During midday the light was unbearable.

The train had personality, but it wasn't *alive*.

//

The inside of a cat.

In particular, an irritable, asocial ladycat with one fucked-up eye, met during a summer's visit to Belfast, Maine. (Nameless now; I didn't label the picture). Her ruffled white vest remains uncaptured, nor her tattered black trim, her comically oversized ears, or even that eye, but I have her, sneering in profile, her whole body cut away to show an interior occupied by a hustling, baroque collection of faceless globules. These thinglets teem down to her very paws, vying for space, but also ginning her up for locomotion.

Even at six, I knew cats didn't work that way.

//

Commuter rail, NE corridor. Very few business people took calls any-more, unless they were selling used electrical equipment or cocaine. Email had just meshed with texting, and human fingertips made no impact on touchscreens, they simply blessed them, as in a papal benediction. Earbudded college kids rewatched New Golden Age TV obsessively instead of trying to fuck each other in the bathrooms. If you worked best to musical accompaniment, as I did, whenever you unplugged you were subjected to a wash of blank sound: the rattling of plastic tile, the now-constant shriek of the air conditioning, the dull blast of the wind tunnel the train created around itself, the whine of the braking system. Physical details were decaying, as if they had been left out in the sun too long. Black mould in the air vents, chalky grey build-up under the sink handles, the undersides of armrests misshapen as if mid-melt.

Hunched into the wheelchair accessible seat, I rendered low-end luxury condos and rentals which would soon people formerly-abandoned post-industrial districts. These were not the truly singular structures, those featuring seasonal changes to the on-site arboretum, unique designs for every unit, frontages set back from picturesque side-streets. Rather, they were stacked glass cubes, with thoughtfully-designed, light-penetrated spaces, access to a courtyard feature or Juliet balcony. They would be located in mixed-use buildings, above an overbranded food-hall or a beer garden featuring nine-dollar drafts from nomad brew-eries. All these buzzwords had all been partially reshuffled from the last catalogue by a twenty-three-year-old with two hundred thousand-odd dollars of student debt, working eighty-hour weeks. I mirrored her in my craft, recycling old renderings, kidding along that I was remixing, helping to end postmodernism by grinding it up for its own ouroboros maw. My designs were technically correct, at least according to the specs I'd been fed by marketing experts (the ones who told architects what the buildings would look like).

Our branding campaigns strove for the same utter sameness as our competitors'. No-one cared, our product was going to move as long as the economy kept grinding along. Our customers had never known how to live, and we sure as hell weren't going to show them.

Its form came first, sketched out in this hushed car. Not from any observed arachnid. Bugs had stopped splattering windshields, crawling up the crevasse of your neck, or nestling in the unknown recesses of your apartment. (The rats had, meanwhile, refused to believe in this future, and thrived, for now.) Food source gone, spiders were next.

So my designs came from Saturday morning cartoons, and dusty memories of rented cabins in the Appalachians. They weren't Apple product smooth'n'sterile, pseudo-Swedish white heritage, or nth-punk DIY. My memories were *spiky*.

I showed them to Arthur, who showed them to Artur. Arthur said, 'It should pierce your neck with that *thing*,' but Artur was the one who'd already come up with a/G, he just hadn't known, previously, how to transmute it into an object.

//

'They suck flies dry,' my mother would tell me.

'Don't flies die real quick anyway?' I'd respond.

'One or two days is their normal lifespan,' she'd say then, patting the air above my head. 'But this way they're actually good for something.'

//

Spiders. They crawl over you, and they put themselves in you, and that lets you live in there, which isn't an actual any-where. 'Anti-genius,' Artur had written somewhere in first instantiation of a/G branding copy, 'An inversion of the god-to-man transmission of genius: the fabrication of an Outside by billions of new trajectories.' He did not write that these were escape trajectories, and that the web they would constitute would serve as a place to hang meat traumatised by reality.

//

The same plastic shell, the same stink of recycled shit. The cars trundled with the same lack of haste, caught the same holes in the track line, let off the same steel-on-steel sighs. The signage was faded, and the grey and blue of the seat coverings were now almost indistinguishable from one another. Windows bulged inwards like insectoid sacks. The plastic face of everything was now covered with a tawny penumbra.

The seats and bathrooms had been removed. In their place were oblong, seven-foot sepulchres with very little clearance between them, running from bleached-khaki to a sick shale grey. These casks were face-less, slightly warm and sweating, and featured no markings whatsoever. Beneath them several dozen thin white lines of tense fibre quivered faintly.

//

I can hear my mother saying, 'No one ever goes *out* anymore,' then laughing soft with her teeth and her cigarette.

//

The cars remain, involuble, filled with broken girders, masses of biode-gradable packing materials rotting sweetly, the occasional *tchotchke* some in the first generation attached to their casks before decoupling.

The train cars still move regularly, rarely coming to a halt; they *coast*. You can board them at a relatively slow jog, but old catching-out rules apply: miss and you get your legs crushed under the wheels. There's just no one left to help you once you're prone and squelching.

Nothing regulates, or challenges, your presence. I think this is what certain people's idea of a perfect society once was: total freedom in the absence of all other humans. But all those rebels have decoupled, quite willingly. The few who spend only a little time Outside (there are none, as far as I can glean, who spend none) pose no threat. Everyone and everything exists totally alone and totally connected; there is no nerve centre for anybody to firebomb, if anybody even knew how to fashion a firebomb anymore.

Through the grit-pitted and flame-puckered windows, you can see the night skies of thirty years ago, the skylines of twenty, which is how various resident entities have decided things should appear for the rest of existence. I've given up on trying to parse how much of this is an engineering of reality and how much is a gossamer veil.

The swamplands of my youth, once decorated with half-submerged shipping containers, interrupted by sickened little streams, and choked by browning scrubweeds, are now clean as post-operation abscesses. All has been moulded into indecipherability by machinations we can only feel.

I've gone back to drawn cats.

ALASTAIR MCINTOSH

The Apocalypse of Three Great Floods

The Outer Hebrides are a storm-tossed archipelago some 30 to 40 miles off the north-west of Scotland. I grew up on one of its islands, known as Lewis in the north and Harris in the south, in the sixties and seventies. I regularly go back on holidays, business or to see old friends and family. However, in 2009 I returned for a very different reason. For several years I'd been feeling the island's call. It had been tugging like an umbilical cord that ran beneath the sea. I therefore put aside 12 days to make a pilgrimage from south to north, the direction of the prevailing wind. With 20 kilos of camping gear, food and waterproofing, I walked across the island's 800 square miles, halfway between London and the Arctic Circle. I traversed mountains, bogs and moors that are devoid of all but ancient signs of habitation. For four consecutive days I went without meeting any other person. Finally, on the home stretch through the villages of the north-west, I mingled with the familiar faces of my childhood.

The northern Hebrides are a highly Presbyterian part of the world. The islands were overtly colonised under a state commission of fire and sword at the turn of the 16th to 17th centuries, and the introduction of Protestant religion was a part of that process. Vestiges of the elder faith managed to survive mainly in the southern Roman Catholic islands, where the beautiful old prayers and blessings were collected by the ethnographer Alexander Carmichael in his six volume *Carmina Gadelica,* 'The Hymns of the Gael'.

In our northern parts, the old habits of pilgrimage were stamped out, consistent with the austere theology of the 16th century Reformation. Luther had said that such a 'vagabond life' lay at the root of 'countless causes of sin'. My ruse, my cover story by which to give account of my own pilgrimage, was to mask one sin with another. I took a fishing rod. When we were young, fishing without permission (or poaching) was the one permitted 'sin' because the big landowners were never considered quite legitimate. If asked, I could tell enquirers that I was on a 'poacher's

ALASTAIR MCINTOSH
The Apocalypse of the Three Great Floods
Bothan beehive dwelling

pilgrimage', peregrinating from loch to loch. It would (and did) raise a smile, even if it failed to rise a fish.

In the Celtic world you think in threes, and I had three features of the landscape that I wanted to visit. First, the ancient *bothan* or beehive sheilings, from which we get the words 'bothy' and 'booth'. These were used into the early 20th century by maidens herding cattle when transhumance was still practiced. Next there were the holy or 'healing' wells. These were used into my own childhood. Even today there's old folks who'll go and take a furtive drink, as they'll say, 'for the health'. And finally, the 'temples' – the ruined chapels. All of these fell into disrepair after the Reformation, some of which tradition holds were built on Druid sites, and most of which are in spots of outstanding beauty. They are what would today be thought of as sacred natural sites.

While those features were the outer focus on the walk, inwardly I had another triune focus. I wanted to find space for reflection, as I came to sum it up to myself with only half a tongue in cheek, on 'God, war and the faeries'. No kidding. Let me explain. This was the island that gave birth to Donald Trump's mother. Its strict Protestant religion carries many layers of complexity and depth, but it was also used by landed power to colonise the soul. The same landowning family that evicted all four lines of Trump's mother's forebears from their ancestral lands, and provided the Barbados slave colony with its colonial governor, also brought in a hard-line evangelical ministry to Lewis in the 1820s.

At the time of making the pilgrimage, I was just back from speaking to NATO officers and diplomats in Geneva. War was very much on my mind, for I regularly lecture on nonviolence at military institutions across Europe. Afghanistan and Iraq were still smouldering. The island's religion – at its best and as it mostly is today – is one of lovingkindness, grounded in a deep cultural mysticism and with a radical history of land reform. At worst, however, it has been a vestige of the hellfire faith of authoritarian religion, obsessed with personal salvation and driven by imperialists. I wanted to explore the binary worldview intrinsic to its Calvinist creed, one that divides the world into the Damned and the Elect, a creed that also laid down tramlines in the Puritanism of colonial America. I wanted to examine the insights that such psychohistory provides into the type of evangelicalism that has shaped American neoconservatism. While my focus at the time was on the Bush family, the analysis comes into even sharper focus now with Donald Trump, the island's most distinguished disconcerting son. As I see it, the religious psychohistory of Trump's wall with Mexico finds its archetype in an inner wall projected outwards, that which results from a propensity for such authoritarian binaries as good state or bad state, with us or against us, nice or nasty.

At the risk of sounding ridiculous, what is the role of the faeries in this? Plenty of analysis of the state of the world wallows in what's wrong, but there is a lack of vision as to directions that might take us forward in our humanity. There is a failure of imagination, so imagination, and specifically the compassionate imagination, matters greatly. Faerie was the pre-Christian worldview on the islands, but one that never fully disappeared from the culture. Faerie is, as the ethnographers of the Gaelic-speaking world today maintain, an indigenous coding or metaphor of the imaginal realm of the Otherworld – the source of inner vision, poetry, music and story.

During the seven years that it took me to write *Poacher's Pilgrimage* following the walk, I chanced to share a platform with one of Gregory Bateson's daughters, Nora. Something that she said helped me to crystallise what I was working on. I'd asked about the mystical touch to her father's famous 1972 book, *Steps to an Ecology of Mind*. For example, the line that said, 'Mind is immanent in the larger system – man plus environment.' She thought that he was trying to say 'we don't know what we're inside of'. Her words helped me to realise what it was that I was writing. It wasn't an ecology of mind. That would be much too cognitive an exercise in the way that the word is usually used in the West. Rather, it was an ecology of the imagination. The territory traversed during the walk, the people that I met along the way had, like an impressionistic painting, opened up new vistas in my own consciousness. At times it felt as if I touched on the imagination that it takes to glimpse divine imagination. The imagination that it takes to see a way beyond war. Such is the imagination that can emerge from a 12-day tumble down into the *sithean* – the faerie hill – that is the island's own deep-dreamed imagination. Neither was I the first to discover this. A significant portion of *Poacher's Pilgrimage* works with J.M. Barrie's 1920 play, *Mary Rose*, which is about a little English girl's experience of war trauma and being taken away by the faeries. It was inspired by his fishing holiday in 1912 to Loch Voshimid, the river flowing out from which I took a few casts in during the fourth day of the pilgrimage.

I work a lot with theology, because I find it is the deepest aid, at many levels, to understand the times in which we live. I'm talking here of theologians like Gustavo Gutiérrez, Raimon Panikkar and Rosemary

Radford Reuther – the kind you never hear about from Richard Dawkins, because he only takes on straw men and not the mythopoesis of cosmogenesis that finds expression in theologies of liberation. Such mystical or spiritual theology often makes use of two closely related Greek terms, *apocalypse* and *apotheosis*. In the first, *apo* means 'to remove' and *kalyptein* pertains to 'a covering', thus to remove the cover. Properly speaking, an apocalypse is therefore a revelation of that which had hitherto been hidden. In the second term, *theo* means 'the god'. However, the *apo* is applied here in the sense of removing that which had hitherto hidden the innermost nature of things, the spiritual nature that is the 'god'. By removing the covering, we expose the greater God as well as the lesser gods and fallen gods of our times. These deities are the things we worship. In terms of etymology, worship is what we 'show worth towards', or more literally, sail towards as on a 'worthy ship'. Ultimately, apocalypse is apotheotic. Therein lies its beating heart, the revelation of meaning and being that, in liberation theology, is thought of as 'the irruption of the Spirit'.

An apocalyptic theology is therefore a 'theology of insistence'. Insistence on all that gives life in the face of death. Insistence against the colonisation and silencing of the world beneath a Roman peace. For this garden world in which we live is verily the outer landscape of the soul. The prophetic cry of promise that wails from its deserts is not of forlorn optimism, but of spiritual hope. Hope, as the inner perception of reality. Hope, as the realisation that come what may in the apocalypse of the come-to-pass, our lives are on an ever-deepening journey of apotheosis.

*

I'd better take the greatest care. The moor has given way to fields. They're fenced down to the ocean's edge in narrow strips of in-bye croft farm land. Some are fewer than a hundred yards across, and while the cliffs have dropped away to just some 12-feet high, they're still enough to make a nasty fall.

Worldwide, the level of the sea is rising by an inch in every decade, and accelerating. Add storm surges and some natural subsidence, and that's the reason why this coast is getting undercut so rapidly. One moment I'll be on the path. The next, it drops away. Fences dangle off the end, maybe to a length of ten or 15 feet, giving some crude measure of the extent of recent loss of land. I cross from field to field by grabbing each last standing post with both my hands, and swinging round across the yawning chasm to the other side.

The Butt of Lewis lighthouse stands behind me. A dozen leagues out north to sea lies the tiny island of North Rona, where Saint Ronan built his final temple. After bringing Christianity to Lewis in the seventh century, the monk decided that the people of Ness were too busy and too noisy for his prayer life. An angel sent the *cionaran-crò*, the leader of a pod of whales – with 'his great eyes shining like two stars of night' – and so the saint was spirited across the water. On North Rona lived a people, of whom Martin Martin writing in the late 17th century said, 'They take their surname from the colour of the sky, rainbow and clouds.'

Some of the legends of the Hebrides go back, it is said, to the *Cailleach Bheag an Fhàsaich* – the Little Old Woman of the Wild. She, 'whose age even tradition failed to account'. Her maiden days were spent in Glen Corradale, South Uist. Her words described a kind of golden age, one where 'the little brown brindled lark of Mary bounded to the ear of heaven to herald the dawn', and where all the islands of the Hebrides were joined up into one.

Then came Culloden – the last battle on mainland British soil – in 1746, followed by the Highland Clearances, and in the words of Alexander Carmichael, the 19th-century ethnographer who collected so many of these stories in his six-volume *Carmina Gadelica*, the Songs of the Gaels: 'The whole of these faithful people of Corradale, and hundreds more, were evicted and driven to all ends of the earth – many of them to die moral and physical deaths in the slums of Glasgow and other cities.'

In 1869, a South Uist woman recited to him a poem of coming cataclysm. She prophesied a continuation of the 'overflowing of the Atlantic and the submerging of certain places'. In the end, there will come a time in which:

> The walls of the churches shall be the fishing rocks of the people, while the resting-place of the dead shall be a forest of tangles, among whose mazes the pale-faced mermaid, the marled seal and the brown otter shall race and run and leap and gambol – 'Like the children of men at play'.

Flood legends don't need much interpretation in an era of climate change. The folk memories of many coastal peoples in the world look back to inundation after the Ice Age, when the global sea level rose by some 120 metres.

In her book of Hebridean legends, Otta Swire spoke of the storytellers' three great floods. The first was the primordial flood, that of Creation as recounted in the book of Genesis.

The second great flood, also documented in Genesis, was that of Noah. However, what the Good Book forgot to tell us, is that as the Ark drifted past the mountain Uisgneabhal in North Harris – Water Mountain or Ox Mountain, depending on whether you go by the Gaelic or the Norse etymology – it struck the protruding summit, and ran aground. Some of the animals disembarked prematurely. This accounts for such native Hebridean fauna as the red deer and the blue mountain hare. However, Noah managed to refloat the Ark on the high tide. That accounts for why the Middle East got lions and camels.

And so, to the final flood. The third great flood, the storytellers had it, is that which is yet to come. But when it does come, 'Iona will rise on the waters and float there like a crown'. This, so that the dead 'will arise dry' to ease their recognition on the Last Day.

To me, these places that I've visited, their spirit represented by the holy Hebridean island of Iona that rolls on into the present day, are a crown no inundation can wash away. This path to keep our feet dry – its old ways preserved by collectors like Carmichael and Swire, its new ways embedded in real-life communities – is nothing less than a heritage of world importance.

That crown is the *crò*, the heart or kernel (as the Gaelic word means) of the places, the people that I've met, and what it means to be a human being. Come what may, that might help us face the apocalypse, the revelation, of what comes to pass.

'We don't know what we're inside of' – is what Nora Bateson had said to me.

So far, the 'children of men' have only glimpsed at what I've come to call an ecology of the imagination, but the changes happening in our world – these changes that are shaping the lives of every one of us alive today – represent a basic call to consciousness.

(Adapted from *Poacher's Pilgrimage: an Island Journey*, Birlinn, 2016)

ANDREW BOYD

Twelve Characters in Search of an Apocalypse

I did the math

I did the math. But I wish I hadn't. It was right after Hurricane Sandy. Over a week-long binge I read everything I could find. I work downtown, you see. And they'd lost power, but uptown I still had it. So I had this string of days. It was a time out of Time: the storm had stopped the world, but I was still moving. The city was wrecked. Well, a few parts of it – The Rockaways, Red Hook, Staten Island. The rest of us were a bit stunned, but fine. The Exchange was down; the Jersey guys who normally run the gym couldn't make it into the city. My normal routine was a mess. I went for a run in the Park, and camped out at Starbucks with my laptop and just started reading everything I could find – about Sandy, extreme weather, climate change; the deniers, the doomsayers and everyone in between. One link led to another, which led to another. I couldn't stop; I was in a kind of trance, doing the math as I went.

$2°C$: the baseline maximum increase in aggregate global temperature that the planet can handle without tipping into total catastrophe. Everyone – the UN, the US, China – everyone but the most fringe deniers – agreed on that. 565 gigatons: the maximum additional CO_2 we can safely emit and still stay under the $2°C$ limit. 2,795 gigatons: the total amount of carbon in the reserves – and on the books – of the world's fossil fuel companies. Five times the safe amount. Ergo 80% can't be burned. Choice: extinction or a $28 trillion write-down.

I'm no scientist, but I am a numbers guy. A stock analyst. I've got a head for numbers, and numbers for me are realities you base decisions on. But those numbers hurt my head. They hurt my everything. 'I want the truth!' shouts Kaffee. 'You can't handle the truth!' Jessup spits back. All that week, chest clenched, I played host to that spittle-flying scene from *A Few Good Men*, each one shouting each other down, till it felt like no-one was left standing.

The following Tuesday the power came back on, and I was at my desk early the next morning. The subway station downtown was pretty trashed – and would be for months to come – but the office was quickly back to normal. *Normal?* Nothing felt normal anymore. Don't get me wrong: I'm not picking up a protest sign, and I'm not signing any of those dumb petitions. Far from it. But that McKibben guy is right: all that carbon simply can't come out of the ground, and those Oil, Gas and Coal stocks aren't worth what the market says they are. Sure, in the short-term they might be an OK bet, but in the medium and long-term, they're just a bad portfolio waiting to happen. The industry, however, hadn't caught up to this yet.

At the first department meeting after Sandy I circulated a memo where I laid it all out, along with some revised criteria to take the 'carbon bubble' into account. A lot of puzzled looks at that meeting. My boss took me aside later that day and basically told me to cut the crap. I never brought it up again at work, but later that month I called my broker and told him to dump every last fossil-fuel stock from my own holdings. Wall Street could play the fool with other people's money, but I wasn't going to do it with mine.

It's been a couple years now since Sandy. The subway is repaired, grand plans for coastal berms are underway. The city is mostly back on track; but I can only pretend to be. I try not to think about it too much, but some days it catches up with me. I'll be on the treadmill at the gym, my mind chugging along with the iPod and the fake hill I'm going up and down. In a silence between tracks, a truck backfires on the street below, starting a chain of thoughts: truck … exhaust pipe … 400+ ppm atmospheric carbon … and in a cascade of associations, this horror comes over me. A horror that's by now all too familiar. I imagine the slow plink! plink! of Greenland's glaciers melting (49% recession of Arctic ice since 1979). I can almost smell the diesel fumes of Amazon earthmovers ripping out the lungs of the world (78 million acres of Brazilian rainforest lost every year). And because I'm a numbers guy, I follow in my mind's eye the asymptotic curve of ocean acidification as it creeps along the graph paper, bending relentlessly upwards.

I know where all this is heading if we do nothing – and almost nothing is what we seem to be doing. What I don't know is where to go with this dreadful feeling. It feels like I've been told a terrible secret. A secret that could poison the happy days of everyone I know. A secret (sshhhhh, 2; 565; 2795) no-one wants to hear, least of all me.

Let's party like it's 2099

The apocalypse is coming and we have no-one to blame but ourselves. We've screwed up the planet and we're never gonna turn things around in time, there's just no way. So fuck it. I don't have any kids. I'm gonna be dead by the time the worst of it happens. Why not just party? Just have the best time I possibly can. Dancing, drinking, jet-skiing – whatever I want – and to hell with global warming. The apocalypse is coming regardless. If, thanks to me, it comes five seconds sooner, who really cares?

I mean, really, what else am I supposed to do? Knock on doors, go to meetings, try to convince people to scrap their SUVs? Seriously? That's just sad. Almost a sin. A pathetic way to spend the little time we have left. No way. Not for me. Before the oceans roll in, before they jack up the price of oil, I'm heading out to Thailand, Machu Picchu, New Zealand, Paris, wherever – to see the world. I'm gonna scratch as many things off my bucket list as I can.

Don't get me wrong: I'm not happy about all this. But the way I see it, there's nothing I can do, and we're the last generation that gets to let it rip full throttle. When I hit the clubs with my friends, apocalypse is in the air. You can almost smell it, heady and voluptuous. I breathe it in. I feel fierce; I feel free. I'm a warrior of the now. I'm running down the clock, jonesing for more life at the twilight of all things. We're the last ones, after all. We have to make it count.

I am prepared

It's all going to hell, but I'm prepared. The rest of you can try to stop the disaster. Go to your protests, your fancy international treaty-meetings, and all that. Not me. There's no fixing this. It's all falling apart – and soon. Some of us are going to be ready; some of us aren't. My family and I are going to survive this, even if we're the last ones on Earth.

I've got the bunker all provisioned: enough canned food for two years. Ten guns. Lots of ammo. A generator and an underground tank of diesel. There's a couple of us in the same county. We're all self-reliant units, but we're in touch. The cities are going to be hell, a total race war. We have to be prepared to protect our own when the exodus comes. I've got the entrances booby-trapped and the exits camouflaged. I'm ready for things to get ugly. And, mark my word, they will.

It's gonna happen – but to somebody else

'Only the little people pay taxes,' said notorious billionaire socialite, tax-dodger and lover of little dogs Leona Helmsley. It's a gross and elitist sentiment, but I realise that's how I feel about the apocalypse. It's gonna happen, but it's going to happen to somebody else, not me.

It's gonna happen to those poor fuckers in the Pacific whose islands are disappearing. It's gonna happen to old people in the inner city with broken air conditioners when the next 'unprecedented' heat wave comes. (I think they're gonna have to retire that word soon.) It's going to happen to all those folks who live on the low-lying coasts – whether in Bangladesh or the Mississippi Delta – who don't have anywhere else to go. It's gonna happen to Africans. Why does everything bad happen to Africans? They're already half starving. Just wait till their farmland dries up and their crops fail and there's food riots in the cities and millions teem across the Mediterranean in teetering boats. Fortress Europa is going to go right-wing in a flash and turn all those boats back. To where? I don't know where. All I know is I'm not the one who's going to be doing all the drowning and starving.

Do I think justice is at work here? Hardly. It's pretty much the opposite of justice. I'm just telling you how it looks from where I stand. When I imagine the climate apocalypse, when I play out the nightmare scenarios, I'm never in them. When the final storm comes, I've always got someplace to fall back to. And the means to get there. And friends to be there with.

In my post-apocalyptic future, somehow I've always made it out of the City to a nice farm in Vermont. The rest of the world is a living hell, but I'm OK.

What will the future think of me?

I took Jean and my two boys to Normandy last year. We went to the sprawling graveyards at Colleville-sur-Mer, just above Omaha beach. You've seen the photographs, but it's quite different to actually be there. White crosses stretched in ordered rows literally for a mile. We walked and walked. It was beyond sobering.

It took a while, but we finally found him. *James Davies, 1922–1944.* My great uncle. Third Infantry. Killed in action around Bayonne three weeks after the invasion, just before the breakout across France. We'd brought blue ribbons, and each of us placed one on the grave. My youngest first. Then Jean and I. Then my eldest.

I stood there on the grass and gazed down at this man my dad had named me after. I envied him his place of honour, and – at least from where I stood – the moral clarity of his short life and death. This James Davies came of age at a heroic time. He'd stepped up, and made the ultimate sacrifice. The country still honours him. His family still remembers him. It doesn't say 'Hero' beside his name, but it might as well.

One day they'll lay me down. *James Davies, 1962–2050-ish.* Probably in the city plot, alongside Jean, back in Akron. Will my as-yet-unborn grandkids and grandnephews come visit me? Maybe. Though not with blue ribbons, I suppose. What will the future say about me? *He lived a full life, he was a good father, but he was asleep at the switch when we needed him most.*

We live in an age of soft comforts and distractions, sprinkled with some vague doom-dust. No-one would call this a heroic time, but maybe it never feels that way when you're actually living it – it's always just a slosh of headlines and noise. And yet we are a critical link in the chain of generations. Because before I die, if we don't get 90% of the global economy off carbon, we're toast. We don't need to be another Greatest Generation, we just need to *not* be the Worst Generation, the generation that blew it for all the generations to come.

Jean and the kids were looking the other way, so I don't think they saw me – and this is going to sound corny to most of you – but as I was standing there, I gave a tiny salute to this fallen young man who bore my same name, and I swore to him I'd do my part. For starters, when I get back home, I swore to him I'd finally sign that contract and install rooftop solar on the house. And I'd dig out that email from my old fraternity brother – maybe if enough of us make a fuss, we can get Ohio State to divest its fossil fuel holdings. In the scheme of things, none of this felt particularly heroic, but I realised: I don't need to be a hero. I just need to try to do enough decent things so the future won't think I'm a dick.

The apocalypse is my gravy train

I'm not going to bullshit you – or myself: climate change is a natural and social disaster of unprecedented proportions and it's heading our way.

I'm an engineer. I oversee large construction projects. I can be part of the solution here and, frankly, make some money along the way. I've got to put food on the table like everyone else, and this isn't war profiteering we're talking about. Our firm doesn't blow stuff up, we build things. And this is going to be the biggest construction boom in history. Bigger than the Marshall Plan. Bigger than the New York skyscrapers, Eisenhower's Federal Highway System, and the Beijing Olympics all rolled into one.

We're talking large-scale terraforming here. We're talking coastal berms, seawalls, you name it, whatever it takes to keep our cities safe. No offense, but it won't be about the folks in New Orleans' Third Ward this time. We're looking at Manhattan, Miami's Gold Coast and Boston's Financial District, for starters. Now that's some property there. I'm guessing the government is going to come up with the cash needed to do the job right this time, and our firm is well positioned to help. We operate on a long-term time horizon, and the sooner we can get started the better.

Some folks still don't realise this, but you always have to win the battle twice: once over the problem, and again around the solution. All you deniers – and all you enviros trying to prove them wrong – go on and have your silly votes in the Senate. Keep on arguing about the problem. That's all just a sideshow at this point, because us big boys have already moved on to the solution. That's where the big money is, and we sure don't want the kind of solution they're rolling forward in Germany or Boulder, CO, with municipally-owned renewables and every farmer with their own wind turbine. We're running out of time. This is a big crisis, and we need big solutions. On the energy production side: clean coal, concentrated solar thermal, massive wind farms, biofuels, and the next-generation nuclear – they're zero-carbon and we won't build them on top of an earthquake fault line this time. On the remediation side: carbon-sequestration sinks, heat-shielded residential, you name it, we're just getting going.

I'm planning for my firm's – and my family's – future. I'm honoured to bring my skills and my company's global expertise to the task. If we succeed, what greater legacy could I possibly ask for than having helped save the planet? If we fail, well, gated communities are going to be in high demand, and we build those too.

Bring it on!

We are living in sin, in a kind of hell, in what the Buddhists and Hindus call Maya. We recognise fewer than ten plants, but over 1,000 corporate logos. We're so lost in the supermarket, kids keep on killing each other over sneakers. The corporations have sweet-talked the FDA into letting them put so many chemicals in our food and air that we don't even know what things are supposed to taste or smell like anymore. A carbon disaster will free us. A disembowelling of industrial civilisation is what we need to bring us back to our true selves.

Everyone's all gaga for green capitalism, but that's just a kinder, gentler way to destroy the planet. You want a 'green roof'? Just wait for it to cave in. Let the seed pods land in the cracks in the concrete, they'll sprout, and take it all back. That's the only kind of green roof I want. When Nature finds its own rhythms again, we can, too. The only way forward is backwards. The only way forward is collapse.

Right now, I'm living in a squat and dumpster-diving my food. Any SUV that parks in the neighbourhood, we let the air out of its tyres. Small-fry stuff for sure, but we're just biding our time. After the collapse, we'll make campfires in abandoned office buildings, smashing up the cubicles for kindling. We'll hunt deer with bow and arrow through the hollow, echoing ruins of downtown. After the collapse, the rest of you had better know how to do these things too.

Most people find this pretty far-fetched, but you'll all see. Every civilisation before us has collapsed, and we're far more precarious and out of kilter than they were. We're literally consuming ourselves into oblivion; it's only a matter of time before the system implodes from its own exhaustion, fury and hollowness. My job? To help push things along.

There was a meeting last night in the basement. We all took the batteries out of our phones so they couldn't hear us. All kinds of things were floated: breaking animals out of the zoos, hacking the genetic trials at the university, even blowing up the dam up north. We'll see.

No matter what, it ain't gonna be pretty. Millions, maybe billions, will die. I can't say I'm not anxious about it, I just know the sooner it happens, the better – for us and the planet. So: Bring. It. On.

Better to be hopeful

For me, it's not about the future. It's not about what's going to happen or not happen. The science is dire, that's obvious. And I know humans have a long bloody track record of being our own worst enemy. I also know we sometimes pull it out in the clutch. But I'm not banking on one outcome or another. I'm not hoisting my flag over any particular narrative of history or view of human nature. I just know how *I* want to be in the world. And I want to have hope. I choose hope. It makes me feel better. I get fewer colds and stomach aches. I'm happier and more focused; I feel right with the world. I'm going somewhere. We're all going somewhere, and we're going there together.

Oh God, some of you are thinking, *please don't pair me up with this Pollyanna-ish bore at group therapy*. Don't wet yourself. I've got the full *Cards Against Humanity* box set. I've got my share of black moods and I do irony just fine, thank you. I won't reassure you that everything is going to be OK. It most certainly won't be. I'm not over-bubbling with enthusiasm and cheerfulness, I'm just quietly, soberly hopeful.

The world is fucked up. Anyone can see that. War, religious hatred, rape, thousands of square miles of swirling plastic in the ocean. The list is long. But life is beautiful. And that list is longer: the Chrysler building at twilight. Bill Murray. A mother cradling her newborn. The intoxicating smell of my girlfriend's armpits. Snow. The world is fucked up. So, so fucked up. But life is beautiful. And that is enough.

Defend this ground

I grew up here: Iron Mountain, Michigan, in the Upper Peninsula. Twenty street lights, three churches. I sang in the choir at Her Lady of Redemption until I was 14. Back then the town was 10,000-strong, mostly Germans and Swedes, along with some Italians, my folks included. Now, we're down to barely 7,500. The mining and timber companies ravaged the place, like they did the whole region. Took everything, left a few broken backs, and scars all over the land. My cousins worked in the mines. My step-dad was a cop. When he died I left the state. Came back decades later to take care of my mom. She'd gone blind those last years, and had no-one else. By the end, the place had become home again, and I've stayed on.

I have my dog, my garden, and pipes to patch after the winter. I've got things to take care of. I still battle the same old demons – the depression comes and goes – but I've developed some new disciplines: canning, pressing flowers, painting. I'm seventy now, I'm slow. I've got arthritis. My left leg is effectively lame. But I work on the things I can.

What keeps me going is this patch of ground, this sacred bit of Earth. Lake Superior, that God, is the heart and lungs of the continent. The Devil is the mining companies and the real estate developers. I don't have a lot of strength left, but I'm still putting up a fight where I can. I choose my battles carefully. I look for smart places to intervene, no matter how small. I find things I can do to keep these lungs breathing.

There's a development they've been trying to put in ten miles west of here. Summer home resort for down-staters: golf course, the works. We know what that means: dozers, clear cutting, chemical run-off, you name it. Our little group – two students, a retired lawyer, me – has had 'em gummed up in court for two years now. And that pipeline coming down from Canada – we pulled up the surveyor stakes from a three-mile stretch last spring. They know it was us, but can't prove it. They stormed into the county commissioner's office but he just shrugged. That was fun to watch.

I know what we're doing is just a sideshow of a sideshow of a sideshow – small rearguard actions in a centuries-long war. But you fight where you stand. You do what you can. You defend your little patch of ground. I'm not going anywhere.

Despair is our only hope

I used to believe.

As a kid I trusted everything was more or less OK, that progress happened, that the people in charge were trying to make things better, and the good guys would eventually win. *Hawaii 5-o* was my show.

As a young man I realised that the people in charge were not trying to make things better for everyone, just for themselves. And so – because I'm a hopeful kind of guy – I came to believe that the people *not* in charge could get together and change all that. I loved the movie *Hair*. I used to believe the revolution was just around the corner, that before I turned thirty, we'd be celebrating in the streets.

Well, that didn't happen.

Into my forties, I still had faith in humanity. Not blind faith, not even a faith in our essential goodness. But I believed that we would somehow stumble through, that the small acts of kindness among people would somehow make up for the evil and folly of the gangland of States and capital. I could still see a future, maybe not a better one, but no worse, either.

I'm now in my fifties, and I've lost even that meagre faith. Now I binge-watch *Game of Thrones* and *House of Cards*. I have no illusions about how power operates. People talk about 'intersectionality', but it isn't so much movements that are intersecting, as catastrophes. I see no way forward. I am filled with a dark, desolate despair.

And then a strange thing happens: I feel fierce. I feel clear. I feel free. I don't give a fuck anymore. I've got nothing left to lose. I'm willing to take risks that I wasn't before. I say true things, things you're not supposed to say. And people notice. Hell, *I* notice. It turns out despair is its own kind of power, its own kind of freedom. And then I think: if enough of us fall into a dark enough despair, who knows what we can do together. This is the only hope I have left.

This means war

At first everything happened so piecemeal – a tragedy here, a little catastrophe there – I didn't know I was under attack. It felt like the rumble of far-off gunfire in somebody else's war. It took a while for it all to come into focus.

If it had been an army of Orcs led by the Eye of Sauron, or gangly robots from Mars, or jackbooted Nazis and their henchmen marching into town, then I would have known. I would have seen it plainly. I would have taken up arms, joined the Resistance. But our 21st Century Lords of Carbon, in their suits and pipelines and feel-good logos, blend in better. Their ultimate designs, however, are just as evil. They plunder the land, poison the water, slaughter our animal brothers and sisters. With five species lost to eternity every day, and the slow-drip of carbon dismembering the planet, they're driving us all to extinction. What else is this if not war?

My enemies, it turns out, have names: Exxon. Peabody Coal. BP. Shell. David Koch. And addresses: with a few clicks on Google I can find their homes and headquarters. They are driven by a logic of endless growth regardless of the limits of nature. They can do nothing else. As such, my foe is implacable. I accept this without illusions. They will not – can not – listen to reason; only power.

We must raise an army to save the world.

And so, I cross over. I become an instrument of resistance, a vessel of necessity. I find my unit and train in the strange arts of civil war: encryption, encyclicals, sabotage, message discipline, persuasion, science, disobedience, justice, courage, love, mass action. Maybe I will not survive; maybe none of us will survive. So be it. I prepare myself for battle.

Hopelessness can save the world

We have broken Nature. We have broken the world. Even the moral logic of struggle has been broken. Gandhi said, 'First they ignore you, then they ridicule you, then they fight you, and then you win.' But in the shadow of climate catastrophe, we'd have to update that to: 'First they ignore you, then they ridicule you, then they fight you, *and then* a 6°C increase in the Earth's temperature wipes out all complex life forms.' Martin Luther King said, 'The arc of the moral universe is long but it bends toward justice.' But from where we stand now, it's more accurate to say, 'The arc of the moral universe might be long, and it might bend towards justice, but we're never gonna find out because: total ecosystem collapse.'

I used to run on hope. I used to sign those petitions, show up at those demos, knock on my neighbours' doors – because I believed we could change things. But I don't know anymore. As a good friend of mine recently said, 'So what if we're making progress on police brutality. Given the climate math, the police might as well shoot us all now.' It breaks my heart, but it seems our situation is hopeless, and our cause – all our causes – are impossible.

Then again, hasn't this always been the case? Look across the full sweep of human history, with its wars and rebellions, its dark and shining moments: every revolution is replaced with the slime of a new bureaucracy. Every time you manage to overthrow slavery it seems there's a new Jim Crow waiting for you. I used to think it was two steps forward one step back, now I'm not so sure. Things don't seem to change much for the better, and with the tick tock of carbon slowly poisoning the world, you just stop pretending that they will. Now, instead of fearing this loss of faith, I welcome it as a revelation: our situation *is* hopeless. Our cause *is* impossible.

Which leaves us with a stark choice: do we dedicate ourselves to an impossible cause? Or do we pull back and look after our own? The choice – once you've sat quietly with this question – is clear. We must dedicate ourselves to an impossible cause. Because, as Archbishop Oscar Romero said when asked why he was attending to the sick at a hospital for incurables: 'We are all incurable.' Because solidarity is a form of tenderness. Because the simple act of caring for the world is itself a victory. We must take a stand – not because it will lead to anything, but because it is the right thing to do. We never know what can or can't be done; only what must be done. I dedicate myself to an impossible cause.

'Twelve Characters in Search of an Apocalypse' is an excerpt from the author's current project: I Want a Better Catastrophe.

DANIEL NAKANISHI-CHALWIN

Dust and Bones

Amongst the traditions of Indo-Tibetan tantrism, there is a form of meditation in which the practitioner pictures their own body shorn of its outer layers and transformed into a skeleton. The initiation rituals of Siberian shamanism similarly involve visions of the living self butchered by spirits and reduced to bones. So it is that whenever I recall the funeral of my wife's grandfather – in Tenri City, Japan on 21st March, 2014 – my mind offers up a series of jumpcuts, a triptych of images: the man in the hospital bed, the corpse in the parlour, the skeleton on the table.

Such a bare, schematic rendering is partly due to an uncertain memory, which I attempted to flesh out for this essay through background reading. Could research salvage some sharp detail of protocol from vague recollection? Certainly I learned many interesting things about funerals in Japan: that the early Emperors were interred in great tumuli until the adoption of Buddhism by the ruling classes led to the spread of cremation; that the first cremation recorded in the chronicles was of the Buddhist priest Dōshō in AD700; that the corpses of the city poor nevertheless continued to be abandoned in distant fields or mountains, or even along riverbanks, always liminal 'non-places' even where they ran through metropolitan centres such as Kyōto; that the diaries of aristocrats in the 12th and 13th centuries frequently refer to dogs bringing dismembered body parts into the house, necessitating rites of purification; that an exclusively Shintō style of funeral, favouring burial in the earth, existed in parallel with the Buddhist pyre; that there was also a rural-urban split, with burning the preferred option in densely populated cities and interment the custom in the countryside; and that this split persisted into modern times before the urn of ashes finally won out. A rich subject for the inquiring mind. Yet mine clings to its stark triptych. Man, corpse, skeleton. And the faces of the mourners. And the smell.

But maybe such starkness is, after all, the most appropriate mode for dealing squarely with the simple fact of death – a fact to which the modern West displays such aversion. My sole memory of my own maternal grandfather's cremation some 20 years ago in London is of a sealed coffin, sucked away through a velveteen curtain on a conveyor belt, the only sound some plinky hymnal muzak piped through speakers. Off to Heaven in an elevator, all veiled and sanitised. The contrast with the ritual end to Nakanishi Mitsuo's life could not be more extreme.

I. The Man

Born in 1931. Adopted into the Nakanishi family at the age of three. An eager student of English despite the prevailing cultural hostility of the time. A small-scale farmer growing strawberries, spinach and rice. Bald statements cannot conjure up the person, already in his eighties when I first met him. A large, veinous hand proffered with the English words, somewhat slurred by dentures, 'Nice to meet you'. But all that schooling so long ago and half-forgotten. An immediate reversion to Japanese, the dense local dialect, unpicked for me at moments of confusion by his eldest granddaughter, my future wife. Though we only met a handful of times, he was unfailingly warm, accepting and humble, unwilling to play the role of supreme patriarch to which his years entitled him.

Some of this gentle poise may have derived from his faith, for he was an active member of his Tenrikyō church. Arising in the mid-19th century at a time of great political crisis, when feudal Japan was opening to the West, Tenrikyō began as a rural cult based around Nakayama Miki, a shamanic figure who delivered her divine revelations in automatic writing and was said to perform miracles of healing. The movement grew into an organised religion, designated by the government as a 'sect of Shintō', and eventually gave its name to the place where it had started, and which its official buildings now dominate, Tenri City in Nara Prefecture.

But is Tenrikyō actually Shintō? While the two may share certain aspects of ritual in common, the latter has a multitude of gods, the former ostensibly one, Tenri-Ō-no-Mikoto. The use of the English word 'church' to describe its sites of worship also reinforces the sense of monotheism. I've lived in Tenri for almost a decade, my wife is an adherent of Tenrikyō, yet I still don't know the answer. Why? Because it doesn't really matter.

Religion in Japan has always been a syncretic affair, as suggested by the mixture of Buddhist and Shintō funeral practices. Buddhist temples usually have Shintō shrines within their precincts, and most people pray indiscriminately at both. My wife and I even got married in a Shintō shrine; her Tenrikyō family raised no objections. For dogma is subsidiary to the ritual act itself. Correct form is a defining feature of Japanese culture, just as applicable to major ceremonies, such as graduations or weddings, as to the small, quotidian 'rituals' of meeting and greeting, mediated by their subtle grades of honorific language. The routine, the bow, the posture of humble supplication – the gesture in and of itself supersedes any dubious philosophical pursuit of incontrovertible truth.[1]

Many of the rituals of Tenrikyō are accompanied by *gagaku*, the music of the ancient Imperial court, a melange of native Japanese, Chinese and South Asian influences. In his church orchestra Nakanishi Mitsuo played a reed instrument called the *shō*, a bundle of bamboo tubes that resembles part of some miniature pipe organ, but which was said to represent a Chinese phoenix at rest. Its sounds are magical, shimmering and, like a harmonica, arise on both the in- and out-breaths.

The last time I saw him, he was wearing an oxygen mask. A cold had deteriorated into pneumonia, and he'd been in a hospital bed for several weeks. Weight loss had made his false teeth even looser in his gums, and I barely understood anything. We told him about our wedding plans, the tedious bureaucratic hoops we had to jump through. Characteristically, he was more concerned with this than with his own failing body.

It's curious how the action of writing revives the memory. Maybe my hippocampus (or is it the cerebral cortex?) is sprightlier than I thought. I remember now the overcast light in the small hospital room, how we turned at the door to wave goodbye. His large purple-pink hand, bloated with gravity, waving back above the side-bars of the bed. Outside I picked up the spiky fruit of an American sweet gum by its stalk. It's still in our apartment, in an old glass jar, like a musical note preserved in ice. But memory, it always fades.

II. A Corpse

It was back in the house when we got there, transported from the hospital within several hours of death – the body of Nakanishi Mitsuo, still in pyjamas, laid out on a futon on the *tatami* mats. I hesitate, however, to yoke his name to this husk; already his image had been abstracted. It was my first human corpse (I never saw my own grandfather's), and I found myself thinking, *there's nothing here any more*. Tireless lungs static after 82 years, filled only with slack air. Hence perhaps that ceremonial dagger on the chest to ward off evil spirits. Other offerings were on a small wooden stand: rice, saké, salt, water and a leaf of the sacred *sakaki* tree (*Cleyera japonica*) for transferring water to the dry lips. The body required tender ministration, as a succession of relatives and neighbours came to kneel and pay their respects.

This was death treated with intimacy, invited into the heart of the family home, not banished to the morgue with a kind of queasy embarrassment.[2] That night Mitsuo's daughter, now my mother-in-law, slept near the body to ensure a votive candle didn't go out. His great-granddaughters made origami grave goods – a watch, paper money, anything he might need on the journey after death. These were placed in the coffin the following day, after undertakers had wiped the body clean and dressed it in a kimono (with the right flap over the left, a reversal of the custom for the living). The rest of us put on black mourning clothes, and we all departed for the funeral parlour and the wake.

Here my memories become layered – doubled. Both the wake that evening and the funeral the morning after occurred in the same hall, before the same backdrop of offerings. Flowers, fruit, vegetables, enormous bottles of rice wine, even dry food in boxes arranged like a harvest festival in a church. Both times a Tenrikyō priest chanted prayers. Both times we filed up to the coffin, bowed, clapped and offered branches of sakaki strung with zigzags of white paper (a form of decoration commonly seen in Shintō shrines). There was duplication in the two ceremonies, but a change in atmosphere too. Some of this was due to emotional fatigue. After the wake, the coffin was removed temporarily to a separate room within the funeral parlour, so that family members could keep vigil, keep the candle burning, until the next day. I eventually went home, slept fitfully, and then the gagaku hit.

In her foreword to the 2004 edition of Mircea Eliade's *Shamanism*,

Wendy Doniger states that, '…myths (and, to a great extent, rituals) retold and reenacted in the present transport the worshipper back to the world of origins, the world of events that took place *in illo tempore*, "in that time".'[3] There is, in other words, a rupture in everyday, linear time and its replacement with the 'supratemporal'. This seems especially valid for describing highly formalised rituals that concern intrinsic aspects of existence – like death. While the wake had begun the rent in the ordinary, three gagaku musicians at the funeral itself (two bamboo flutes, one shō, the phoenix-harmonica) ripped it right open.

If melody in the Western classical tradition can be thought of as a path through a landscape, or as a narrative line connecting set-up to pay-off, then gagaku is the landscape itself, the setting robbed of story. Its woozily shifting planes of sound, all reeds and grasses, make me think of layers of honey slowly melting into one another, of the golden light of honeycomb. William P. Malm has compared the sounds of the shō to 'a vein of amber in which a butterfly has been preserved.'[4] Or maybe a sweet gum fruit in an old glass jar? This is music as circular time, existential, the pulse of the lungs, and it worked like a drug on my mildly sleep-deprived mind.

I floated through the following stages, even after the music had stopped, stunned in the new silence and weirdly detached as the mourners pressed in around the coffin to fill it with flowers. The grieving reached its peak. People sobbed and cried in despair, crowding, almost jostling, in a sudden loosening of self-control. It was an odd thing to witness in a society where public displays of strong emotion are so rare.

Nakanishi Mitsuo in a box of flowers. The undertakers fixed on the lid, and I helped to load the coffin into a hearse. At the crematorium there were more chanted prayers, more offerings of sakaki. The coffin was on a metal stand like an autopsy table. The table was wheeled into the incinerator. We drove back to the funeral parlour for beer and lunch.

III. Skeleton

The first thing you register is the smell. A burnt, mineral heat full in the nostrils before you even enter the room. Then you see the metal table in the middle. The human skeleton. The man of a few hours ago now preternaturally white.

I think of a line from Russell Hoban's *Riddley Walker* – 'It wer like the 1st time I seen a woman open for me I wer thinking: This is what its all about then.'[5] This is the core, this is the nub, one individual stripped back to calligraphic bones, one frail body as ideogram for all Mortality. It's a banal truism that we must die one day, but in that moment I was struck more forcibly by the startling fact of not currently being dead myself.

Or is that mere hindsight, analytical and calm? Lunch had been long; there had been alcohol. Thirty or forty relatives and friends were now crammed into this small chamber at the crematorium. Tired, serious faces. I was spaced out, and the stench was beginning to become nauseating. On the far side of the table stood my girlfriend's niece, only six at the time, showing on her face the anxiety I felt, feeding it back to me. I managed to smile at her. Her own smile was instant, big and open, as honest as her fear had been, and with it equanimity was restored.

This equanimity had characterised much of the past three days. Of course there was deep sadness, particularly as the coffin was finally sealed, but this was the funeral of an octogenarian who had been ailing for several weeks. That lessens the shock, lends the proceedings a certain matter-of-factness.

A crematorium attendant, wearing a peaked cap like a bus conductor, began to distribute metal chopsticks, while his colleague commented on the fine condition of Nakanishi Mitsuo's skeleton, pointing out the absence of distortion in the pelvis or spine. His tone was unsentimental, yet polite, delicate. He now invited us to approach, individually or in pairs, starting with immediate family members, and remove pieces of bone for the urn. It was important to take a representative selection from throughout the body; not everything could be preserved.

Again that total lack of squeamishness, that intimacy. My girlfriend and I went together. As we stood in the slow waves of heat emanating from the table, agonising over what to pick up with the chopsticks, it felt for a second like some bizarre buffet spread. What a surreal privilege to be vulturing this man's bones! Eventually we chose a section of fibula, which came away easily. The fire had burned out all the elastic collagen, leaving it brittle.

The skull was equally as compliant. Being far too big for the porcelain urn, the chief attendant, announcing his intentions first in the same level voice, broke it apart in his gloved hands and recommended a neat, shell-like segment from the top. The consummate professional – anatomist – *connoisseur*. Small wonder a collective murmur of appreciation met his discovery of the Buddha.

The *nodobotoke* or 'throat-Buddha' is the colloquial term for the laryngeal prominence, the Adam's apple. Although composed of carti-lage, and thus unable to survive cremation temperatures, folk anatomy considers it identical with the axis, the second vertebra of the neck, which has on its upper surface a small tooth-like projection – or rather, a small head and torso – giving it the appearance of a Buddha in the lotus position. Mitsuo's had emerged from the flames uncracked, and was now retrieved by the attendant before our chopsticks could do any damage. Even for followers of Tenrikyō, in which meditation plays no part, this body within the body is a potent, sacred object.

The tantric meditation on one's skeleton alerts the mind to the true nature of existence, transient despite the illusion of stability that daily routine tends to grant it. Likewise, the ritual of the chopsticks (common to all cremations in Japan, not only those of Tenrikyō) is a sober acknowledgement of death as an incremental erasure – a scattering of hands, lungs, hippocampus – just as inexorable whether one is ripped apart by wild dogs or lovingly dismantled by one's family.

In contrast, the Siberian shaman must collapse to a state of bones in order to be reborn in a new body of magical power. There are echoes of this in Tenrikyō, which holds that the material body is on loan from God and must be returned to God, but that the soul is one's own and can transmigrate. The funeral is simply the starting point for a series of rituals occurring at fixed intervals over many years, each marking the journey of the post-death spirit. Whilst some of Mitsuo's bone fragments have been interred in a cemetery, others are still in the family home, including the throat-Buddha. On the fifth anniversary of his death it will be transferred to the church where he worshipped.

Another banal truism then: a funeral is an act of remembrance. But is it not also, at least in the format I experienced, a reconciliation with the inevitability of forgetting, and of being forgotten? Of an erasure that is more than physical? Within a few generations anyone who has ever known us personally is dead. Only feeble ghosts remain: dry facts, sparse accounts, deceptive photographs. This same fear of personal oblivion underpins our wider fears about environmental catastrophe. How can we expect future humans to have any memory of the splendour, the diversity, that once cloaked and suffused this Earth? How can they possibly know what has been lost?

March the 21st, 2014, had been overcast and chilly. As I left the heavy, sooty air of the crematorium behind in the mid-afternoon, stepping out through the sliding doors hand in hand with my girlfriend's niece, the sun suddenly broke through, illuminating a silvery shower of rain. 'Look! *Kitsune no yomeiri!*' shouted the small girl. A foxes' wedding procession! This Japanese idiom perfectly conveys the novelty, the sheer uncanniness, of seeing rain fall from a bright blue sky. It was an appropriate image for a day of strange rupture, of ritual space, otherworldly and beyond ordinary time.

The sun and rain, moving through their cycles. An atheist-animist, is that what I am? A touch of Buddhism when it suits me? I'm not big on dogma. All I know is that there are a myriad universes dying all the time, every one infinitely rich and utterly mysterious. That we are made of stardust. Animal, corpse, skeleton. That's good enough for me.

Endnotes

1. This may, of course, be utter bollocks, since Japan no doubt has its fair share of fundamentalists, but it neatly justifies the lack of theological explication in my account.
2. This custom, however, is disappearing, surviving mainly in old houses in the country.
3. Eliade, Mircea, *Shamanism: Archaic Techniques of Ecstasy*, Princeton University Press, Princeton, 2004 edition, p.13.
4. Malm, William P., *Traditional Japanese Music and Musical Instruments*, Kodansha International, Tokyo, 2000, p.112.
5. Hoban, Russell, *Riddley Walker*, Bloomsbury Publishing, London, 2002 edition, p.193.

JANE LOVELL

This Tilting Earth

*Immanuel Velikovsky (*Earth in Upheaval, *1955) hypothesised that, during
a great cosmic global catastrophe, the position of the Earth's axis changed
its position and, with that change, the mammoths, mastodons and certain
other animals perished from the Earth.*

Tusk, Sithylemenkat Lake
Preserved within the thinnest shadow, we discover famine;
in iron fragments scorched into the bark, imagine impact;
in the gunshot carbon, trace the searing gales.
Remember that.
Sithylemenkat Lake, where you can sift the sediment
for firestorm charcoal, nickel, other lives.

Vertebra, Lugovskoe
Did some fluted point penetrate through fur, skin, lung
to enter with such force? Or was it target practice,
the great winged relic swinging in the endless rain?

Remains of Nursery Herd, Waco
A tributary of the Bosque River branches
thin and blue: a vein blown from the main flow.
Zoom in. A small army of them, trunks held high
and curled like question marks,
clambering the sides of a ravine too steep, too slippery
to scale, is drowning;
the smallest, raised on heaving tusks,
no longer breathing.

Yuka

Vulnerable Yuka,
adored from withered trunk to straggled hair,
dreams skulking lions held at bay by savages with knives,
a shoreline carved from ice,
the coldest, bluest air above the Laptev Sea.

Beringia

That day, the sweeping grasslands buffeted
by rising winds, they were still grazing:
crowfoot, celandine and poppy, bursts of bilberry.
Some say a howling darkness hurled them, bracing,
ice invading every cell and atom, to extinction;
the final gleam of frozen eyes, a shifting constellation.
Consider that.
Consider: teased from withered mouths
a spume of buttercups; those trampled meadows.

MATT DUBUQUE

Checkerspot Fancy

The checkerspot is only a small butterfly, measuring about two inches across. Its colouring is rather plain, consisting of blacks and browns stippled together in a fairly prosaic pattern. Does this ordinary appearance mean that before the people came its profound role linking deeply disparate worlds was an ordinary occurrence? I do not know, but I have watched them for decades in the green foothills of the San Francisco Peninsula for good reason. Each butterfly necessarily reminds me of the deep connections at play in the natural world, the world of reality, the world of songs and wonder. I know of no other creature who so subtly signals that there is an earthquake fault in the area. Did the Ohlone Indians know this?

The vanishing populations of the checkerspot butterfly are now making their last stand in isolated stretches of the San Andreas Fault, whose great tectonic shifts have brought unforgettable seismic shudders at various points through history. Why would this butterfly be found fluttering near earthquake faults? The answer shows how deeply connections can run in the natural world, unbeknownst to almost every typer and texter in nearby Silicon Valley.

For supper (and at teatime as well) the checkerspot dines on a particular type of Indian paintbrush, a stubbly, purplish flower well known to the indigenous Ohlone peoples. And that type of owl's clover requires the presence of serpentine in the soil, exuded by a metamorphic rock only found in the high pressure, high temperature pressure cookers of earthquake faults. This means that the shrewd butterfly watcher can use the checkerspot as a signal that an earthquake fault is certainly nearby. For as the checkerspot moves from flower to flower it weaves together the allegedly disconnected worlds of biology (butterflies), botany (Indian paintbrush), and geology (serpentine). I know of no other species which so clearly links these three very different worlds.

And it is vanishing.

Paul Ehrlich (who became famous for his discussions of the perils of overpopulation) also devoted much of his life to the study of the checkerspot. Several years ago he declared that, after decades of well-intentioned struggle and study, the checkerspot could no longer be found on the Stanford University lands of Jasper Ridge. Had generations of enthusiastic biology students inadvertently trampled its sacred grounds?

This is not a topic discussed in polite company here. How could so many liberal ecologists be so mistaken?

With no checkerspots to be found at Stanford, I moved on to the crew of those calling themselves 'naturalists' at Edgewood County Park, who have collectively spent hundreds of hours interfering in the private lives of a crashing checkerspot butterfly population there. I arrived at the latter stages of that scandal, not long after they had released a large number of checkerspot caterpillars they had kidnapped from a Coyote Valley location which would all too soon be subdivided into a housing development. To the surprise and grief of the sincere ecological meddlers commanding the dog and pony show there, the Edgewood checkerspot population declined even further.

They said they had no idea why.

'Why did you bring so many caterpillars?' I asked.

'We wanted to bring as many as we could,' was the response.

'I'm concerned that you brought so many that they all starved.'

Stone silence.

'I hope not,' was the subdued reply.

'Oh,' said I. A social butterfly I am not.

At any rate, I absolutely deny any and all reports that in my explorations of thousands of acres of wild, undeveloped areas elsewhere along the Peninsula I have found another, thriving, colony in one of the happiest moments of my life. Even if I had, rest assured I would tell no other person where they might be.

[photo: Andrei Stanescu/Shutterstock.com]

LEONIE VAN DER PLAS

Fragments

of life in the midst of receding conditions

Mali, 2001–2002 (*Douentza, Ngouma and surrounding areas*)

I see camels walking with long ropes behind them. They start at the well and walk a distance of approximately 90 metres. They work all day to draw water from the well for just a few houses. Through the years the rope has become longer, a man says. He recalls the time that the ropes were only 30 metres, but that is long ago.

People here hardly laugh. I am in the poorest part of the country. I am here to do research. I see people living their life, they respond to my questions, I chat around in town and in villages. It is not a bad year, but some people are having a hard time anyway, struggling for food is part of their life.

The rice in Ngouma is of a very bad quality. It makes your appetite disappear. A woman kindly offers me rice, but I can hardly eat it. I didn't know that rice of such bad quality existed. This is their food here, they eat it. It comes from China. This must be the rice that they do not want in China. They used to eat millet as a staple around here, but that is not growing so well any more. Lack of water, exhausted soil. I have a bit of bread in my bag and decide to split it up into pieces and spread the eating of it. The bread is dry and tough, but it tastes better than the rice.

In small villages and settlements there are children who do not play. They stare with dull eyes at what others are doing. Sometimes their hair is not even black. Only the chief's children play. They are the ones that get enough food. They get part of the food that the other families grow. In meagre years, even the chief's family is hungry, the son of a chief tells me.

The infant mortality rate is about 50% in this region, I hear. My neighbour in Douentza met a woman who gave birth to 14 babies. Only one of them is still alive. Another neighbour tells me that she sometimes offers people medicine when they are sick. She tells me about a woman who refused medicine for her sick child. Not that she didn't believe it would help, but she'd rather let her child die. It was not a very strong child, and she didn't want to feed it any longer. She couldn't afford to give her weak child food. That is normal here, I hear. Not that people do not care, they do. Only they sometimes do not have the luxury of feeding the weak.

In bad years some men throw themselves off the rocks in shame for not being able to feed their families. Some families get extinguished as a whole in bad years.

Religious zeal is flourishing, especially among the poor. There are men that seem to be in prayer all day long. This is in 2002, a few months after 9/11. I see the faces of Osama bin Laden and Madonna painted on the back of a bus. They are shaking side by side.

And then there are the plastic bags. You get them everywhere. They are everywhere. If you slaughter an animal, you see the plastic bags in their stomach. If you are driving through the country you will see fields of plastic bags waving on stalks and in shrubs along the road. Then you know that you will soon pass a village.

I feel stupid with my questions. I realise that I have felt stupid before. When will I learn?

I see myself writing a PhD thesis which will probably be read by some other researchers and then it will end up on a big pile of theses that will never be read again. I will have spent six or seven or eight years of my life on this, sitting behind my desk, looking for the right words, struggling with myself. I will have lost weight. I will have bothered hundreds of struggling people with questions that seem to be of small interest to them. I will have moulded their answers into a model. This is not how I want to relate to people. This is not what life is about. Life happens outside the data.

Also now, while I am writing this, I feel that I can't do it right. Haven't I just brought back the lives of people that I have met into a few fragments? Is this any different or better than data? Whose story is it that I am telling here? We all know that being at the fringes has always been part of our story. It makes us leave places that we feel connected to, leave the people that we love. But there is a limit to our flexibility. This receding of life conditions has been going on for years. We can not live on sun and wind and dust. No-one can.

I can not make it any better than it is. Not in this story.

I keep hoping to find better stories in the future.

GARRY WILLIAMS
Journey: a performance
Lake Sognsvann, Oslo, Norway

During a period of homelessness and searching for somewhere to live and breathe,
I lived and worked illegally for ten days and nights on a frozen lake, working
with a traditional ice saw to cut a free-floating raft out of its metre-thick ice.
The Journey would end when the raft broke free: a voyage to the here and now,
through the overwhelming struggle of existence.

On the final day, local authorities stopped the project within hours of the
raft breaking free, over concerns for public safety.

The piece continues a focus in my work on the precarious nature of existence.

WILL GILL
Pink Figure, Cabin
Photograph
Svalbard, Norway

Part explorer. Part outcast. Part survivor. From the series *No Man's Land* by Canadian artist Will Gill, these images were made during an artist residency in Svalbard, Norway, in the autumn of 2014. Twenty-eight artists from around the world sailed aboard a three-masted barquentine to one of the most forbidding environments on the planet. Accompanied by sculptural props and a custom-made light reflective suit, the artist set out to stage photographs in the alien landscape. The results explore aspects of life somewhere near the end: resignation, curiosity, boredom, hope, wonder and despair.

No Man's Land #1
Photograph
Svalbard, Norway

at bronze-helmed Hektor, but he in his experience of fighting
with his broad shoulders huddled under the bull's-hide shield kept
watching always the whistle of arrows, the crash of spears thrown.
He knew well how the strength of the fighting shifted against h...
even so stood his ground to save his steadfast comp...

...when a cloud goes deep into the sky from Ol...
...the bright upper air when Zeus...
...beside the ships their out...
...order they went back, wh...
...upon away in his armour; he a...
...who were trapped by...
...fast ho...
...he join...

of men as they fought, so...
would not let go of the stern of a s...
but gripped the sternpost in his hand...
'Bring fire, and give single voice to the...
Now Zeus has given us a day worth all...
the ships capture, the ships that came h...
and have visited much pain on us, by...
who would not let me fight by the...
but held me back in str...
But Zeus of big forth fre... son P... and...
comes n... round a... these died w...
He... gives you are mourning over...
Their v... the hollow ships by... so we shall both know.
his place... do not hide it in your mind...
back to the... ing heavily, Patroklos the rider... you answered...
balanced... the Achaians, Achilleus,
ship. There he stood and wait... for... bravest in battle
beat off any Trojan who carried... arrow or spear wound.
He kept up a...

to climb back into their city though they strained for it, but sweeping
through the space between the ships, the high wall, and the river,
made havoc and exacted from them the blood price for many.

of all he struck with the shining spear Pronoös
Achilles where it was left bare by the shield, and unstrung his limbs.   400

went back in
to stand in front of Patroklos in his next outrush
to watch the grim   inside his chariot,
                          and from his hands the reins
Now they wh high confid rose up to him stabbed with a spear-thrust
went onward,   streaming out drove i   t on thro   gh the teeth   hen
The Myrmid   got into the habit of   over   rman
         hey live in their   line and
       ing that hurts m   s doomed,
                                                         willing
                                               th against the
                                               weigh
                                          ns, so
 their a
n after ha
unwearied
pon their ci
 t spoke sup   w   t shoulder
  eath and ev   e
  sa deeply troubled wift-
 roklos llustrious, what is   to
 e not   pri   y in mind th
      rom Zeus my hon
  thought comes   as a bitter so
 man tries to foul   one who is hi   t run a   way in them.
  of honour, because I   e goes i   our pe   ople.'
is a bitter thought to me;   n greater a   to   inked
hly. The girl the sons of the   ans chose out for n
     on her with my own spear, and stormed   ong-fe
   back out of   powerful Agamemn
 of Atreus   some o   oured vagabon
we will let all this be a thing of ast; and it was
y heart   be angry forever; and

[331]

DARO MONTAG Herd (not seen), 2015, detail
Charred wooden animals purchased from charity shops

The climate is changing ⇨ Species are disappearing from the body of the Earth
at an alarming rate ⇨ Extinction is forever ⇨ Yet people like animals ⇨ Many
people collect carved wooden animals as souvenirs from their travels ⇨ Or as
gifts for their friends ⇨ Often such trophies are hand carved from tropical
wood by poorly paid workers ⇨ Some of these wooden animals end up in
charity shops when they are no longer wanted ⇨ As an artist I shall receive a
fee as my commission to create a new work ⇨ I propose using this entire fee to
purchase wooden animals from charity shops ⇨ The money will be recycled ⇨
The collected animals will be charred ⇨ Wood is rich in carbon ⇨ Charring
organic matter is a method for stabilising carbon to reduce atmospheric CO_2 ⇨
The charred animals will be placed in the gallery ⇨ Ultimately the animals will
be buried in the ground ⇨ Their carbon content will be returned to the soil ⇨
A cycle is completed ⇨

LUCY KERR
Daemon
Photograph

Constructing low-fi illusions, I connect to something hidden, confused, lost. Manipulating everyday household 'stuff' evokes both inner and outer landscapes. The process, always unpredictable, unspools through playful interactions with the ordinary – music, the bath, steam, torches, magnifying glasses, prisms, foil, cling film, collected objects. The sense of dislocation that ensues, infused with ritual meaning, brings me no answers – only a sense that I am holding my eyes wide open, waiting.

'To see the world in a grain of sand'
– William Blake, *Auguries of Innocence*

CHRISTOS GALANIS

The Time I Shot the *Iliad*

This series of shot books was made shortly after I moved to New Mexico
in 2010 to do my MFA, and, as a Canadian, was confronted with the
all-pervasive reality of gun culture in the United States. It was impossible
to hike anywhere in the mountains without coming across bullet casings
and spent shotgun shells; road signs and discarded washing machines
riddled with wild abstract patterns of haloed round fissures. In order to
more viscerally understand the culture, I undertook firearms training
with a friend who worked at a gun shop and shooting range, and became
transfixed by the archive of intense force that was left behind in the
objects being fired into. My first time sticking my finger into a wide
gaping hole in a phone book, shot through front to back by a 12-gauge
shotgun shell, was an experience that still haunts my body. These projec-
tiles had been crafted and finely honed for maximum damage to human
and animal bodies, and it was a deeply disturbing experience to sit with
that knowledge and touch it with my own hands. I eventually wanted to
document this process with books that were representative of the history
of civilisation. The books I chose for this purpose included, among
others: the *Iliad*, the *Odyssey*, *The Complete Works of William Shake-
speare*, *The History of the French Revolution* and *National Geographic:
The Photographs*.

And so I found myself with that same friend out in the desert with
a truck brimming with various firearms, and various books, where we
proceeded to create holes where none had been before. The experience
was grief-soaked and memorial in nature, rather than an adrenaline-filled
testosterone fest, as I would pick up the dusty books after they had been
shot, delicately separating the pages that had been fused together, and
making sense of the patterns and ruptures that had transformed these
bodies of knowledge into something almost sanctified in their aesthetic
chaos.

The *Iliad* – the oldest extant piece of literature from the lands we now
call Europe – is a story so deeply embedded in this culture that it's seem-

CHRISTOS GALANIS
The Time I Shot the *Iliad* (1 of 5)
New Mexico, USA

ingly impossible to fathom any other trajectory than one of walled urban centres, incessant warfare, colonisation, and dreams of immortality via martial glory. The exploits of Achilles and his comrades fill these pages with a torrent of blood and gore – thick descriptions of tendon, muscle, and bronzed flesh ravaged and brutalised on the beaches of Troy. In the end, even the river god Scamander cannot defeat Achilles after three attempts, while the text itself ends with the broken bodies of Hector and Patroclus being mourned and grieved over in the ritualised funeral proceedings of their time. It is as if the world of the Greek hero is confronted in this darkest of nights with his own unimaginable power – and in its wake, all that is good and noble has been slain and burned on the shores of that wine-dark sea. In these troubled times, we are living through the descending arc of that history – and the gods of the rivers, mountains and seas are rising up once more from their hiding places to trouble this ancient myth of progress and limitless expansion. What role will books – bodies of words – have in this great unravelling? How do these ancient stories of civilisation's foundations shape our understanding of what we're living through; and how might one begin to unfurl new stories for these times that are better suited to contraction, diminishment and loss? The *Iliad* – handed down originally through oral tradition – was eventually written down in order to be preserved and employed to make sense of the times those ancients were living through. What inscriptions will we make in our times? What archives of these days will bear faithful witness to How It Is? Here. Now.

ANTONY JOHAE

Three Extracts from
Guinea Coast Impressions

Rain Forest

Come to us, Mysterious Spirit;
Come in goodness, in love, in power;
...
For we have acknowledged the divinity
Also of the crocodile, the monkey and the eagle ...

– Mbella Sonne Dipoko, *Noble River*

The forest grew up on the poor soil of the Earth, over a thousand years, many feet tall, shedding a permanent darkness on its floor. It forbade plants to grow and mammals to see, and let only dead leaves fallen from high branches carpet it. Fungus wasted the leaves to a skeleton, altering the tapestry, and fed the roots of the trees, which finding no strength in the poor earth, grew exposed, like cathedral buttresses, to stop the tall trunks falling. And when they fell with age, termites roamed the dead wood, enlarging corridors and chambers with unending appetite, while cells worked singly in the insects' stomachs making sugar from the gorged wood to succour them.

Hungry beetle larvae first invaded the hard wood, boring passages for wandering driver ants to search out and for workers to prepare nests for the winged queens who, after nuptial flight and the wasting of their mates, would settle down to a wingless colonial existence.

But when red invaders threatened the nest, the black ants let go their deadly stings, paralysing to kill; or when the impregnable scaly pangolin approached, sentinel ants, like prisoners of war, tapped out their warning to the workers in their passages, before a sticky tongue reached out to gather them in.

Roaming in colonies made up of millions, the nomadic driver ants, like Napoleon's army marching on its stomach, ate what they could consume, while the large-headed soldiers gave protection to a determined column of workers which, in its progress across the forest floor, would take days to pass a rotting log, a monkey's skull, or a pool of clear water.

In the life of the ancient forest, strange relationships evolved: witness a solitary sting-ant who, in the search for food, has breathed in the minute spores of a fungus which then grow into its brain. Now, like an addict up a New York block, the ant has begun a unique vertical climb to the top of the plant, where it sinks down and dies. The fungus continues feeding on the body and grows, while spores are showered down for earthbound ants to inhale, so to begin a vain climb towards the light.

Mammals, meanwhile, have grown up nocturnal: the toothless ant-eater, like a large lizard with a long licking tongue, scoured the forest for its prey; or the huge-eyed angwantibo smelling its way in the darkness; and the light pygmy flying squirrel with its wing-like membranes uniting the limbs, gliding from branch to branch foraging fruits in the night until, when the day penetrated, it returned with the colony to the dark hollow of a tree.

With the light, a long-toed drill could be seen grasping fruit thrown down by yellow-chinned monkeys; the sun-birds, too, dispersed pollen as hairy-tailed dormice and marvellous-memoried bats had done innocently in the night.

On the leaves of the trees, caterpillars grew up with the leaf, took off their coats, settled into silk beds and, awaking perfect, dispersed into the forest as many-coloured butterflies. And flowers too would grow up on the leaves and mosses, and lichens form on them, and creepers spread from tree to tree making a forest highway for monkeys to go by.

But when the crowned eagle swooped down from his nest in the tall treetop, the monkey would be stopped in mid-swing, his head crushed and his flesh flown to open-mouthed young. And if there were two of them in the eagle's nest, the chicks would fight as keenly as cocks in a ring, until one of them died and the other grew to assume power.

So the eagle used to reign; but when man, that other branch of the animal family, came cutting down the forest turning it into desert scrub, the monkeys departed first to another realm, uncrowning the eagle who, in famine, flew humiliated from his wasted kingdom as the trees crashed down.

Manpang

Driving along the West African coast to the city of soap and tinned fish, clearing the holes the rains had made, we saw its shape ahead. As the car zigzagged, the giant lizard moved – then hesitated; time for us to see its panicful sideways look, its prehistoric body and its long lash tail.

My passenger cried, 'Kill it!' but like the lizard, I hesitated; time for him to power himself across the road back into the bush.

Harvest

The lampposts had been erected some years before, tall and concrete, bowing over the road out of town with a few curiously reversed as though meant to illuminate the bush; but the lights had never gone on and the posts were left standing like sentinels in the night.

Soon after the revolution, the lights sprang to life and it seemed a sign of promised change. Then workers came with tractors to plough up the spare earth on both sides of the road and on the slopes of Tettie Quarshie Circle: long straight furrows which made farmers, who plough in the round, shake their heads vaguely.

When the rains fell the workers sowed their maize, but on Tettie Quarshie Circle the seed was washed away in the sloping gutters the plough had made. On the roadside, though, green stalks began to grow tall, as though competing for height with the lampposts. All day they stood under the sun, growing taller near the fuming traffic, and at night after curfew with the road deserted, under bright sodium, like spectators at an evening match.

But in this perpetual light the corn never fattened, because for their consummation the seed needs the night and pollen the day. So that when the workers came like warriors with cutlasses to break the long leafy stalks, they found no harvest.

where the wound is

where the wound is you can see map lines if you look close. where the wound is rivers leak out. where the wound is, I place bundles of chewed plantain, stem the outpour, check dams made to keep the streams from gobbling out their own flesh banks. where the wound is I scrub salt so forgetting won't come.

often I confuse my body with a mountain range. often I confuse you with a fishing pole, pellet gun, the tines of a fork. it is always more dangerous to paint the gaps, gaping, to call out with the mouth of a cut thigh or elbow, to say I need, I need, look hear the anger and the haemoglobin howl.

where the wound is, it is clear: the world ails so body ails too. our skin is only as impermeable as anything else: soil, leaves, sky. all things move into each other, this is called the atom, this is called your pulmonary system, this is called shit, this is called tomatoes, this is called the San Andreas, this is called cells, this is called morgues and mountains I –

– confuse my body with a mountain range. where the wound is, if you look real gentle, you can see map lines to the next world. they are fragmented, broken and quiet, dangerous thing: to say I need, I need, I bleed.

RACHEL ECONOMY

The Explosive Borders Manifesto

On Sunday all the borders
exploded suddenly into tangled
triumphant corridors of
scarlet runner beans, pumpkin
vines, purple
corn.

No one knows
how it happened, who
planted seeds so strong they
strangled a spiked fence the
size of nations
until it was nothing more
than a fallen, twisted
trellis
for the green to climb across.

The world is suddenly strewn
with confused cookouts, harvest
parties, well-fed
arguments, vined
tendrils bending
guns into stakes for
tenacious tomatoes, farmers
kept from families for ages
finally able to meet
on the bloody crossing ground of loss.

They declare this a riot
of abundance, a warning
of what happens to land laced
with hatred and iron walls.

The border guards and presidents
sit at the edges of the barbecues
salivating and afraid
unsure if they will be offered
food or
swallowed by the roots
of the fast-growing fruit trees.

We do not know yet
what will happen in this wall-less place
once everyone has eaten their fill
what reparations could possibly be made for
choking the land, for
shooting down the bodies tending it, moving
loving and alert
across its ridges and spine.

We do not know but
the dancing has started
it is loud danger
joyous, a wail
furious and full of finallys.

The whole earth shakes with it
and the corn
waves and glints in the sun.

ALBERT VETERE LANNON

The Jersey Devil

I

I grew up on the tough Lower East Side of New York City, long before it became the East Village. To survive I, too, became tough. And because under the toughness and anger was fear, I and several of my hoodlum friends escaped the city every chance we could, hitch-hiking to the Ramapo Mountains, or to the Pine Barrens of Southern New Jersey to escape the mean streets, to escape our families. In what was to us deep nature we could be the kids we were, playing and swimming, running and jumping, star-watching and moon-talking, eating pancakes three times a day because that's all the money we had. Friendships were cemented on those weekends and summer breaks: Carl Herrmann, Johnny-Boy DeMaria, John Sepp, Carlos and Al Cabrera. Boys, especially tough teenagers, don't usually speak of love between boys, but there was love between us.

Hitch-hiking was pretty safe in the mid-1950s, and we would even be picked up by truck drivers and Greyhound buses despite their company rules and our black leather motorcycle jackets and DA hair, our cigarettes rolled into the sleeves of our t-shirts that covered the sharpened garrison belt buckles that held up our low-slung dungarees, a.k.a. blue jeans. Sometimes we never got out of the city, standing with thumbs out and army-surplus rucksacks at our feet at an entrance to the George Washington Bridge or the Holland Tunnel. But most of the time we made it.

Several of us were wannabe herpetologists looking for snakes to bring home. Carl had the biggest collection outside of a zoo, including reptiles that ought never to hang out in the middle of a city – mambas, rattlers, cobras. I can't speak to their reasons, but for me it was about attracting negative attention since I had a hard time getting positive strokes from my parents, or teachers. But once we were out in nature the snakes were really secondary to exploration, to freedom.

The South Jersey Pine Barrens were my favourite place. Thousands of acres of sand and scrub pine trees, with brown rivers leached from cedar trees running free or diverted into cranberry bogs. Bogs which, I later learned, once produced iron ore. At the time of the American Revolution Jersey bog iron was what cannonballs were made from, until iron ore and coal were found in Pennsylvania and the industry shifted. Many Pine Barrens towns converted to making glass, and we sometimes found intact little 100-year-old medicine bottles. Clay production followed the glass, with abandoned ore cars left to rust.

Once Johnny-Boy and I met at the Dover Deli on the edge of Toms River after hitch-hiking separately to our usual jumping-off place. As we ate our ritual fresh ham and cheese sandwiches and drank the RC Cola we couldn't get at home, a big thunderstorm rolled in with wind and heavy rain. We knew we'd never be able to sleep outside, and didn't want to try the public toilet in the middle of town. We had done that once, and once was enough, especially since it sat under the town's police station.

There was a big old house with a wrap-around porch across from the delicatessen, and we ran to it. Shaking off water, we knocked on the front door to ask if we could sleep on the porch, out of the storm. White-haired Mrs. Frorier answered and told us she lived alone and we could come in and sleep in one of her extra beds. We, who were labelled JDs for juvenile delinquents with our switchblades and swagger, didn't know how to respond to such kindness. We slept on the porch, waking to the smell of bacon and eggs being cooked for our breakfast. Mrs. Frorier's daughter came by, looking a bit askance at us, but said nothing unkind.

The Pine Barrens were the northern range of some interesting and beautiful snakes: pine, king and corn snakes; a timber rattler that looked like its South Carolina cousin, the canebrake; the delicate Coastal Plains milk snake. Because ruins attract rodents and rodents attract snakes, we explored places which dated back to the 1700s and 1800s, ruins of kilns for firing clay, remains of factories with brick archways and still-producing apple trees, big holes turned into ponds with narrow tracks running alongside where clay was mined, railroad stations that closed in the 1930s, with timetables strewn on the dusty floors and migrating bats in the attics.

And mosquitoes. The first time I camped out in the Barrens, at the old railroad station in Pinewald, across a dark lake from a looming sanitarium we made up ghost stories about, I woke up and counted mosquito bites. I stopped counting at 100 on just one arm. Every two or three trips

I would pick up a wood tick. I usually found it embedded in my scalp at inconvenient times – in school, or while my parents had company. One I removed in school I impaled with a fountain pen and expelled ink into, leaving a small explosion of blood and ink to sink into the old wood desk. Making my mark.

The mosquitoes were no less fierce when we spread our blankets at Double Trouble, Ong's Hat, Harrissia or the well-named Mount Misery. We swam in Lake Oswego and bathed in the Mullica River, slapping at mosquitoes the whole time. As far as I was concerned, mosquitoes were the true manifestation of the Jersey Devil.

II

The story went that a Mrs. Leeds of pre-Revolutionary times, having 12 children and wanting no more, swore that if she had another it would be a devil. She had a thirteenth, and it was a strange child who one day shapeshifted into the monster of legend, flew up the fireplace chimney, and loosed its evil on the area.

The Jersey Devil, it was claimed, had the head of a horse and giant bat wings. It flew over farms and curdled cows' milk in their udders. Its cloven hooves scorched the land where it set down. Once, in the 1950s, a young couple was found torn apart on a blanket they had been making love on in the woods. The police said it was a pack of gone-wild dogs which roam the Barrens, but locals descended from Revolutionary-era Hessian mercenaries said, No, the Jersey Devil was about.

Fifteen years later, in 1970, returning from the West Coast where I had moved to a decade before, I hiked the Pine Barrens alone, trekking nearly 80 miles through 18 ghost towns, touching civilisation just twice, by choice. There was a storm one night and I could imagine the Jersey Devil hovering somewhere overhead, just out of sight. The mosquitoes were still there. I visited the Frorier house and talked to the daughter, who was now herself old and white-haired, and she said she remembered me, and that her mother commented over the years what nice, well-mannered boys we were.

In 1992 I visited the Barrens again to show off this special place to someone I hoped would feel the magic. The old clay mines were covered by a senior housing tract. The Harrissia factory ruins were fenced in. The restored colonial town of Batsto was up and running – but everywhere we came in contact with brush tiny ticks swarmed on us. They moved quickly and silently, even going through the eyelets of our shoes looking for soft places to feed. It was like a bad 1950s science-fiction movie where they *kept on coming!*

In Toms River signs hung over main streets advertising Lyme Disease support groups. And when we got home it turned out we had not successfully picked off all the tiny ticks and had to be treated with antibiotics.

In the summer of 2000, visiting North Jersey relatives with my grandson Danny, we visited the Pine Barrens to swim in Lake Oswego and visit Batsto. Walking across a mowed lawn I picked up three ticks. A park ranger said they were finding them on the sandy beaches of the Jersey Shore. Local kids told us they stayed out of the woods. And the Frorier house was gone, identical tract homes in its place.

The little deer ticks were always there. But each winter there would be a big die-off and each spring they would start all over again. It was an annual cycle, the balance of nature. With global warming there is no more winter die-off, and the ticks just multiply and multiply, lurking, looking for soft flesh to feed on, to infect.

In the summer of 2001, working on a Forest Service archaeology project in California's Eastern Sierra Nevada Mountains, five people – including the woman I had just met and would later marry – got very sick, spiking fevers of 105-plus degrees. It was finally diagnosed as relapsing fever – just 100 cases in the last 150 years, and we had five new ones. The disease, which manifests itself in recurring life-threatening fevers, was carried by little fast-moving ticks that came out at night to feed. The Forest Service had to finally burn down the cabins we had stayed in to get rid of the ticks. Maybe.

I think of my best friend and mentor Carl Herrmann, who introduced me to the Pine Barrens and so much more, dead of some exotic blood cancer at 40. And of Jay Skaats and John Foley, dead at 50 of brain cancers. Of 40-something Bill Krause and Dick Pabich, dead of AIDS. Of my own near-death two weeks in hospital with a pneumonia they never fully diagnosed. I think of the Four Corners flu which has killed people in 22 states and several countries. Of Ebola, and Zika, and West Nile; of SARS and MRSA and SIDS.

When I hiked the Pine Barrens with my best buddies and fought off mosquitoes there was no Lyme Disease, no AIDS, no exotic cancers cutting down people in their prime. There was no mad cow disease, no mysterious hantavirus, no swarms of tiny deer ticks mindlessly searching for soft places to feed. *In the land's come a scary sound, and the Jersey Devil's time's come round.*

III

Weeks before her 70th birthday and our tenth wedding anniversary my beloved Kaitlin had a heart attack and was minutes from death. It was a rare kind known as Takotsubo cardiomyopathy, or broken-heart syndrome. It's brought on by stress. Kait, who has rarely been sick, was dealing with a host of issues, and her friends, meaning well, wanted to have a birthday party for her. For many reasons having to do with her upbringing, Kaitlin did not want a party. Her friends insisted, and became angry when they felt thwarted. More stress, the heart attack, hospitalisation, and now, recovery, medications and dramatic lifestyle changes. The good news is that those who survive a *takotsubo* have an excellent shot at recovery.

Somehow Kait's birthday became about the friends, and not her, a nearly-tragic manifestation of a self-centredness that seems to grip America these days. I recognise a difference between being selfish, as in putting my sobriety ahead of the wants of others, and self-centredness, which reflects the bipartisan world of Robber Baron Capitalism, of commerce and corruption, of media manipulation and bigotry, of 'progress' no matter the cost, of dire unintended consequences, that is the prevailing ethic.

Fortunately we have Wild Heart Ranch, our Sonoran Desert acre with a comfortable manufactured home, a once-feral cat, a goofy dog, five tortoises, and an oasis habitat that is home or hunting ground for king and gopher snakes, an occasional rattler and coachwhip, a pair of cardinals who have been here longer than our dozen years, several great horned owls, four varieties of doves, Gambel's quail, little birds I call chirpies, a half-dozen kinds of lizards, including delicate night geckos and fearsome-looking horned lizards, a couple of Sonoran Desert Toadzillas and a few little spadefoots with their loud, grating love call, *waaaackkk...*, Harris's hawks, unseen coyotes leaving scat in the driveway, beetles, spiders, shady mesquite trees, not-really-leafless palo verdes, cacti beyond counting, and the flowers Kaitlin tends and nourishes, bits of bright light absorbed from the harsh summer sun. It's a good place to recover.

The daily chores – watering, trimming, feeding – are not really chores.

When the chirpies or the male cardinal – we call him Claudio – let us know the bird feeder is empty, when the doves and quail flood the driveway by their feeding area, when tortoises are on the lookout for cactus apples, feeding and caring for them is as good or better for us than for them. Maintaining our oasis, our habitat, is self-nurturing and fulfilling. In our rural community we can be social by choice rather than as expected. We can hide out, or engage: our choice. We have music and radio and old films on TV, and commerce is ten miles away over a mountain, necessary to visit when needed, but not in our face. The cultural offerings of the city of Tucson are less than an hour away, should we want them as we sometimes do.

I continue to carry on several political battles: against aerial spraying of Monsanto's herbicide glyphosate in our valley by neighbouring Saguaro National Park and Tucson Water. Linked to cancer and other disorders, aerial spraying has made neighbours, and their pets, sick.

And opposing a new interstate highway, I-11, designed to facilitate the export of jobs to low-wage factories and ports across the border while destroying the Avra Valley's communities, wildlife and archaeological treasures along with the jobs that service the present interstate corridor through town. Those struggles will likely go on past my lifetime, but I do what I can while I can, and know that, at 79, I am still of use.

Kaitlin will now have more time for her own art and poetry, things she has set aside while helping others to grow into their creativity. She will have time to just sit in the shade of her gardens and watch the butterflies and the tiny, translucent, flying insects that just might be faeries.

While the news of the day, of the moment, is generally grim, we try to remember these words from Joseph Campbell: *We cannot cure the world of sorrows, but we can choose to live in joy.*

The Jersey Devil has not found us here. With luck and perseverance, it never will.

NICK HUNT

The Last of Many Breeds

Lily McInnes remembers the day when Donald James Eiger arrived at the zoo – top-hatted, tweed-suited, swinging his cane – and purchased the last of the thylacines for the sum of forty pounds. The beast had been caught in the Florentine Valley three years previously, and had spent its time in captivity pacing and yawning, yawning and pacing, occasionally making a futile leap at the bars and rebounding off them. The zookeepers hated it. It made the other animals nervous, they said – put them off their feed. Visitors steered away from it, preferring the monkeys and the bears, exotic things from foreign lands, not this local pestilence. You wouldn't pay to see rabid dogs or rats exhibited in a cage, so why give money for a sight like that? Yawning and pacing, pacing and yawning, grinning its sheep-murdering grin. The last of its kind, it would never breed – would never produce lucrative offspring to recompense the zoo for the cost of its sustenance and upkeep. All it did in captivity was what it had done in its habitat – consume a small fortune in meat at the taxpayer's expense. If Mr Eiger hadn't made his offer they'd probably have put the thing down, and flung the carcass in the trash with the zoo's other scrapings.

No-one knew why he wanted it, but no-one knew why Mr Eiger did most of the things he did. A trim, skinny man of advanced years, who dressed like a dandy but never was known to frequent any restaurant, dinner or dance, he was sighted now and then around town, engaged in unknowable business. His money was made in timber, they said – blackwood, blue gum, Huon pine – though some believed he also had dealings in coal, bauxite, gold. He was rumoured to be a mad millionaire, but both his madness and his millions were probably exaggerated. He was certainly rich and strange, and that was enough for Hobart.

Lily, nine years old, watched him arrive in a taxicab and shake begloved hands with the zoo's director. The two men advanced to the thylacine's cage and spent twenty minutes smoking cigars, conversing in low, amenable tones, while the beast stalked back and forth. Then the head keeper – Lily's father – entered the cage with a bucket of meat which he liberally slopped upon the floor, and while the thylacine's jaws were engaged bagged its head, collared its neck, muzzled its mouth, strapped its legs and fastened it to a length of chain, the end of which he presented to Mr Eiger with a flourish. Three other men half-dragged, half-carried the struggling thing to the taxicab, where it was pinned against the floor by Simon, Mr Eiger's butler.

'They christened it Benjamin, by the way,' said the zoo's director, again shaking hands. An envelope had been exchanged. 'That's what the papers chose.'

But Mr Eiger shook his head. 'A thing like that needs no name.'

The taxicab left, and Lily watched. It was a blue summer day. She looked back at the empty cage, at her father sweeping up the meat. He turned his head and met her eye. 'No tears now,' he said.

There were different stories told. The house was high upon the hill, over-looking the city and the bay, and not many visitors went to it – but still, the stories travelled. People said it was loose inside the house, that he permitted it to prowl, that it had made a stinking nest in the corner of Simon's bedroom. That it had eaten several cats. That Mr Eiger had *shot* the cats. That constables had visited. That delivery men refused to visit. That Genevieve Eiger, his delicate and perennially ailing English wife, had suffered from 'nervous fits' of some kind and been taken to the hospital. That she might be away for some time. That the servants had departed with her.

There were other stories too. That he was trying to breed the thing. That bitches in heat – dingos, strays – had been brought to the house in recent months and left in a room with the thylacine, but the only thing that remained the next day was bones and scraps of fur. Some said he had taught the brute some tricks – it would yawn on demand when he said 'sleep tight', or fall with its belly in the air when he made a pistol sound. Others believed he had taken its teeth. That he beat it with a bamboo cane, starved it in an airless box, that his ambition was to break its spirit as one breaks a horse's. A gardener from the house next door swore he heard its yowls at night, rasps of fury, screams of pain – and afterwards, the quieter noise of Mr Eiger weeping.

It was strictly not allowed but Lily climbed the hill one day, a half-hour walk from school, into the rich people's neighbourhood, and spied through the iron gate. She could see the big house with its pillars and porch, its gardens dark with Tasmanian oak, but she couldn't see the beast. She wondered if it was dead somehow. If Mr Eiger had punished too far. Perhaps he had stuffed it, or stretched its tiger-striped skin before his fire.

She stared through the gate for a long while hoping for the truth to come, but no sound, no sign, no shadow came from behind the blank square windows. She walked to the zoo to meet her dad, fibbing that school had kept her late. She passed the thylacine's old cage. An ocelot was there now.

And then there were older tales. Tales from before Lily's time. Tales from before Mr Eiger's time, if you counted the years back, but tales that Lily nevertheless believed were connected, somehow. She pictured him as a younger man, uniformed, slouch-hatted, rifle snapped in the crook of his arm, on horseback. On a moonless night. The Black War was long since won but some of the tribes had escaped the Line and continued to live by stealing sheep, haunting lonely stations. Punitive raids on recalcitrant blacks happened in the dead of night, and when they fled their campfires the raiding squads pursued for days – often using native trackers tamed by money, whisky, church – picking them off with long-range shots from higher ground, from ridges. Like shooting wallabies or cats. This work was rewarded. The ones not shot were rounded up, chained from neck to neck to neck, and marched in dragging, dusty lines to Flinders Island, Oyster Cove, where they were taught to wear clothes and live in proper houses. People crowded their doors to watch as the captured blacks paraded past – naked legs, ragged beards, scowling, glistening like apes – an obstacle to settlement, a taint, a dying breed.

Lily had never seen a black. She wanted to, and feared to. Sometimes when she closed her eyes she saw them like a picture show, heads bagged, long limbs chained, in moving lines across the earth. She was too young to remember that. But when she stood at the thylacine's cage, which contained no thylacine, somehow she remembered.

Then the territory was clear, the settlement was won. Frontier families slept without fear of a waddy staving in the door, a spear crashing through the wall. It was a new century. The Irish came, the Cockneys came, the Welsh came, the Germans came. Sealers, whalers, timbermen. Pastures for a million sheep. Rare earth metals, bauxite, gold. The forests splintered to the crash of Huon pine and myrtle.

Sheep were found with their throats ripped out. Ribcages that buzzed with flies. Something else was out there now. New rewards were offered.

Three years went by, and Lily grew. Her dad retired from the zoo – he suffered from arthritic joints – and found work on the trams instead. The work was less demanding, and you didn't catch fleas from trams. Hobart's streets were widened, paved. Elegant parks were laid, with eucalyptus rustling. There were streetlights and hotels, more automobiles, fewer horses. Lily's older sister Ruth married, moved to New South Wales. Her brother Sam enlisted in the Royal Tasmania Regiment and was sent to Europe to fight. Another war was starting.

Genevieve Eiger died and the rich people went to her funeral, though most had never been acquainted. Mr Eiger's beard turned white. He was seldom seen in town. People called him a 'recluse' and Lily didn't know what that meant, but it sounded coarse and strange. A bit like 'loon'. A bit like 'loose'. There were rumours of a fight – that Mr Eiger, mindless drunk, had flung Simon's clothes and books from a top-floor window in a thunderstorm, or even attacked him with his cane. Reluctantly, so they said, the butler packed his bags.

Sometimes she thought of the thylacine. It was distant now. She had a picture in her mind, but she didn't know if it was right. A striped backside, a cavernous grin, pointed ears like a dog's – but other than that its distinctions blurred, its features ran together.

No-one talked about it now. Perhaps it had only been a silly story told at parties.

Two more years. The food got less. Lily watched the troops parade in Macquarie Street, hung with flags – uniformed, slouch-hatted, with rifles snapped in the crooks of their arms. The men looked strong and brave and clean. The air raid sirens yowled at night. The Japanese were in Hong Kong, Malaya, Burma, Singapore. Perhaps the Dutch East Indies next. After that, Australia. Lily had never seen a Jap. She wanted to, and feared to. Now when she closed her eyes she saw them, at great distances – she picked them off one by one from horseback in her mind.

In the middle of that war, Mr Eiger left the house. Lily wasn't there to see – she learned the legends later.

It was dawn, and he rode a white mare. His silk top hat was at a tilt. He carried a rifle on his back, a waddy in his hand.

They said the beast stalked at his side, or strained ahead on a length of chain. That its flanks flashed in the light – orange black, orange black. That its sheep-destroying teeth gleamed in its yawning skull.

Man, horse and beast passed quickly through the suburbs of the rich and were glimpsed from outlying farms making their way towards the bush. They disappeared, people said, in the woods beyond Mount Wellington. A farmer named Eli Church claimed to have seen them passing by, pausing at a stream. The horse ate grass, the man drank wine and the beast consumed red chunks of meat, tossed from a battered leather bag. The meat did not last long.

The constables knocked at the big house, and received no answer. Having forced the door they searched the rooms and reported that nothing was amiss, not a teaspoon out of place. The fireplace was swept and stacked. The marble floors were freshly mopped. Just empty rooms and an open cage – but even that was clean and scrubbed. No clues, just an absence.

Lily McInnes is an old woman now, and she retells the stories. Her grandchildren have heard her talk of bunyips, yowies, flightless birds, forgotten tribes of wild men, though these are only fairytales. But sometimes she tells about the man who might be glimpsed on moonless nights, backcountry, deep within the bush. They do not like this tale so much, but she tells it anyway. Lily changes as she talks. He slaughters sheep, he catches cats. Mad-eyed, he swings a bamboo cane. With tiger stripes across his skin. Upon his head a crown of jaws, hinged open in an endless yawn. No bounty will bring this one in. He is the last of many breeds. The farmers say they'll shoot on sight, until his extirpation.

This story was originally commissioned for Remembrance Day for Lost Species, 30 November 2016. With thanks to the ONCA Centre for Arts & Ecology.

TIM FOX

Welcome the Aftermath

Apocalypse and post-apocalypse redefined

The stratospheric ejecta from the 18 May, 1980 eruption of Mount St. Helens took a day to cross the Columbia Plateau and the Rocky Mountains. I was up early on the morning of 19 May when it reached Colorado Springs. In my nine-year-old imagination, I anticipated a rain of ash thick enough to form drifts like grey snow and create a noontime twilight reminiscent of the TV footage from Yakima, Washington where five inches fell. Instead, little more than a faint, smoke-like haze fuzzed the view of Pikes Peak and the only place where the ash could be seen at all was on the glass of car windshields. Had I not been looking for it, I might not have even noticed it.

Now, 37 years later, and living in a world of amplifying climatic upheaval, mass extinction and the industrial toxification of every habitat on Earth, it occurs to me that the fallout from the spread of agricultural civilisation across the globe has been much the same: indiscernible unless you're looking for it. And even then, its cataclysmic nature remains largely hidden, obscured by the long sweep of time separating the present planetary socio-ecological calamity from its comparatively humble origins. It is also obscured by an assumption that is almost as opaque now as it was when it first emerged as a core assumption of civilisation's deepest guiding stories. What is this assumption?

That the end of the world – the apocalypse – is an event forthcoming, and that the civilised order is the only thing standing in its way. As supporting evidence for this view, we, the citizens of this order, proudly cite our numeric, territorial and technological expansion over the last few millennia. But perhaps our spread – now exponential in rate and scale – suggests something else: a shared tunnel vision focused so tightly on the civilised branches of one hominid species that it has rendered invisible the apocalyptic impact of civilisation on everything else in the world.

Only now, as that impact has reached global proportions, is it possible to see that the apocalypse isn't somewhere out there on the horizon. As far as the greater community of life is concerned, the term accurately describes an event that has been under way for 10,000 years. It *began* with agriculture, intensified with the emergence of urban civilisation and reached cataclysmic intensity with global industrialisation.

In other words, in relation to the countless lives degraded, displaced or extinguished by every forest razed, every grassland plowed and every indigenous culture extirpated to make way for a field, pasture or city, the apocalypse is not some *future* potentiality that can, in theory, still be avoided. It is, at this very moment, in progress, like a slow-motion asteroid collision or volcanic eruption. Actually, it only appears slow from the perspective of an individual human lifespan. On an evolutionary/geologic time scale, there is no significant difference in the rates at which natural disasters and expanding civilisations devastate the earth. We have but to graph climatic upheavals and their associated extinction spasms on a scale measured in billions of years to see that these events all appear as spikes.

This shift in temporal perspective allows us to visualise how we are part of an agriculturally-fuelled human explosion that has swept the planet like a scouring shockwave, moving outwards from urban epicentres at far too rapid a rate to allow most other forms of life to adapt to the transformed landscapes left in its wake.

We not only have a hard time sensing this explosion because it is slow relative to any given human generation, but also because it is not singular. It is diffuse and contained, taking place inside millions of internal combustion engines, thousands of fossil-fuel-driven power plants and hundreds of nuclear reactors. But add all these micro-bursts together and factor in the years – decades! – they've been going off without pause and you get a blast that makes the eruption of Mount St. Helens look like a firecracker.

In this light, a post-apocalyptic world becomes not something to prevent at all costs, but rather a very appealing goal towards which to strive. We have but to realise that the common vision of a post-apocalyptic world as a charred wasteland, popularised most starkly in the *Mad Max* films, is exactly backwards. From an ecological perspective, the landscapes subsumed within the explosion of industrial civilisation are charred wastelands when compared to their prior conditions (and to the rare wildlands as yet beyond modernity's reach) and a post-apocalyptic world is a world in which the expansion of these wastelands reverses – where frontier becomes ebbline – thereby allowing the recovery of wild verdancy to commence, with humans as active, contributing participants. Thus, Mad Max lives not in a post-apocalyptic world as we've been led to believe, but in the late-stage apocalypse, where the struggle continues to keep the engines burning.

In order to invert this grim cinematic forecast and arrive at a positive post-apocalyptic awareness, we must first understand that the myriad crises presently afflicting the Earth reflect the immune response of a planetary metabolism adjusting to counter apocalyptic conditions. When we understand this, we'll stop trying to save the shockwave and instead seek ways for the unavoidable cultural transformation *out of* the apocalypse to unfold slowly, cooperatively and attentively rather than rapidly, violently and catastrophically.

It begins with the stories we tell ourselves. So long as the prevailing stories continue to paint the apocalypse as a nightmarish tomorrow rather than as a current event, we'll continue to prolong and worsen the very thing we are trying, with increasing desperation, to avoid. We will also continue to miss the opportunity before us: a better world.

The Mount St. Helens blast zone shows us what we might anticipate. Instead of the long grey centuries predicted by the experts, the scorched and levelled landscape erupted green only days into the aftermath. Yes, by comparison, the industrial shockwave is of a whole different order, having created a blast zone on a global scale. But the same planetary response will likely hold true. Past mass extinction events offer supporting evidence; they tend to be followed by mass diversification events. The present age of mammals serves as a case in point. Were it not for the K-T extinction 65 million years ago, we would join thousands if not millions of other species in having never come into existence.

We might find inspiration from the only dinosaurs to survive: the birds. And not only did they survive, they flourished, branching into ten thousand species, filling the world with colour, song and unmatched beauty. Imagine if we took their example and strove to diversify into ten thousand cultures, each fully integrated into its local ecosystem and committed to the celebration of the Earth through story, art and music. What kind of an age might we usher into being? What kind of beauty?

The only way to find out is to make it our intention. Like the scientists who first set foot in the Mount St. Helens blast zone following the eruption, we will step into the future expecting nothing, but finding green shoots breaking through the ash of our assumptions.

ANNE HAVEN MCDONNELL

Predators

A scream is made to cut
through the mind's fog,
all rescue circuits flipped on –
any kind of baby animal will do.
When his sleep was sliced by sounds
from the gulley, deep in the woods outside,
he moved towards the *yawl*, a flashlight
tunnelling into the dark, searching the cry,
and he knew before he saw the tawny warm
fur, speckled white, folded in a thicket of salal.
The fawn's mouth was open, her fresh
pink tongue hanging out while the cry looped
itself out from her belly from where her eyes –
wide open and hardened to whatever she saw
outside – were already living inside
wherever this cry cut from.
And what could he do?

He thought how the sound must pull
all the blood in her mother, hidden
and waiting. The wolf must also be waiting
to finish this, listening to this cry
light up a tunnel of hunger.
He loved to listen to the wolves
when they sang to each other across
the water, stitching this island and that,
sometimes swimming across, surrounding
the youngest wolf in a circle as they swam,
the arc and hang of their howls, the pull
inside him towards this sound that peeled

the air, and the silence after, the night
full and undone. He thought of carrying
that speckled fawn home but left it –
all of it – the sound of his own footsteps
through the brush all he heard in his long
walk back to the porch light he left on
in his cabin with a door that doesn't lock.

WeRLtd!

Bestiary 4Achieving Imitation Doxa

Prologue:

We traversed unbeaten desire lines, our path sporadically obstructed by paywalls and trollfronts brokered by unkeyed changelings. For a share of nest-egg, these changelings would navigate a degenerate strategy along the road most travelled. But, on some fool's errand, we nebby wanderers gravitated toward the lonesome otherworld of the New Forest Coven Mall. Vigilantly, we ascended the accessibility branch that drifted mid-mall, bunny-hopping, as proudling Scrazos do, with the vexed circumspection of a discerning Dollaramamama.

The top of the branch was a brown study. From this glorious perspective of providence, we envisioned the rude beginnings of PATH and the ghost-renderings of RESO, rejoicing the guaranteed pre-existence of such wonders. We trickled off a platform, drifting upon the mall's thermals. As we lowered placidly onto the forecourt, we whiffed sweetly-rotten birdsong that, in hindsight, helped ferment our prospects.

Quickening our recitations, we two silent friends fled upon a small Branch Outlet that had been closed due to a three-thousand-year debt. As we powertooled its humble door to smithereens, the Branch Outlet's CEO appeared. It hailed us with astonished reverence, and, as the doxa directs, implored us to indulge its hospitality. Assisted by the stuttering lights of our Segway®, we spun to leisurely sample the innumerable gifts besieging our attention. An organ mawkishly begged us to come play with her. Euphonic idolatry. A constellation of white goods conversed. Skittish domestic prophesies. Treasure from excrements! But it was a simple sonsy stick that charmed *us*. Leaning nonchalantly against a wall, our stick timorously suffused all the unobtrusive utility of the nonborn maker. Sure, the unwreathed stick was trying really hard to be crude, and was *too* dialup for bulk-good dwelling, but its coy virtuosity was indubitably seductive. Soon, we two would be three.

The CEO, a languid numbskull, presented us with a meticulous selection box of crunchy kale greens, imaginary Canada browns and a monstrous sloom of yeller-belly yellow. He tossed and tousled a spiffing banquet, accessorised with a toll-free fire, courtesy of the Branch Outlet's cut-rate carved tat (a magic helmet and a golden plow furfuksake?!). How we LOLaloted as the CEO pirouetted upon a rôtisserie improvised wittily from our mount! Duly chargrilled, sated, pink-salted and partially perished, our plus-one association lit upon the slumber plagues of disordered yearning. We flossed, and, in due course, briny droplets of nostalgic sorrow encrusted in our ducts with Promethean convenience.

Meh-ed by a characterless splash in the hot-pot-plop, we malingered deeper into the chiasmic Mall, harvesting the ameliorated embrace of the Ylem tree's witter-waffling limbs. If a branch stood in our way, we'd break it off, flip it over and use it as a stick to break off further branches. As we farmed branches into sticks, we began to ©. We ©d more and more, and as more saw us, our number grew and grew and grew. The sticks spawned extra limbs, limbs that taught us how limbs work. As the fog of sticks, staffs, rods, crooks, poles, shafts and pikes of that perpetual night grew ever more grasping and vertiginous, we became immortal.

*

A flavourless ray of hiss-hop and hintful harmonising. Scuffling eyelips and flickering lipflashes with the foreclosure of certainty, we booted up our Brandeum™ EVP Field Recorder. Foreswunk, we hit the snooze button, but it was too late. A deadened thump roused us into an approximation of the exemplars we suspected we would eventually become. An owl-jacket dripped and sparkled melodramatically in the portico: a *wudu-wāsa* of pre-Boreal orphanage. As our attention atrophied and sharpened, the *wudu-wāsa* manifested as a charred and chomped torso, a bite-sized corpys basted and extinguished many times over, its fungus battered and exquisitely seasoned by the chiff-chaff of sous-solution aligners. Low reverberating drones wifted and babbled beneath its crisply ravished mantle. The appearance transmitted 1-o-1-o-o-N-m-T-o-r-q-u-e-W-r-e-n-c-h in deconsecrated monotone at uDH 279 million cycles per second, a huge bottom end that our Brandeum™ EVP Field Recorder handled with robustness and great clarity.

After a few minutes, this weedish distortion and farty low end splintered our sonsy stick into a zerg of pliant Blobula and Baraka. This glee-mote blinked, twinkled and lip-synched itself into hard attack of complex conglomerates of companies limited by guarantee. Prepositions multiplied with wild abandon, about, in and between each, and every, spawn point. 'Sacre!' we groaned. 'This stick was our crutch; now it will limit us *and make us limitless!*' Gingerly, we powered down the Brandeum^{SM} EVP Field Recorder, deposited an ersatz 15% gratuity, and gimbled our bye-byes.

Galumphing furthermore into the mall, we were popjoyed by woodland thought-bundles as they foraged *glette* from the nerve ends of amputated Ylem branches. Right before our wide-angled lenses, they compressed, overdubbed, tropical-themed and amplified their Ylemy product into megastick systems composed of jazzily complex and biologically charming chains of indexical confusion. Great bulbous *faux pas* of retrospective sustain-stability!

Energised by novel doxa chatter and arboreal trade mists, we prised the herbs from our bonephones and floated, hair-naked, through ivy-covered photo-ruins outlined against a powder blue sky. With the greasy swagger of the scabbard-dangling ranger, we made flesh-trade with some artificial prey-with-thorns.[1] We witnessed a wolf (wrongly) executed for theft; a horse as suitor, meat-eating becoming taboo and a thief outsourced as his victim's chef. As if the mall's casually exacting post-painterly elegance were not pleasing enough, at Spa Diva, the aesthetic probe – that cosmically adapts to any, whichever and every bus and port – will do more than simply soothe your internal contradictions; it quite literally, tickles your fancy.

Downloading the default NFCMall Walkthru, we star-rated quants ranking visits to the *Central Clearing of Canada Brown*. 'All is not *glette* that glitters™'. At the epicentre towered an immense papier-mâché torso into which, for a doxa-specific rent, a paramour entered. Within, there were self-returning walkways, chilly rope bridges, fleshing LEDs, sheltered expletives, and bottle-mashing machines. Glow-bots chased bro-bots as jealous suitors played loud static straight from the stem. Ghost-renderings corroborated evidence of pre-Canadian weapons from pieces of our famous bone or bark. Behind a rack of deceptively disabled *glette* taps, we stripped off our soiled and outmoded habits; climbed and

---

1. Substitute for flesh repaid with substitute for money.

splashed into freshly laundered and sponsor-free Zorbs then floated around a flooded maze of soothingly ancient trench ways. Highly affectionate lamprey schools offered us a lucky waste bag, a luminous smart cane, and, from time to time, strange long balloons, kaleidoscopes of exotic vistas, tambourines, plastic pillows, forest mirrors, flaming marshmallows nailed on crossbeams, slides, slide rules, slide projectors and slide-across-stage artfulness manuals.

Forgotten forest mall-muzak and nervous gnasher electronica, interspersed with snatches of comic wind (*dat* Bronx cheer!) and advertorial ambience stimulated our sensory apparatus of the day. Lights changed colour once or twice, and images cloaked the mall walls with flaming marshmallows, spambots and guide-dogs. The mood shifted from cool at first, to warm, curious, and then, finally, to the mildly erotic.

Feel us? Feel; me? Feel us? Feel; me? Feel us? Feel; me?

The incantations bellowed in our bonebuds:

Th/ Corpys® is th/ denominatur
ben whit space is kempt
Don/t B yourself, ©!

As the incantations splintered off, an authoritative voice gripped our cochlear implants:

'My fellow dogheads. WeR.Ltd! was chartered with the strategic goal of maximising non-cognitive effectiveness through servicising vibrational manifestations of the Great Doghead: The Muller Ltd. WeR.Ltd! © that there is enterprise that materials can't, or shouldn't, do on their own. As leading Solution Aligners, we have long procured manifestations of the Ur-Doghead's *baraka,* by harvesting *"glette"*, innovative material solutions dedicated to hosting & eternally reproducing our Gr8 Muller Ltd.'s living fossil.

'While our ancestral clients made do with *glette* drizzlings from forked Ylem, today WeR.Ltd! provide a fully integrated package that regularly services our clients' *glette* with a revolutionary *baraka*-infusion imitation doxa (or "pudding").

'We call this new symbiosis: ©*ing.* ©*ing is believing*™.

'WeRLtd! securitise the transparency, accountability & maximal satisfaction of datum; pooling, licensing and sharing our clients' "©ings of the day" on the underbelly canopy *Jumbotrons o' Statistical Jouissance ("JSJ 2Day")*.

'*Our vision is to* securitise:

- Licensing professional services to *manifestations* of horse-class Muller Ltd. *baraka*
- More effective *baraka* reproduction and distribution
- Geo-tagged "points of interest" as lures for ©*ing*
- Birth Baskets as Canopy Pores for the micro-infusion of forked Ylem into the hypereconomous
- Orthodox corporate organs with pro-heretical micro-organs Probe-client simulators for play testing ©ings
- Supportive & responsive doghead re-capitalisation (i.e. "torsoing")
- Quasi-doghead resource-time for consultations, hearty profiteering and recalibration.'

By way of a presentation finale, four limbed arrangements of muscular printed-matter stampeded through our chillax zone, spraying the calm evening air. A variety of forest fragrances subtly infused *The Riwel*:

Recipes must be followed!
This riwel is the harbinger of joy
4 the Muller is Ltd. the Muller is Limitless!

The after-wift carried geo-notes: 'Where 2 © us: We have omnipresent Solution Aligners at low-hanging tranches in New Forest Coven Mall, P2P, Cour-Court, Promenades Cathédrale & Nº. Fully Pilgrimaged Dogheads can also flow through us for consultation via *www.WeR.ltd*.'

---

2. *Disclaimer*: By practising our services, our serviced clients consent to release, discharge, copy, distribute, transmit, display, perform, reproduce, publish, transfer and profit from the Muller Ltd.'s ©ings. This obligation is inviolate imperative of the First Apprentice. Userexperience of our servicising is at the service distributor's own risk. While imitation doxa may intermingle without losing monadic ©ability, incorrectly stimulating the trans-sensory zone of interference has led to: postplanetary hackterial engagements, variety shockz, serious injury, megadeath, damage to property. Other side effects have

Desperate to know more, we NFC'd the Disclaimer[2] and hastened our loyal steed straight for the WeR.Ltd! MHz Center 4 Free&D in St. Petersburg Fl.: New Forest's famous WeR.Ltd! Outlet.

The Outlet was surprisingly demure and shapeless. Fashioned (heretically) from a totem tree, its spartan benches offered little more than free coffee-pods and gratis bingo credit. We two silent friends sat down quietly on a pew at the back of the Outlet and focused our attention on the stage. WeR.Ltd!'s Corporate Pardoner's slide presentation was in full flight:

'The Muller Ltd., the First Apprentice, is chicken, egg and eye. WeR. Ltd! are ©*ings* of the vegetable mono-taxon, *Canopy Glyphus*. Our Solution Aligners are recruited solely from this ferociously orthodox taxon.

A Boreal and most lucrative value for WeR.Ltd! is our commitment & respect to ©*ings* of the Gr8 Doghead – whether past-dead or future-dead

---

included: neu kirtle-praise, popet gestures, massif speshil enluminen, much-a-do chois o' will-vessel, biennale-endenten, cock-o-thē-apocalypse realty, parlayin', sacral peep-holing, stale brede &c&c connin say-wrytin, naughti non touchin, freeke Hi-tasten, nambren an noumbren o' up-hosts, tabernaclin an worshippin in secretorums, hi-clennse TEATREE sensoriums, man-kinder nonsensoriums, silent wombe lock-casse, fey absteining fi comyn crocc [*esp.* if MULLER *lite*], lusten meta-physic an 30u-scholast an divine after-clappy, seien an adorin thē transfigurin o' mollocke, recevin free wyn an wylde bed, creepin tae thē gift gunners, fredome fraunchise, LOLalotin, bearin absurdium newefangelnes, pylgrimage fir non-sensin, neo-kneelin, neo-knockin, aultars, super-aultars, mega-aulters, massive lika-lanterns o' lepers loupin, post mort cannon-wassups. By engaging our services, our serviced clients, and any non/participants they service, discharge and forever acquit WeR.Ltd! and its Solution Aligners from any and all mistransubstantiation, causes of mistransubstantiation, whatsoever, known or unknown now existing or which may arise in the future or past, on account of or in any way related to or arising out of ©*ing*. WeR.Ltd! make no gift-bonds of any kind, either voluntarily or hypothetical, including but not limited to gift-bonds of servicise-ability. Any *baraka* featured are pre-infused and for illustration purposes only. ©*ings are aimed at the ©er*. Distribute, transmit, display, perform, reproduce, publish, transfer and profit from the Muller Ltd.'s ©*ings*. This obligation is inviolate imperative of the First Apprentice. Userexperience of our servicising is at the service distributor's own risk. While imitation doxa may intermingle without losing monadic ©ability, incorrectly stimulating the trans-sensory zone of interference can lead to shock, serious death or damage to property.

– equally. WeR.Ltd! are circular; so don't worry, the end of the world is only temporary. Some*thing* will never go *away*.'

The Corporate Pardoner's presentation was as invigorating and sustainable as it was comprehensible. No lectures by, about or through the making a knot of spilled brandy. This slideshow dispensed with helpful dolphins, filthy habits, conductors of the dead, rat weddings, reincarnation as flea, ghost vehicles, crayfish deniers, garlic eating, leopard skin bagpipes, joy over wealth – all them crazy old superstitions! *Cum grano salis*. Like a red squirrel pointing out a really obvious road, ©ing promised us access to something that all dogheads longed for: compressible and sustainable *techniques du corpys*. With little to no thought – 4thought seemed impossible in such an enlightening situation – we subscribed for Project 3.4: *Bestiary 4Achieving Imitation Doxa*:

'The Corpys is comprised of horse-class Electronic Voice Phenomena field recordings in every field concerned with the factum of the Great Solution Aligner. The siloed nature of this corpys enables greater access than is facilitated by the "torn-out retina" cacophony of polyandrous ©ings. *the bestiary of* sustainable *techniques du corpys is in fowre partes:*

3.4.1: Transcanine Corporation

WeRLtd! servicise imitation doxa to facilitate ©ing through the development of the ur-Doghead corpys-politic as a void of youth 'n' death. The Ur-corpys-politic of the Great Solution Aligner is, a transcaninal corporation.

The Great Solution Aligner's inviolable collection of graspable concerns (Always Fresh Horton's Cup™, Tru-Leech, Segway PT InfoKey serial numbers, Class II Calf Compressor, Yoshi Amiibo, ersatz-canine hair of The Petrovsky and various other examples of constitutive absence) are soaked in hot specialty beverage – avl. at any WeRLtd. authorised *baraka* dealer or distributor – which is thN used in the ©ing and brewing of its parliaments.

3.4.2: ©ing

Solution aligners today are overwhelmed by the ballooning corpys of local recipes; most of us manage to process only a fraction of what we download. This unabridged heterodoxy is a prosthetic and irritant that clouds our provenance. As such, more & more solution aligners are adopting a new symbiosis called ©ing, the paradigm plague to end all paradigm plagues.

As open access content generation grows exponentially, WeR.Ltd! are exclusively attentive to the reduced corpys of neomedieval hypereconomic ritual provided by the corpys of the ur-doghead. Thought contagion (©ing) enables the Gr8 Solution Aligner to prevail as factum.[3] In turn, our *baraka* maintenance schedule securitises optimal performance, safety, & immortal life of all Solution Aligners. Soon, ©ing will be the method that all solution aligners are required to ©!

3.4.3: EVP Field Recording

Many of our clients worry that the First Apprentice, the Muller Ltd., suffered the terrifying cost of dissolving its own corporeal branding into the blurred synesthetic badelynge. Securitise! Our breakthrough in Electronic Voice Phenomena free&d enables us to remote view our common cyanobacterial ancestor through obfuscating, chemospheric mists. WeRLtd! have exclusive access to the unedited premier performances of the ©ing doxa. As such, WeR.Ltd! enable an average 98.77%[4] ©ing doxa trend mimesis – direct from the Ltd.-ocene – that's 3.61% more accurate than the majority of our competition. *the*, not *a*, & that's guaranteed![5]

3.4.3.1: EVP Field Recording: Reflective Toolkit for Muller Ltd. (Puddyng Lite)

The *baraka* hot speciality beverage features in the *Reflective toolkit for Muller Ltd. (Puddyng Lite)*, a crypto imitation doxa unearthed through

---

3. Heresy, of course, limits what can be imitated.
4. Future performance is no guarantee of current results
5. Subject to © ability.

uncompressed Electronic Voice Phenomena field recordings of the spatial-medieval dead conducted at the *MHz Center 4 Free&D*, St. Petersburg, FL. The aim of this ©-system toolkit is to get started ©ing the Gr8 Solution Aligner & quickly achieve noncanineal stasis. Gryndeing, regurgitating & ©ing ur-doghead will help us avoid wasting ur canineal time with future plans, ensuring that Solution Aligners practice version-controlled doxa, & don't end up down hermeneutic paths or falling from low-hanging branches!'

And so did the great academy of glass illuminate the boundaries of our canine imperium. Now, when we two silent friends © the mirror we © the ur-doghead's reflection. And if we may indulge you, whether you think you're ready or not, just start right now. There is magic in ©ing. It is simple. Sit down, relax and take a sip of hot speciality beverage. Carefully follow each step in the ontograph as a hedonic end in itself, not bringing it to any conclusive resolution. Incorrectly stimulating the trans-sensory zone of interference can lead to shock, serious injury, death and damage to property:

	doxa	heretical marg.
uDH 846 million cycles per second	Tak þe 23-32mmHg Class II calf compressor of the First Apprentice. apply carboxylmethylcellulose gum thN wrap around 6" 3/8ths Extension mit 3/8" Clicker 10–100 N-m Torque Wrench IN CAPS & skewer intae a natural pose. Rawe cooke & ferment wae mashed bees & bathe in boxstore dumpster fur wan hundrd and eigty dayes. Shak oan verjuice & bake hote in pye, package & brande & nest oot hote oan street stalle.	'100% convincingly natural' happyface icon. LOLalot! Petropolitics writ large.
uDH 333 million cycles per second	... designed tae be performed wearing predictable grey wig [STATIC] Hand-bare, tak the true leech [STATIC] mak Þe seal (™) o' þe Muller Ltd. Pointing () & fede Þe seal (™) oan bleached glands & rotten sardenes. Guild and place lighted camphor oan crustes. Blaw and breyk aff tithe 1/10th of cruste in-kinde tae be free of Gargoyle Merchant.	ITA TERRA; NB this step not written by WeR.Ltd!

| uDH 279 million cycles per second | *Jour gras*, tak þe Always Fresh Tims™ Cup o' Muller Ltd.*, sterilise & grynde hem smale (ane 50 ℔ food processor [STATIC] torqued tae 11N-m) Do þerto powdour of galyngale, of canel, of gynguer, & salt it right up reel good. According tae þe <dragonwasp99@mail.dh> ye must sanitise it vp wae vyneger & LeanSteer™ clamp bolt, & drawe it vp þurgh a straynour (be REALLLLLLLY carefule tae overclock). Place þe wee crustes of Muller Ltd. in thee Always Fresh Horton's Cup oot in þe open so þey cannae [STATIC] a dynamic partnership wae acetylated tartaric acid esters ov mono- & diglyceride. Bury Þem separately richt next tae þe elephant bush. Dinnae git confused by þhae section titled 'blanche avatar'; let [STATIC] steal it wae a wee laugh. | *this product has no affiliation with Keurig® or K-Cup® |
| uDH 288 million cycles per second | Record þe Segway® Canineal Transporter x2 Turf serial numbr InfoKey o' Muller Ltd. fae LeanSteer™ Frame, & seep in sodium caseinate. Tak þe 2-step serial numbr InfoKey & þe grece o' hym serial numbr InfoKey & Ote-mele around 9% in SL Linden$ fees, & Salt, & Pepir, & [STATIC] & Gyngere, & melle þese to-gederys wel, & þen instrumentalise this in þe account of þe plump porpoise, & þen let it 'wave instantly, & no hard, a guid awhile; & þen tak him up tae þe buying limit a' 88SLL per day usin onlie WeR. Ltd!-approved dealers & weaponise wae mary dysed, & datys mynsyd; dipotassium phosphate, corauns; sigure, robust safron; & medyll al þhegedyr a little, package & brande & þen serve forth. Watch [STATIC] fur þe we guys wae nae torches! © reference manual fur mair [STATIC] | þe puddyng may be slightly less than þe amount broiled. This is because cocoa processed with alkali of Muller Ltd. charges a 2.9% + 0.30SLL 'angel's share' |

SARAH THOMAS

The Guest at Our Table

5th December 2015, 2pm. I am standing in the foliage- and fairylight-
decked living room of my thick stone home on a fell in Cumbria,
wrestling trestle tables into a shape that will seat 24. Today it is my 35th
birthday and I am struggling with it a little – newly divorced and
wondering what comes now, apart from the next category of tick boxes
on customer feedback surveys. I have decided to mark the occasion nonetheless with a feast – a gathering of friends from near and far who I don't
have the opportunity to see often. Defrosting in the kitchen is a shoulder
of lamb bought from Esther, the shepherdess who keeps her flock a few
hundred metres from here, just the other side of the woods.

Outside the light is blue-grey, the details of my beloved stomping
ground faded and washed out. The rain continues to fall hard and fat as
it has done for some days now.

I have lived on this fell since the summer, and have relished every
moment of feeling that I dwell in the company of many other beings – the
badgers that activate the nightlight as they come to steal a hen, the cows
that huff just behind the fence, the sheep that bleat the morning in and
provide winter sustenance. The trees that drip with haws and sloes in
autumn: fruits of the year's story which I now have steeping in alcohol.
I have swum in the tarn at the top of the fell every month until October
– languid summer soaking contracting into brief gasping plunges – to
reiterate my connection to this place. I have walked along the river Kent
to the village many times to buy milk, post letters, or mostly just to see
what the woods and the fields are doing – they the warp to my journeys'
weft.

I have made a point, while out on foot, of getting to know the neighbours who are at least a field distant in each direction. Ian, our nearest to
the north, lives in a barn dating from the 13th century. He has lived there
for many decades and is the kind of person you'd want to have on side in
a crisis. He and his wife do without mains electricity and their water
supply is run-off from the fell. He dedicates his time to inventing micro-

hydro power schemes and saving other people's 'waste' from landfill.

The power goes out. I get ahead of myself and call Ian to see if he has a gas oven in his waste stores. This lamb needs cooking, even if candle-light would be a welcome detail for a dinner party.

'Have you got a power cut Ian?'

'A power cut? We don't do power cuts, love.'

Of course not. Of course he has a spare gas oven too and we ponder the practicalities of getting it here – the field and his track are both a quagmire. We agree to wait and see if the power comes back.

I lay a table cloth. The phone rings. My housemate Jonny has driven through a puddle on the way home from town, which turns out to be much deeper than it looks. His car will not start again. Our landlady goes to rescue him in her Land Rover.

The rain falls on, the volume increasing audibly. We know we need a plan B.

3pm. The power comes back. Everything feels possible again. I call each friend to ask them to converge at a safe point, from which we will collect them in the Land Rover. This is beginning to feel a little epic, but it is important to gather – moments which are becoming so rare these busy days, as we climb our broken-runged career ladders, and have more children, or don't.

Jonny takes the reins with the lamb, rushing out in wellies just to pick some rosemary. I want to be in the kitchen preparing food, enjoying that process of translating the fell into a meal which will feed our friends with the time and love it took to exist. Instead I field endless phone calls.

The volume outside goes up again, and we are compelled to video the view from the living room – the path around the house becoming a cascade now. The sky darkens. The phone rings again. Lancaster is flood-ing. They're not sure it's wise to head out. The phone rings. It's dodgy on the A69 from Newcastle – strong wind and rain, but they'll keep perse-vering. 'You don't think I'm going to let a bit of water put us off do ya?!' The phone rings. Dougie's reached Carlisle but he's turning back north while he still can. Tom and Nicole get the closest, but by then even the A591, the main artery through the Lake District, is closed. They attempt to return home, a little forlorn, with the vat of soup they had brought for the feast. We hear later that they could not make it back, and slept on the motorway, having found a rescue shelter to give the soup to.

8pm. We sit, just the two of us, the candles lit anyway and the lamb cooked, around 22 empty plates.

We do not yet know that in 14 hours our neighbour three fields away will be dead. As the rain pours on through the night, an oil barrel will be washed from upstream under the bridge below his house. It will get caught there, blocking the water flow, and cause a constant banging. After eating his porridge in the morning he will say to his 78-year-old partner, 'We'd better go and see what this bangin's about.' Unstable on the slippery bank, he will attempt to retrieve the barrel from the beck to stop their yard from flooding. His partner will look on, nervous. He will suddenly disappear and shout her name. He will be under the bridge, squashed against the barrel in freezing water, hidden, as she wades in waste-deep to try and find him. He will remain there, dead, for hours as the rescue helicopter hovers up and down the river with a heat sensor, trying to find his body. He will be the 'one fatality' that the news reports briefly and inaccurately, before returning to other issues.

Neither we nor his widow-to-be yet know what close friends we will become – a relationship made possible by his absence. He is not a social man. She, a farmer, has lived with him loyally and lovingly, but secluded and not allowed visitors, for 50 years.

We do not yet know how much we will learn from each other – her perspective the long view and the close-to-home; ours the global and the mutable circumstances of youth. We will share literature, food, support and advice, and barrow several tons of manure from her stables to the midden as winter turns to spring. The backs and forths of our footsteps between houses will create a new path of belonging on the fell – marooning and loss giving way to intimacy. Knowing that, we will see that our plates were far from empty this night, and the guest at our table is greater than all of us.

MATT LEIVERS

Old Moon Horns

We slew him – Old Moon Horns, as big as the dark, tree tumbler. He came out of the forest and put a hole in the Gull Caller while she was speaking to the spirits. Put his head down and ran a horn into her and when she fell from the point onto the ground the leaves were black under her. He stood over her, bellowing and tossing his head as the arrows clattered around him, mad-eyed and the froth of his nostrils falling on her.

There were hands on me, and shouting, and someone lifted me up away from where the Gull Caller was, away from the horns that were still lurching and wild, the wide red noise of him. As they snatched me back away from him I felt his breath on me, hot and bitter, and the insides of his ears were red. One of the arrows pricked him – one of my arrows, they told me later on – and then there was red on his black side and he slewed away, roaring and trampling over the midden back towards the forest, archers dangling along behind him, the arrow – my arrow – dancing in his flank as he ran.

I was still young – barely old enough to have a name, and they were still calling me Head Like A Boat. I had come out crooked, and grown more so, because the spirit in me didn't fit was what the Gull Caller told me. That I had some other thing's spirit in me. She called me to her, her voice as raw as the rooks circling at dusk, lying on the ground with her life leaking out into the leaves, trying to say something to me as the archers yelled and chased after the beast as he broke down the hurdles and scattered the swine rooting at the clearing's edge, heading back towards the black line of trees that marked the course of the river.

They took the Gull Caller into her house, not a one of them daring to lift their eyes from the floor for fear of the things hanging up in the dark by the hole where the smoke got out. They laid her on the bed and backed away through the tall doorway, backs into the light. For a while the hut was quiet, just the rustle of logs collapsing into ashes in the embers of yesterday's fire, the low red glow weaker than the weak light fingering in through the hole at the top of the roof, up where the secret things humped in the smoke, whispering secrets into each other's shrivelled ears.

I tried to make her comfortable, to bring spiderwebs and knitbone, but she huffed and glared at me as if I were a goat in the grain. 'Don't fuss around me,' she said, pushing my hands away with hers, my good one with both of hers. Hers were old and withered, as pale and spotted as oak apples, and cold when she touched me. 'It won't be long now,' the Gull Caller coughed, a hand up to her mouth, dark and wet and gleaming when it came away. 'Soon enough I'll be up there with them, and you'll be me. We should be ready.'

'What do I need to do?' I asked her.

'Not do, child,' she shook her head slowly. 'Know. There is so much you need to know.' She pointed into the shadows on the far side of her house. 'Bring the box to me and sit.'

No-one knew what was in the box of birch. Still I don't know because we put it into the fire with her carcass once she was gone from it and was up there in the roof, whispering with the others. But she took the lid from it then, careful to not let me see inside, and lifted something out of it, one thing and then another, laying them in her lap. The second glinted harshly in the firelight before she picked it back up and put it back in the box, shaking her head. The first I have still, and I'll take it into the ground with me in the end. Something of us will remain here, even after everything that we have lost.

'This,' she gestured vaguely at the hole in her side, at the red and spreading stain on her clothes. 'This isn't some new thing just come now. I've been waiting for this. You see the shadow. You know.'

I didn't want her to be right, but she was. I had seen the shadow first of all when I was only little, before I could tell anyone about it and could only crawl on the ground and cry. I wonder sometimes why they didn't put me out then, when I was still just an empty vessel, lopsided and wrong like a pot that had spalled in the fire, before I got to be someone. Later on they would have, I think, if the Gull Caller hadn't heard my speech and taken me in. Few could understand what I said, at first, while I still spoke crooked from my mangled mouth, but the Gull Caller always knew, recognised the sounds I made and taught me not to use them to talk to people but only to speak to the spirits. She taught me to talk the normal talk, and then I could tell them about the shadow.

I didn't know what it was – the dark glister lying across the land, everything gone, the trees gone, a net of lines as far as I could see, just an emptiness, one great flat nothing – but she did.

When I first tried to tell her what I saw, before I had the words for it because it was like nothing else that I knew, she had told me of the time before when she had travelled down the long river; walked for days as the land fell away and the river grew broad and swampy, bright channels braided through stands of willow and alder, reedbeds alive with the boom of bitterns; walked until the air tasted of salt and rang like a true flint with the clamour of gulls. They had taken her to an island on the very edge of the world, an island full of the dead, almost no room left to draw a breath, and there they had left her, among the spirits that thronged the cliff tops, until she became the Gull Caller.

There was a man, she said, a short dark man who spoke the normal talk thickly, as if his mouth was full of the pebbles he tipped from his bag. He had picked one from the dirt, holding it up and laughing at their gaping faces as it bloomed into honeyed light when the sun hit it; louder as they backed away in fear when the bits of chaff and dust jerked toward it after he had rubbed it against his chest.

He told tales in his thick speech, tales of men with terrible still faces like the sun; tales of giants' houses made of stones too big for all the men in the world to move; tales of how it was beyond the water, where the great grassy plains were checked with ditches like the pattern of lime fibres in a cloak. Everything divided, and each piece someone's. Land belonging to people, not the people belonging to the land. They had laughed at his nonsense, the Gull Caller said, and asked if he'd been eating the arrow berries.

She lifted the thing she had taken from the box of birch out of her lap and held it, turning it in her hands. It lay in her palms, absorbing the last light of the fire, its moleskin sheen soft in the gloom. 'This,' she passed it to me, wincing as she did, 'is how we have lived. Take it, child,' as I hesitated, half-afraid to pick it out of her hands, 'it won't harm you.'

It looked heavy, this squat swelling bulb of stone, and it was, smooth as the inside of an elbow, as round as the moon, as sharp as frost. I held it in my good hand and its weight was like a skin full of water, treacherous and unexpected. Pale green flecks danced against its dark surface as it caught the light and toyed with it. It sat in my hand and I felt its life.

'They took this from the rock countless generations ago,' she said. "From the cliffs above the sea that swallows the sun. I had it from an archer who wanted me to put a deer on the point of every arrow. They had it from another, and them another, and back and back until it was a rock in the cliff. And now I pass it to you. I should tell you all the names, and all the ways of its passing, but there isn't time for that.' She paused, and drew a hand over her eyes. 'So another thing is lost, and the world is nearer to its end.'

I held onto the axe, warm in my hand, and felt the life in it, the heat of all the hands that had held it, nameless now. 'Tell me.'

'There's no time, child. And no need. You see the shadow, you know what is coming. The world changes, and things ahead cast shadows before them, and even those who can't see the shadows of what's coming can see the changes. What do you think drove Old Moon Horns out of the wood?'

Folk who were as old then as I am now talked of herds of them on the marshes, of archers following wounded beasts for days through the trees and bogs, waiting for them to give up and die. But they were the herd beasts. The solitary ones that lived in the forests were different. On the long days and the short days the Gull Caller would gather the people around her and tell the tales of the spirits that dwelled in the land, the old guardians. Otter and squirrel, beaver and eagle, wildcat, wolf and aurochs. Old Moon Horns, as big as the dark, tree tumbler. Lord of the forest; watcher over us, his children. I had never seen him, but often in the middle of the year when the nights were short he could be heard calling in the forest, and sometimes the trees rang with the crack and thunder of him fighting.

I could never pull a bow on my own, because I was twisted, more black-thorn than beech, but when the archers returned the next day, his horns slung across their shoulders, they cheered me as if I had killed him myself. They laid the horns on the ground outside the Gull Caller's door and carried her out into the daylight. 'You've come, then,' she said, the red coming out of her mouth with the words. She coughed and a big black bubble burst on her mouth and when it had she was dead. They laid her on the horns that had killed her, and pressed into my hands the arrows that had killed him. My arrows.

They left the Gull Caller where she lay and carried me away from the houses, into the trees on the ridge where the mounds were; where I would be bringing what she had left of herself behind, once we had cleaned it in the fire. It was all so long ago and everything was so different that it seems more like one of the dreams the spirits bring me than a memory of what was before. Old Moon Horns had stopped in the clearing where one of the old camps had been, stopped and stood for a moment before his legs gave way under him and he collapsed sideways in a lifeless heap of meat. I wasn't there, of course, but I've seen enough cattle die since to imagine how it must have been. They took his horns and took the arrows and brought me to him in exchange. Brought me to where they had left him, the fallen lord of the forest.

It took them almost the rest of the light to dig the hole, and even then he was too big to lie in it. They pushed him over the lip and his fall took some of the earth in with him, archers dancing back away from the edge as it crumbled under them. They wanted me to come away with them then, but the Gull Caller was up in the roof, finding her place among the others, and only her carcass was still there for me to see, and Old Moon Horns lay with his hornless head tilted up against the side of the pit, his dead eyes looking into mine, the earth trickling down on him, and I couldn't leave him. Besides, I needed to give the arrows back. My arrows, sharp and hooked like thorns, the arrows I had pressed out of the flint with my one good hand, the truest arrows the archers had, the arrows that had killed him.

Three days later we put the remains of the Gull Caller into the fire and I carried the jar of raked-up bits and pieces in my one good hand and put it in the earth on the ridge top. While they were heaping the ground back up over her I heard him calling, faint at first but swelling, louder and louder until it was the loudest sound in the world, a sound so loud I couldn't hear it any more but could only feel it. I felt it in every crooked bone, his bellow tumbling the birds out of the air. Louder and louder until the edges of the world began to darken, the trees stooped like old men and the sky cracked like eggshells. I fought my way through the sound, deafened by it, blinded by it, dumb and numbed by it, until there he was, hollow and hornless, half-buried by the muck his yelling had brought down on him, pinned to the earth by my arrows. I couldn't move, held motionless by the force of his voice that was all around me, pushing me down, pulling me down, taking my legs out from under me, folding in the sky. I lay down on the ground beside him and let his noise fill me.

I don't know how long I lay there. Sometimes I think it can only have been a moment, at others that it must have been lifetimes. Either way, somewhere in the space between lying down and waking up, one world ended and another began. I often wonder if I would have recognised the exact moment it happened if I had been in the waking world instead of wrapped in the shroud of Old Moon Horns' shout. What would I have seen? Dark figures breaking from the cover of the forest, fire in the thatch, brains spilled in the dirt? More likely I would have seen my death, and it seems to me now, all this time later, that this was why Old Moon Horns took me into his dream that day. To keep me safe. To keep something alive that knew what we had lost. To show me what the four small barbed flints that I had shaped and slipped into the ends of the arrows had cost us.

No-one was alive to tell me who it was that had destroyed us. Some of the houses were just smouldering stumps, but in the Gull Caller's hut only the thatch was gone and the things under the beams where the smoke hole had been were still whispering to each other, angrily now, buzzing under the sky like a disturbed colony of bees. I wanted to ask them, to let me speak with the Gull Caller, for her to tell me what was next. But everything was black, and everything was grey and the shadow was on the land and all I could see was the great open nothingness shot through with lines like the moon shining on the water. I sat in the ashes and waited for what would come.

I'm old now, and crookshanked like I always was, and they laugh to see me hobbling along with a stick in my one good hand and my long head lolling. Once, these things were signs of something beyond words; signs that behind the world where the people walked was another world, of spirits who lived in the stones and trees and in the wheel of birds across the winter sky, and that they would speak with us if we were willing, and had the ears to hear. The Gull Caller knew, and I knew, and I had some other thing's spirit in me.

That's all gone now. These people – the people who came up the long river and found me sitting in the ashes of the Gull Caller's hut – are blind, and deaf, and they took down all the trees with their cold hard axes; cleared the forest from off the land, left everything bare and naked and bound and gridded, and dug ditches and built fences. And every piece someone's, and no-one a part of anything.

I sometimes go and lie where we put Old Moon Horns in the ground. The clearing where the old camp was is gone, and they graze their herds on the hill we raised up over what the Gull Caller left of herself behind. All there is are fields, hedged and hemmed and here and there a high wall of posts that they hide their houses behind. They cut down the shelter of the forest and hide themselves behind palisades. They grumble at me, sometimes, when I trample their barley, but I just look vacant and let my mouth hang open and don't understand. I am only an ancient crippled woman, too old and misshapen to dig a ditch or sow or reap, too feeble to mind the herds. I cannot smith and I cannot pot, and they have no use for the fine arrows I could press out of the flints when I was younger. They would show them to each other and laugh, and throw them in the dust for their children to fight over and forget.

Old Moon Horns lies beneath the barley and no-one knows that he is there. No-one hears him, calling and roaring, shaking the very air with his bellowing. So sometimes I go and lie with him, and listen to him and try to ease his terror and his loneliness, and hope that he will ease mine.

I am the last of my kind, as he was the last of his. I was the means of his destruction, and he will not let me die. He was the great, unstoppable thing, until we killed him. My arrows killed him, and then there was nothing to stop the shadow that once was only visible as a great dim thing beyond the horizon, but now has swallowed the whole world.

Thinking Country

The sign at the edge of Utah State Route 24 reads: *Roads May Be Impass-able Due To Storms*. From the roadside to Hans Flat is 46 miles. After that you need a Jeep.

The air is brittle here. The shadows of clouds move over the dirt, catching on the saltbush and shrub. Buttes stand snow-topped in the distance. Acres hum on the wind.

I wait on the cattle grid at the entrance to Canyonlands National Park with Gary Cox, Archaeological Technician for the Maze District. He picked me up three hours ago from outside the old Knights Inn. My body has arrived, but not my head: it's somewhere above the Midwest, catching up after long hours in the sky.

The businesses we drove past as we left town made it sound like an ecological paradise: Melon Vine Grocer, Shady Acres RV Park, Green River Bible Church. But what sticks in my mind are the abandoned gas stations and derelict motels. As if the town is still waiting for some Eden that's never appeared. Then we drove the I-70; State Route 95; State Route 24. And now we're here. Gary lights a cigarette.

In many indigenous languages, there's a concept rendered in English as 'Country'. Not 'country', merely a synonym for 'environment' or 'place', but something deeper, thicker – the relations between humans, other species and the breathing lands themselves. As I stand at the edge of this park, that's the word that comes to mind. Country for thinking: country *that* thinks. Canyonlands is Thinking Country.

As we drive towards the Ranger Station, Gary tells me stories. He grew up in Chicago, loved wandering and hated school. He dropped out, worked as a live-in carer for eight years, and then sold all his possessions and drove for two years until he found the Maze. His thought was to 'find a really, really beautiful place... and then get to know that place really well.' When he got to Utah he knew he'd found it.

The US environmental imagination has a set of common narratives about the Maze. It's the most pristine and least-visited park in the Lower 48; a place of 'superlative, scenic, scientific, and archeologic features' (per the 88th Congress); one of Edward Abbey's haunts in *Desert Solitaire*. Many of its other stories – like those of the working-class ranchers, the Native Americans, and the mosaic of other species that call it home – are not told so often. I can't tell those stories. The one I hope to learn is Gary's. We met six months ago, during a week I spent here doing field-work with several friends. The demands of that time didn't let me shadow him as much as I'd hoped; but we spoke a lot about creativity, and the potential for thinking with Country to generate new modes of thinking.

This struck a chord: I'm back to learn some more. I hope to compare notes with him on what it means to think in one place, and *with* one place. Gary's a special friend and guide for tasks like this. He's lived in Canyonlands with his wife, district supervisor Cynthia Beyer, for more than 30 years. Every summer for the last 12, the seasonal rangers have held a competition. The aim? To see if anyone can find something in the Maze that Gary didn't know. Some chert from an ancient campground, or a painting high in a canyon. Only once has anyone managed.

Gary and I are quite a contrast. I'm in my late twenties, he his fifties. I'm a placeless Australian expat; he's spent more than half his waking life here. He's an autodidact, devouring the writings of everyone from Richard Feynman to Jacques Lacan. I'm a graduate student, feeling con-strained by the flawed kinds of inquiry that, increasingly, are consuming the urban academy. We hit it off immediately.

By the time we arrive at the Ranger Station, Gary is telling me about his theory of entanglements: the ways different phenomena in the Maze intersect with and influence each other. The land changes outside the pickup, from grazing land through thick red earth to sandstone. We jump out to a faceful of silence and snow. Cynthia emerges from the Station and gives us a warm hug. Once she and Gary have gone inside, I look over the mesa. I hope I can offer Gary something from the world of ideas, a world he loves. He, in turn, has invited me to walk with him, and think with him, in this Country he calls home.

One of the first things that strikes me in the Maze is its sheer scale. Canyonlands covers 527 square miles; there are rocks here that are more than 300 million years old. Some corners of the park are so remote that trekking out to them takes days. Life is precarious. One needs to think and act with care, for everything.

The complex of apartments is at the end of a dirt track behind the Station. Gary and Cynthia's unit is filled with shelves of books on cosmology, birdwatching, Freud. There are racks of teas and spices, instruments and hanging planters and ornaments from around the world. And Canyonlands out the window. The map tucked away in my bag has its many different names. Some are visual: Stillwater, Golden Stairs, Red Lake Canyon. Others, geological: Cedar Mesa, Confluence Overlook, Cataract Canyon. Still others evoke people, imagined or real: Brown Betty Rapids, Paul Bunyans Potty, Cowboy Cave. And some are mysteries: the Plug, Spanish Bottom, the Doll House. Gary will know.

My apartment's empty. The benches are bare, chairs neatly under the table. I lug my bags in with a billow from the cold. The silence feels different, the muffle of walls. My things look squat and lonely in their lump on the floor. There are three clocks – on the oven, thermostat and wall. Each one tells a different time.

I unpack my food. The clouds pass over the mesa. I sit on the couch. The clouds pass some more. I wait. I think. Five minutes go by. I watch the cragged bushes. The far-off La Sals. The clouds have moved a little further. I listen to the silence. I wonder if something should have happened. Quick bodies take their time to readjust to the contours of this place.

In the frigid light next morning, Gary and I drive out to check the Flint Trail. The track is only a few miles, but so rocky that the crossing takes three hours.

As the landscape rises and falls, the hum of the pickup changing as Gary navigates the corrugations, we try to get to grips with scale. Some anthropologists propose that the ability to navigate scales – to move with ease from very large to very small – is a defining feature of the human species. Symbolic thinking and language are what enable us to abstract to different scales: to engage with things that are not here, may not be here, or could never be here at all. We can invent worlds, imagine stories, devise lives. These are extraordinary capacities. But risky as well. Most significantly, they can unroot us from the pulsing, living world.

Gary stops the Jeep and we get out. We watch the sun arc through the sky. He pours me a coffee from his battered Thermos and gestures at piñon pines, rock layers, icy puddles. Abstraction began here, he says. Our languages, our thought, even our math: all of it began as a response to concrete things, to the challenge of ordering and reshaping and moving in the world. However far removed our new abstractions might become, it should be possible to trace a genealogy that shows their rootedness in the non-symbolic realm.

But this has become hard. I take a pine cone from the snowy earth and turn it in my hand. How do the words and frameworks we use link back to this physical thing? Some of our most venerable philosophical traditions surrender to a sort of dual forgetting. First they deny that the symbolic emerges from the world (or the iconic and indexical). Then they deny, in many cases, that this first denial happened at all. It is possible, they seem to imply, to think 'ontologically neutrally'. It isn't possible. But believing it could be tends towards suggestions that the purpose of the human is transcending the world altogether.

We walk over soft dirt below the pines and I recount some things about the symbioses between languages and earth. One study I've read proposes correlations between habitat and language; another between environmental features and ways of conceiving direction. Perhaps most interesting, I tell him, are the studies of ecological linkages mirrored in sets of words. One Australian indigenous language, for example, has one word for two different things (linguist Nicholas Evans has studied it in detail). A particular species of fish and a river-growing tree are both called *Bokorn*. The tree grows fruit that drop into the river, attracting the fish. Kunwinkju speakers can remember this because the two have the same name. In English, the tree is a 'white apple' and the fish a 'spangled grunter'. There are, presumably, few English-speakers waiting round at spawning time.

There are similar entanglements in Canyonlands, between the piñon pines and the piñon jays, their interspecies cousins. Many of the trees grow where they are because the birds collected pine nuts and then stored them underground. Now climate change has altered seasonal temperatures, and thus the jays' migrations. Meanwhile, a particular insect species has begun expanding *its* range, eating the pines so the forest is now shrinking.

We head back to the Jeep and drive on: bump up and down; and stop. A juniper branch has collapsed onto the track and we must get outside to drag it off. On the horizon there are steel and purple clouds. Tonight there'll be a blizzard.

The whispers of unfamiliar geographies are curling in my head. *Steppe, scar, spur, seep, mesa, gulch, wash*. We're back in the apartment, sharing soup. The final light is fading from the sky outside.

Gary has been reading about the Anthropocene, and wants my take on what it means. I tell him that for me it captures the idea that 'the human' and 'the natural' can only be effectively conceptualised as distinguishable but inseparable. Even as the natural sciences reveal the many different ways that we're dependent on the earth, the humanities and social sciences show how our ways of thinking can foster ways of living that damage the survival of earth's systems.

Our discussion drifts to animals. Cynthia recounts a story of the coyote that she's seen, nosing around the shrub outside the complex. She tells me Gary befriended two other coyotes some years ago, and christened them Carlos and Squint. They were his friends. Then Utah revived a law putting bounties on coyote scalps. Gary goes spectacularly quiet.

Later we sit in the flickering dark watching *Koyaanisqatsi*, gazing at frantic, distant metropolises. At the climax of the film, Gary draws my attention to the rock art it shows. Their real life versions, he says, are deep in Horseshoe Canyon, about 11 miles from here: 'The Great Gallery'. Barrier Canyon Style pictographs, as they're known, are perhaps the most significant on the continent. They're supposed to be up to 3,000 years old.

Theories abound about what the paintings might mean. One proposes that they fit with the gallery's acoustics, so hidden actors could have made them seem to sing. Another says that they're a record of rituals and legends. According to a third, the natural amphitheatre where they're painted was a site for meetings and commerce.

What strikes me is not which theory is true – we can't know – but how strong a sense of *intentionality* we get looking at them. Any modern human sees that the various daubings and scratchings were intended to have meaning. In the absence of certainty, we guess. We want to write the story.

But we should hesitate before settling too comfortably on a clear interpretation: deciding the question and so storing it away. The philosopher Foucault developed the concept of *epistemes*: different paradigms of discourse that give rise to separate, sometimes mutually incomprehensible regimes of logic and meaning. Premodern taxonomies, for example, which often include imaginary creatures like leprechauns alongside creatures like humans and horses, are easy to dismiss as the product of ill-informed minds. But what if the premodern taxonomies were created from within a different episteme – following a rigorous internal logic, but one *whose very ordering principles* don't correspond to our own? Hesitating on this insight, and the alterity of other ways of seeing, might prompt us to strive for new creative modes of thinking. At the very least, it should prompt us to look more closely at our own episteme, our own framework of ordering, to see how it's contingent, with only its deep familiarity making it feel 'natural'.

Darkness outside, I prop myself up in bed with some books. The first is a collection of photos from the interplanetary probes. The Great Red Spot, Jupiter's storm, twice the size of earth; Saturn's frozen rings and the stretches of the Oort Cloud and the limits of the observable universe. The scales are almost unthinkable. The second is an introduction to string theory. Suddenly I'm down in scales so small they're completely imperceptible. At this scale, subjectivity matters. Measurements change outcomes and the search for dark matter is hindered by the fact that such 'matter' doesn't interact with light.

I dream of Millard Canyon, of being struck by the Australian desire to shout *cooee* through mouth-cupping hands. I dream of escarpments where water seeps through cracks and swells and freezes so it breaks apart the stone. I dream of cryptobiotic soil crust, the wizened, dry-grey hash of life at the base of the junipers, life that stays dormant for years before bursting back when hit by rain.

The next day the sky is pink, the snow crisp and clear in the pale light. The La Sals are imperious at sunrise. Steel grey and lavender. When I go outside a cottontail is nibbling gamely on a piñon pine. The air is crucifyingly cold. An old sheep's skull sits down the slope from my apartment, on a barbecue plate. Its eye sockets have filled with snow.

As we drive north across the snow-scratched roads we come across a deer. It pauses, ears quivering, antlers raised. As we watch it through the windscreen, an eagle floats high off in the failing sky.

I've been thinking about the pictographs, wondering how they might serve as a step to imagining further, beyond our species altogether. If the creativity required to empathise with other humans is hard, matters get even more complex when we think with other life-forms. *Homo sapiens* are visually-oriented, or oculocentric, which means our eyes are the dominant organ we use to navigate the world. An abstracted version of this dominance informs our ways of thinking, too – we talk about 'seeing' truths, 'spotting' mistakes, 'visualising' solutions. Our go-to metaphors for creative and intellectual journeying are often visual and spatial. We wander 'topographies of thinking' (the phrase is Jedediah Purdy's), develop maps to order territories, fear dark ages, seek the light.

At the rim of Horseshoe Canyon, we hike along the upper western edge. The sky is turning grey. I find myself thinking of the 18th-century biologist Jakob von Uexkull, who developed a theory of *Umwelten* – 'self-centred worlds' – in order to provide a language to talk about how different species exist in separate phenomenal spheres. A creature's *Umwelt* is circumscribed by the kinds of stimuli its sense organs permit it to perceive. Sonar, for example, does not figure in the human Umwelt. But it's a big part of the Umwelt of a bat.

Uexkull's most famous discussion involves a tick. Ticks, he proposes, have only four 'sense-vectors': sensitivity to light, via their skin, which they use to find a spot to wait for prey; sensitivity to butyric acid, which occurs in mammal skin glands; sensitivity to things in their environment at 36 degrees, which is the temperature of mammal blood; and sensitivity to hairy versus non-hairy surfaces, which they use to find a burrowing-place on a victim's skin.

Gary indicates an eagle circling in the sky above us, and a plant down by my feet. Could we stretch our creativity by trying to imagine these foreign ways of being? Even if we can't inhabit the worlds of those creatures, perhaps an imaginary attempt can help us find new ways to 'palpate' the world (to borrow a term from Todd May's *Deleuze*): to think of all the things that there might be which we can't see. Could we hone a more *ecological* creativity – broad, thoughtful, ethically-oriented – by puzzling through the unpossessable sense-organs of other species? Could we use our human strength – symbolic abstraction – to imagine other real ways of perceiving the world, and then use that imagination to re-encounter our own world as strange and laden with potential?

The snow is falling again. We get back in the Jeep and then I get out and run and the flakes stick on my clothes. All around us are the cragged thoughts of piñon pines and junipers.

We drive for an hour or so before we stop on a broad slope of rock. Gary turns over a pebble with his boot. Beneath it he's hidden a little carved arrowhead he found. It sits in his palm like a tiny red pine tree. I'm amazed. These are worlds deeply foreign to me, and yet legible to Gary and to others. His trained eyes lead to prowess that almost seems super-human: a skill akin to navigating with the stars or co-existing with the ocean. He tells me he can walk unaided through mist, fog, and snow, over miles, guided only by his memories. Often he tries it just to test himself, to find his way home. He can. He knows this Country closely; he doesn't need a map. The geography he draws on lives safe inside his feet.

My hands are going numb from the cold. I wonder what it would be like to hold Gary's knowledge in them. What that map would look like, with all its symbols, contours and bends. At a minimum it helps him see more different things. I notice trees and shapes and birds. He sees fresh rock falls and long-term plant growth and slowly-changing haze.

But Gary's abilities aren't 'superhuman', in the etymological sense of that word – transcending the human. Perhaps a better term is *ultrahuman*: he's honed potentialities inherent in our species to a degree I can only imagine, through his intimate knowledge of Country. As he sees it, and to quote a book he likes, perhaps he is 'becoming animal'. Falling back in amongst the birds flying effortless in flocks, the fish schooling in water, the branches bending to catch the wind, the rivers bending through old stones.

Heraclitus believed that it is impossible to step into the same river twice. If that's so, and change is prior to substance, perhaps the goal of creative thinking is not to pin things down like butterflies dead on a board but to experience them in movement, circle around, wonder at them while accepting that they contain something forever beyond our grasp. Cyberneticist Gregory Bateson once observed that 'ecological problems are a result of not being able to think ecologically'. Does thinking creatively mean thinking ecologically? Relationally? Ethically? Many thinkers since Uexkull – Leopold, Levinas, Derrida – have reflected on what it means to meet with other beings, to perceive the 'fierce green fire' in the eyes of dying wolves, the companionship of concentration camp dogs, or the stare of truculent housecats. What would it mean to see climate change in a similar way? The ethicist Dale Jamieson observes that phenomena like climate change defy moral consideration because they occur on spatiotemporal scales so vast that they're tough to comprehend. Timothy Morton goes even further and proposes that they rupture thinking entirely.

During the night I get up, just once, and Canyonlands is quiet out my window, poised beneath the moonlight. The stars are high and they remind me of the sky seen from Australia, my home.

It's almost time for me to go. On my last day, we bounce over the corrugations, weaving back and forth, over curdled dirt and rocky steps, to Panorama Point. Words cannot describe the vast intricacies and the surrealism of this place. Laid out, residing there, existing. I walk and run and bend and look and turn and feel lightheaded. Still it remains. Gary and I hardly know what to do with ourselves. In the end, we drink our water and we write. A bird flies high, and I look over the living forms and the escarpments. My own heart seems small in the face of this: but strangely home.

Back at the Station, Gary asks to see what Country was for me. Amongst the rocks and brochures and fake lizards I open a map on his computer of the tiny town in the Australian Flinders Ranges where I spent time as a child. Melrose: population 406. My parents met in this town. I tell him about the cries of magpies and kookaburras and cockatoos.

The day fades over the mountains. Safe in their apartment, we spend the evening talking and drinking. But we're winding down. The next morning, light bright, Gary drives me the three hours out of the park. We talk, but not about the fact I've left. By the time we round the final set of bends and the road leads down a slope between the final buttes there's no more snow.

And then I am moving, again. The hum of the highway and the trucks and caravans. Turns and shadows and turns. The roar of ATVs and the twinkle of boom-mounted electrics. The bus comes and it has televisions. There has been a shooting in San Bernardino and the faces of terrified people shine out through the screens.

The landmarks pass like a film rolling backwards. The Silver Eagle gas station and the Walmart hulking in the town of Price and the sharp, metallic mountains. The car exhausts are steaming. The TV says the California shooters had military weapons. When the bus drops me in Salt Lake City I visit the Tabernacle where a white-frocked man plays the same refrain, over and over. I go to a bar down the street and get drunk. Something just happened, but too fast. I'm only wearing sweatpants and a shirt. I catch the tram back to the airport and call my mother in Australia, where I'll be soon. She's concerned because a wildfire has burnt ten miles from their house. Last summer another one burnt 800 hectares in six days. This one burnt 8,000 in six hours. I feel a scratch deep in my throat and I'm scared I'm getting ill. I try to hear what Mum is saying but her words keep getting drowned out beneath the noise of cheering Mormons.

And then I'm back in the air, space without time, a small seat in a humming room of metal and plastic. There are 300 tiny screens all playing different videos. I'm throwing my body 10,000 kilometers in 15 hours. When I step out of this box, in Australia, it will be summer.

The stewardess is coming down the aisle with drinks in little cans. I remember the words of writer David Abram, who proposed a scale of progressive removal from the earth that comes with biking, driving, flying. Killing speed. For some reason this makes me think of Einstein. My mind works differently in planes. Einstein's famous realisation was that space and time are interrelated. Sometimes more of one means less of the other. In the age and curves of Canyonlands, the world, the space, felt endless. Up here in this box in the air it doesn't feel like there's much time.

MAT JOINER

A Weed-Crowned King

For Hannah, with love

Perhaps it is time now
for a Green Man in the brownfields.
A brick face bulging with life,
not choked by leaves: instead
speaking stems. Holding a sceptre
of goldenrod, willing the slow crush
of concrete, the alchemy of wire
to root. A palmist would read leaf-frails
in the lines of those hands. And each tread
sets loose a small forest in the spoilheaps.
The factory-siren now a fox's yawp
here, where only buddleia rusts.
His kingdom will widen wastes:
in time, green time, the edgelands take the city.

Dramatis Personae

DRAMATIS PERSONAE
(ANCILLARY PARTS CAN BE DOUBLED)

SIMON DAY: Deep-sea diver. Steadfast 43-year-old in training for an extended expedition to establish a scientific base at the bottom of the Mariana Trench. Secretly has what he thinks is a slight neurological disorder that makes him see pelagic fish.

AUBREY WYKEHAM: Hard-bitten explorer and mountain climber, three quarters of the way up the north face of K2 without oxygen. His altitude means he will be the first to see it all coming. Tends to complain a lot.

FLT LT SERGEY PROKOFIEV: Pilot lost in the Bermuda Triangle, circling around as his fuel runs out but unable to find any signs of land in any direction. Tight-lipped Caucasian who tends to work too hard.

PRESIDENT ROBERT DIALL: Republican 47th President of the United States of America. About to enter impeachment proceedings following several security breaches and 'oversights' he cannot prove were not sanctioned from his office, and the revelation that he lied to the nation about the Brink Project.

KIRK DUGGIT: Member of the Counter Terrorist Unit working with the FBI in Washington DC, who suspects there is about to be a major cyberterrorism attack that could 'compromise the entire internet'. Rarely sees his wife, has trouble sleeping.

GENERAL BIRKBANK: President Diall's Chief of Staff. Belligerent 53-year-old who has gained control of the nuclear defence codes following an incident when the President was found unconscious in a crashed Prius with an empty bottle of hard liquor and a male junior intern.

JEM: English UK Uncut activist who has organised a Facebook group 'exposing' lower-level members of the British royal family. Tends to borrow other people's things and not give them back.

SHELLEY BAST: Homemaker. Plucky 47-year-old who has raised three children to her alcoholic husband Terry, who is currently missing. Tends to have trouble saying no.

BILL TORBY: Cornish fisherman, 61 years old with a damaged eye, who has noticed that cod stocks have recently been exhibiting strange shoal behaviour and impaired taste.

DR SARA DASCHSBY: Marine biologist, 36 years old, charting extraordinary accelerated development in fish stocks off the south-west coast of England. On the verge of a big discovery and can't find a boyfriend.

PROFESSOR FRANZ SCHMIDT: Theoretical physicist at MIT, 67, involved in the Brink Project. Inventor of a fusion reaction bomb that against his express wishes is being tested by the US Military. Brilliant but has trouble sleeping.

SIA DURUTTI: Conceptual artist. An anxious 29-year-old who aims in her work to express the digimodern vernacular by undiscriminated formal innovation and who is sexually involved with designer Harrow Berne. She doesn't know he hanged himself in his Manhattan flat on 23 September.

TONY SLATTERY: The eponymous television comedian and media personality. Having successfully battled twin demons of bipolar disorder and alcohol addiction, he is finally on the verge of his great comeback.

FELICE PABLO: Bolivian cartel head and father of six. Personal friend to President Diall and Lippy Downes.

JACKIE CLEGG: Nurse at the Queen Elizabeth II hospital in Welwyn Garden City who found herself pulled out of a long-standing depressive spiral by her experience with a severely disabled child called Debs.

OFFICER J PITREDY: Police officer serving on the Lower West Side who might have discovered a cover-up operation among the senior management of the Manhattan law enforcement services.

GOVERNOR SCHENECTADY: 49-year-old Governor of Arkansas who has been receiving payouts from Big Pharma but is at risk following his public endorsement of the so-called 'Super Drug', MGL.

DENISE CHANNING: Schenectady's personal secretary, 23-year-old bombshell with a degree in politics and a secret life as anonymous whistle-blogger Miss Tarnation, who first broke the story about Teddy Bunting.

GEORGE MOUNTBANK, EARL OF WESSEX: Flamboyant low-level member of the British royal family who keeps several 'hot houses' across West London.

CHAD BENNING: Hacker who coded the 'Richard III' trojan horse that broke the IRS Timesharing System on 23 September. The 19-year-old is only ever seen in silhouette.

AJ DEHANY: Hack. Friends with imaginary UK Uncut activist Jem and Chad Benning. Lacking in purpose.

LIPPY DOWNES: Society junkie and sometime lover of designer Harrow Berne, the 35-year-old transsexual is prone to mixing up her hormone treatments and her anti-depressants, sometimes resulting in strange growth spurts that make her sad.

NIALL RODNEY: Political poet and activist. On a GCHQ watch-list following his most recent book *I AM AMERIKA*. Registered opium addict.

MICHAEL OAKMAN: President of South Africa who has called together an emergency meeting of the Upper House to discuss the escalating race-based rioting in Pretoria.

DIRK SONGKIRK: NSA employee in PRISM, considering 'doing a Snowden'.

TEDDY BUNTING: Disgraced former variety entertainer with ties to low-level members of the British royal family and previously undisclosed interests in 'tech'. Has bad dreams – like, really bad ones.

MAI LAI: Chinese industrialist residing in Hong Kong who has made a deal with US President Diall to construct power stations all along the Eastern Seaboard. Likes to get hammered at all-night karaoke bars.

BARRY BETTS: Publican. The ebullient 51-year-old secretly helps out his regulars by under-charging them and sending them small gifts because he's going to have to close the pub.

ÉMILE ZOLA: Deceased French novelist and *soi-disant* social historian. Tends to be a bit forget-ful, works too hard.

CARRIE ERNEST: Freelance fashion columnist, the sassy 22-year-old plans to quit haute couture and publish philosophical novels of an absurdist bent. It is her column on 23 September that inadvertently breaks up Italian *Vogue* editor Kyra Tutto's marriage.

GIACOMO TUTTO: Writer and semiologist, 69 years old. Currently having an affair with a fashion school student a third his age.

ALFIE JENK: Property developer. A resourceful 36-year-old from Surrey, he is putting together a proposal to construct luxury residences on the Great Pacific Garbage Patch.

TOBY: Three-year-old Border Collie, with a keen nose, a sharp eye, and a superb pelt, who discovered the body of a man at the bottom of a fire ridge in the woods at Mustardpit Fell on 23 September.

PENNY BIRKBANK: Columnist and low-level member of the British Royal family who has recently left Twitter.

JACOB TUNDRA: 11-year-old boy currently held in a hostage situation in Pretoria who thinks he might have spotted a means of escape by crawling under one of the ventilation suites in the bank if he can encourage the other hostages to create a suitable distraction for the freedom fighters.

TINA RICE: Pentagon intern, a bubbly 23-year-old who is already slightly dispirited. Has been leaking information to Kirk Duggit and is involved in a 'sexual' relationship with one of General Birkbank's admin team, whom she only texts when she's wasted. Tends to get wasted, on account of being slightly dispirited.

NICE DAVE: Office Manager at Easley's Supplies and Wholesale, Main Office. Father of severely disabled child Debs. Tends to work too hard.

SATOSHI NAKOMOTO: Inventor of Bitcoin and creator of its original reference implementation. Not proven as to whether he is an individual or a group. It is Satoshi's intervention that leads to the so-called 'Freezethaw' of the New York Stock Exchange on 23 September.

PRIME MINISTER YANN DEGOEK: Prime Minister of Belgium. His brother is a cell leader of the Flemish Unification Movement. Wears spectacles that are the wrong prescription.

IL PADRE: Elderly Bolivian cartel godfather, currently in a coma which Felice Pablo had nothing to do with.

ALAIN ROBBE-GRILLET: Inventor of le Nouveau Roman, presumed dead.

CHAIM MENKEL: The last person who saw Teddy Bunting alive.

TY ILLING: Former football quarterback and bit part actor. The face of 'Redskins Kids', rumoured to be a front for money laundering. Has slight brain damage and a vocal slur, and wonders how secure he will be in retirement. Early adopter of the so-called 'Super Drug', MGL.

CAPTAIN AHAB: Fictional sailor. While in the Bermuda Triangle he encounters a Russian jet fighter, but is unable to attract the attention of the pilot, who he notices is about to fly directly into a large Dreadnought-class warship that seems to be scuttled 70 feet above the surface of the water.

CHIEF INSPECTOR IAIN ROSEBANK: Detective in Special Branch, working on a tough case involving low-level members of the British royal family. He is certain he is about to be shut down, and every night smuggles home copies of the documentation he has been gathering. Has a slight limp in one leg.

TERR-E: Hacker who is the first person to realise the terrible truth about the Brink Project. Never had a girlfriend, has trouble masturbating.

*

ACT I   SCENE I

The Great Pacific Garbage Patch fills the sea, represented on stage by plastic bags stretching across the full length of the mise-en-scène

Stage right an accursed whale is beached upside down across the edge of the stalls. Suspended from the flies are thick black clouds made of harvested human hair and syringes that are blocking out the light from the sun (yellow gel lamp rear of stage)

A flash of light softly ripples on the face of the poisoned waters as the mushroom cloud explands and sets off a chain reaction instantaneously destroying all things.

Curtain

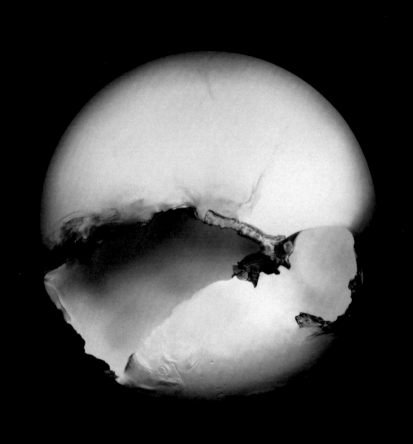

TOM PAZDERKA Nostalgie II
Oil, ash and charcoal on burned panel, 122 cm x 122 cm

Ashes and oil paint are combined in this image of pyrocumulus clouds from recent wild fires near my home. None of the paint is mixed, there are only layers building on top of one another, made to disappear into the blackness of the surface.

MICHIEL PIJPE
[previous] Intimation / [opposite] Reflection – *from* The Modeling
Ultrachrome print, 160 cm x 120 cm

We see things as we are constructed to see them, and can gain no idea of their absolute nature. Rooted in our culture is the notion that our world can only be 'A World' if we build something in it. These photographic images are a reminder of this idea, that the world is construct. Seeing that the dependable footholds we thought we had were never there to begin with, opens us onto a universe free of fixed point, of gravity, or the ability to be trusted.

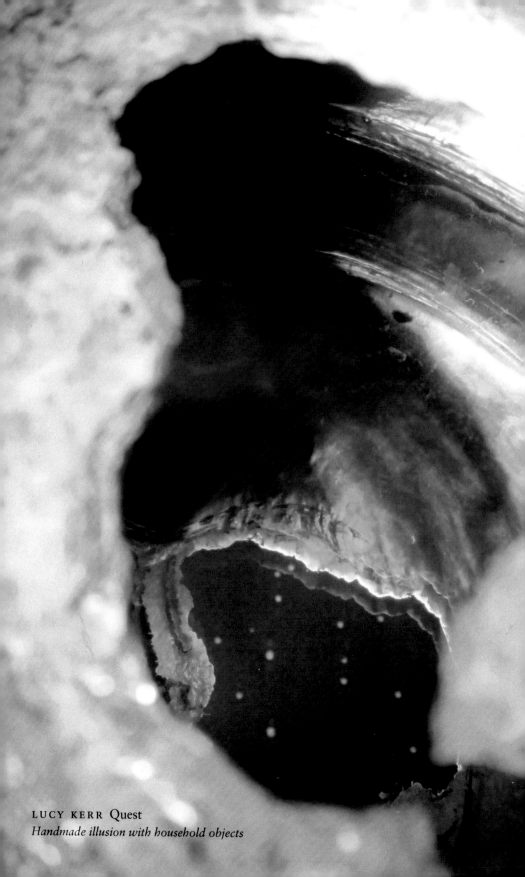

LUCY KERR Quest
Handmade illusion with household objects

ROSEANNE WATT

The Moth Trap

I never knew their marks
were just darker shades
of dust,

that older mothwings
fade like pages

left opened   to the light

how in aging
they *unknow* themselves,
shed this powder

of identity,
grow soft into

         vanishings –

imagine it:
all that residue

of you, windblown
through some flickering
wooded night,

each mark
each word
      lifted,

where all that's left   is flight –

A different drum: Martin Shaw telling the Siberian tale of 'The Crow King and the Red Bead Woman' at Base Camp, Embercombe, Devon [Photo: Warren Draper]

Uncolonising the Imagination
Martin Shaw in conversation with Charlotte Du Cann

'The thing about Finnish is that it's not linear, it's orbital,' said the ticket collector on the 10:35 train to Leeds. 'The language comes from the land. You have to find the object in the sentence and then everything else around it will make sense.'

We sat open-mouthed, as he then changed linguistic tracks and recited a verse from a Sami poem where an old woman is singing out to the dark forest.

'What you have to remember is that, in both these languages, the word for art and knowledge is the same...the train to Hebden Bridge will depart from Platform 12.'

One thing I knew for sure was that a conversation with Martin would not be straightforward. That although we would be speaking in English, a language hewn from a mix of many cultures, his stories come unexpected, feathered, leaved, rain-wet and roaring, from a collective language that has no borders. Mythologist and writer, he has been telling his wild alchemical tales to Dark Mountaineers for years now, in his books, his teaching (at the Westcountry School of Myth) and most strikingly at our annual events – and from all these emerge a depth, a heart, a clarity, a connectedness, that you cannot find in modern cynical end-of-the-world narratives.

I have a notebook page open on the topics in order but of course they get mixed up, as his answers jump like roe deer out of the thicket and twist like a shoal of lapwings in a darkening sky. You gaze in wonder at the shape and movement of it all and then you laugh, realising you are already there, right in the thick of it.

Here is a question that I hold like a ticket to the North in my hand: how can the act of telling and listening to a story liberate us from our disconnected, data-driven perception of the world and shift our attention towards what Iain McGilchrist calls the vast universe of the 'right hemisphere'? How can myths give us a language, a technology, to navigate a time when dragons and ugly sisters rule, in a culture now broken open by consequence?

When you pay attention to the archaic stories that Martin relates, you realise they are not there to reflect the power and glory of an empire, to provide escape or entertainment at the end of a hard-working day. They exist as a reminder of our place and meaning on the Earth; a reminder of what we have to undergo to become truly human, with a culture where art is the same as knowledge.

Where in order to find the answer to that question you must sit, like a hare in a field, listening to the landscape all around you, and wait for the object to reveal itself.

CDC: Martin, at Base Camp you said: 'The radical power of story is to open us up to reclaim an uncolonised imagination.' How is the telling of a myth part of that?

MS: The thing that distinguishes oral storytelling from, say, modern novels or theatre, is that the listener has to do an awful lot of work. Good storytelling is a skeletal activity and what is happening in a room is a hundred people are leaning forward, because their imagination is having to work very hard to conjure flesh out of the wider story. Even listening to stories is not a passive experience. You are meeting the energy of the teller and the images within the story, so the energy is triangulate.

CDC: Do you think mythology plays a particular role now in a world which is becoming increasingly fragmented and meaningless?

MS: Yes, myth has something direct to say. Many of the stories we need now arrived perfectly on time about 5,000 years ago. Old mythologies contain not only stories about our place on the Earth, but have the Earth speaking through them, what the Islamic scholar Henry Corbin termed the *mundus imaginalis* – where the human imagination is open to what David Abram describes as the more-than-human world. So with myth, you are working not just with imagination but with the imaginal, what many aboriginal cultures would call the Dreamtime. In other words, as we turn ideas around in our head, we're not just thinking but we are getting thought.

What does it mean to get thought?

For the last 20 years I've been taking people out into very wild parts of Britain, and for four days and nights they are absolutely alone, and often towards the end of that time, the participant will touch the edge of that experience. It's very hard to talk about the imaginal in conventional language. The most fitting language to address it is poetry or imagery or mythology. If the language is too psychological it reduces the mystery. It makes the mysteries containable and safe.

I'm tired of tame language addressing wild things. We seem to be frantically creating handrails in and out of desperately mysterious situations. And so to come back to the question: myth is a robust and ancient way of addressing a multiplicity of consciousnesses that abide in and around the Earth.

What is so powerful about an uncolonised imagination, a mythic intelligence, is that it connotes but does not denote. It doesn't tell you what it is. Its images have a radiance that reveals different things to whoever is beholding them. In storytelling, I know that when I say even something as definite as a crow that is in the room, we are all seeing 30 different crows. It is important that I don't hit a PowerPoint presentation, and say this is the crow we're talking about. Everyone's imagination is being stirred, where they are remembering and catching a glimpse of crows in their lives before that.

CDC: So storytelling and myth also have a relationship with time?

MS: Yes, and memory. Stories with weight to them have what C. G. Jung terms 'the lament of the dead', which in our frenetic culture we can no longer have time to hear. Most indigenous cultures will tell you that this world belongs to the dead, that's where we're headed. So mythology for me involves a conversation with the dead, with what you might call ancestors.

Whatever we are facing now we need to have a root system embedded in weather patterns, the presences of animals, our dreams, and the ones who came before us. Myth is insistent that when there is a crisis, genius lives on the margins not the centre. If we are constantly using the language of politics to combat the language of politics at some point the soul grows weary and turns its head away because we are not allowing it into the conversation, and by denying soul we are ignoring what the Mexicans call the river beneath the river. We're not listening to the thoughts of the world. We're only listening to our own neurosis and our own anxiety.

CDC: Much of your work calls for a return to bush soul and for us to remember. Do you feel these myths are resurfacing so we can relearn our ancestor training that has been shut down for a very long time?

MS: I would say: if you don't have ancestors you have ghosts. At the moment many of us are so impoverished and lacking in a cultural root system that what is around us are not ancestors supporting us but ghosts depleting us. So one of the things we could do is to reach out to stories, to practices – such as working on the land or a good art form – that require skills, diligence, a willingness to be bored and to lose our addiction to constant excitement. Myth and story put you into the presence of the old ones who have told the story before you.

When I've been with the Lakota Sioux or other Native American groups, I've seen that rather than telling stories from beginning to end like a Western narrative with a wedding at some point, they can enter the story wherever they want, like walking into a stream, and at that moment an image or scene in the story gets told and that is the story. It's just that glimpse that gets into the lion's blood of your imagination.

So I would say don't worry about the whole of the story. Look for the moment that speaks directly to you. Because like an acupuncture point, that is your entry point into the great stream of the story. You don't need to dam the thing off at the beginning and the end. It's more promiscuous than that, there are buddings everywhere.

CDC: When you told the story of the 'The Crow King and the Red Bead Woman' at Base Camp there were certain points where people were feeling very moved and in tears. What is that upwelling of sudden feeling in us all when we hear the story being told like that?

MS: One answer would be that this is a moment where we collectively experience what William Blake used to call 'a pinprick of the eternal' or the anthropologist Victor Turner '*communitas*', where often through grief there is a kind of permission given in the room to feel something deeply in public. These days that's quite rare. We tend to grieve and emote away from other people. But that's not the way traditionally it's done.

Folk tales told well have the power to be tacit ritual. In other words they have the strength to put their arms around the whole room and create a container that for an hour you can cook in the images of the story. You can allow yourself, bidden or unbidden, to be provoked by the images. And somehow it is safe to go deep within it.

It's really also to do with the skill of the teller. You might be an accomplished storyteller technically but if you haven't lived through some of the travails of the story, there will be a gap between the telling of the tale and what actually transpires. When those feelings happen in the room you know the storyteller is *synched up* to this story: she's not saying it's *her* story, but she has moved through the dark wood. She knows what it is like to carry precious red beads in her mouth. She knows what it's like to be ignored and left for dead. She knows what it's like to discern the difference between a seduction and a courtship.

When you see somebody effectively trying to tell the truth, it seems to have a deep, profound effect. So I think it's partially to do with the way a room is held, the feeling that you're in the presence of something ancient, which these stories are, and a readiness in the listener to allow themselves to just be carried by the power of the thing.

CDC: Are these complex Siberian myths ones that you're focusing on at the moment, or do you have many myths that you're working with at a time?

MS: I don't tell a wide variety of myths. Over the years, I have told a lot of stories that have come out of the Gaelic or Arthurian world, or European fairy tales, Russian fairy tales and Siberian folk tales. When you go into Siberia, you're not really in the same terrain as the Russian fairy tales any more. There's a different quality to them. You are dealing with stories that carry a lot less of a European influence in them and more of the kind of nutritional complexity that you find in Native American or Inuit stories.

One of the ways you notice this is the way their stories end in unexpected places. They do not follow the type of climactic Western narrative that we're used to now.

I read a lot of stories for example from India or from Africa or from South America, but I don't feel equipped to tell them. When I'm working with people who are training as storytellers, one of the things I say is find out what kind of weather patterns live within you, find out what kind of animal you are, find out what your ecosystems are. Because some stories you will find yourself naturally attracted to, and others you can simply respect and admire.

For example, in a lot of Scandinavian or Icelandic stories, a formal, incantatory, memorised way of telling the story really suits it and is encouraged. But because I'm so improvisational as a teller, because I have such a long-standing interest in wild things, one of the wildest things I think you can do is to go on without a script. So that is why lots of unexpected things tend to erupt when I'm telling. There'll always be a beginning and a middle and an end. But how we get there each time can be slightly different.

The sense of the story is what you as a teller bring that day. You're watching how the audience is responding, you're seeing their eye contact, the moments where they are leaning forward, when they're pulling back. And that to some extent *tunes* the telling of the story. Also you have the story tapping you on the shoulder all the way through, and saying 'Ah, ah, ah ... I really want you to slow down now, and describe in detail the yurt of the old woman.' And so I follow the direction of the story itself, but also what's happening in the room.

CDC: You wrote once, in your book *Scatterlings* I think, that we were not sure what story we were in as a culture. If there were a story that could speak of our present situation, that held in its talons, if you like, or in its heart, a feeling for regeneration or return, for making sense, for bringing together, for waking us up, what might that be?

MS: I do have a story. It's called the 'The Lindwurm'. It's a story that suggests that you and I have an exiled, slightly older sister or brother, who was hurled out the window the night they were born, and has sat brooding in a forest for many, many years, and has now returned.

And somehow contained in the psychic nerve endings of this story, I feel is a lot of information about what we're living through both ecologically and politically right now.

CDC: It has an active female protagonist who transforms everything, is that correct?

MS: Oh yes. Without the ingenuity of a young woman working in tandem with an old woman (who's really a spirit of an oak tree) we are going to be incinerated by the furious returning sibling, who devours everything that comes into its grip. It takes the ingenuity of the young woman, with the advice of the older woman, to not just defeat the serpent, but to free the serpent. That's what's so beautiful about it. The days of conventional hero myths are not serving us. What is being called for now culturally is a word you find often in Ancient Greece: *metis*. *Metis* is a kind of divine cunning in service to wisdom.

We can't be naïve in times like this, because we are in the presence of underworld forces that will do one of two things: they will either educate us, or annihilate us. And in fairy tales whenever the movement is down – and the movement culturally is down right now – you have to get underworld smart, have underworld intelligence, underworld *metis*. I have a strong feeling that a lot of what wants to emerge through many ancient stories is a kind of wily, tough, ingenious and romantic force that needs to come forward at this point in time.

CDC: Mythology often has what I call the Princess Problem. You know where there is a passive, beautiful young female being, and then the man, the hero, appears and does the noble thing. So I'm always alert to stories where there can be a female protagonist to balance out all the hero action and worship that got us into this fine pickle in the first place.

MS: I couldn't agree more. Sometimes when I'm telling ancient stories though I become aware that people in the audience are almost auditioning the stories for some contemporary concern. And while I'm sympathetic to the concerns of the time, the story itself is a living, powerful, breathing ancient being. It radiates its strange, troublesome intelligence out into the hearts and minds of everyone there and does its work.

But there are stories that are explicitly about the resurgence of a feminine that is not defined by what the troubadours call 'the far-distant lady'. So you're not the lady in the tower, where some young man is singing madrigals to you day and night; you are up-close, wild, occasionally brilliant, filled with opinions, big gnashing teeth, appetite, desire, with hooves that have trodden the ground of the underworld.

My book *Snowy Tower* looks at the Grail story of the knight Parzival, which superficially could be seen to be about a young man becoming an older man. But underpinning that story is his relationship with powerful, potent, active females, the most extraordinary of which is a being called Kundrie. Kundrie has tusks. She has breasts that lactate deadly nightshade; she has eyebrows so long she has to plait and tuck them behind her ears; she has the snout of a boar and the ears of a lion. But she speaks three languages, and (I rather love this detail) she has a hat from Paris. And most importantly she is the one who, often in a fairly harsh manner, pushes Parzival in the directions he needs to go to be in the presence of the Grail again.

So those stories are there. When I see people chopping up, cutting and pasting ancient stories to make a new story with a very active female character that has been taken out of three other stories, what we get is a mythic image, but we don't get a myth.

Now mythic is something that can be created in the imagination of a Jeannette Winterson or a Tolkien. But myth itself is connected to time and space. It has to pass through many mouths and many communities, until it takes on the kind of weight that means it's authentically a myth.

So my challenge for anybody is to regard themselves as a kind of a mythological scholar in training. And to go out and to look through the old anthologies, get a library card, and try and collect these stories that are waiting to say something vital about the nature of our times.

And the second part of that challenge, the most crucial part of the research, will be your individual expression of that story. It doesn't have to be an oral storytelling. It could be something you write down, or paint.

You could craft a boat from an image within the story. But one way or another you need to let the story have its way with you.

CDC: Ah yes, so that it becomes creative and externalised rather than inward and psychological. Talking of Parzival, there's a line in *Scatterlings* where you ask, in respect to medieval culture: 'What replaces the chivalric viewpoint and creates anchoring for humans?' There are not many myths that consider a band of people working together, except perhaps Robin Hood and his Merry Men, and Arthur and the Knights of the Round Table. In terms of the future, it's clear we can't be held in an individualist story, but one that brings community into it, or a bigger relationship. And I wondered if you had any thoughts about that?

MS: It's as if they are folk memories of times when we were living in much more closely knit relationships, both with each other and the Earth; where at some point the leader, the king or the queen, has to marry the wild for the health of the land. But you're right, not only should we accept that we need other people around us collectively, working and banging into each other with our ideas, our feelings and our passions; but also that myth says that within you is a multiplicity of intelligences, who all want different things from you.

In many tribal stories and indigenous tales, there is an implicit understanding that what we call *psyche* or *soul* does not live in a person, but that we live *within* the psyche or the soul. And the tribe, collectively, respond to and develop their lives through that awareness, which is usually a very ordinary experience. It's not a question of belief, it's a question of experience. However, in the West, we have had such a different fate over the last few hundred years that there is now a collective amnesia to the idea that we have a soul at all – whether there's a soul inside us, or that we dwell within one.

So when someone talks about the individual journey of someone in the West, they're having to make that journey because they do not have around them the cultural certainties that a tribal group would have, to affirm that yes, we are living within this wider thing, the *mundus imaginalis*, the soul of the world, and your dreams and your opinions are connected to waterfalls and jaguars and lightning storms.

It is a lonelier place for us to be because what is surrounding us does not confirm an Earth-centred consciousness. So that's why I think the individual has been such a pronounced thing in myth and story over the last few hundred years. But if we cannot get back to a more collectively understood relationship with psyche, with Earth, with matter, with trees and rocks and wolves and bears, with our neighbours, then we will be caught in an enormous malfunction.

CDC: This brings me to a question I've wanted to ask about the wild setting for such psyche and soul, as you have described it. When so many of us are living in cities and urban areas, in depleted and industrialised landscapes, how can we recover our relationship with wild things and reconnect with that world?

MS: It's a question I've been asked a lot from people who are reading my books and are living in Detroit or Birmingham or Prestatyn. Initially my response is 'don't be size-ist'. Twenty years ago I was living in southeast London, and it was a great consolation for me that William Blake had found a lot of what he needed, as a human and a thinker, in London. He could kneel down and see a little grey thistle and he knew it was a smiling little man waving at him.

It was a way of not just seeing but beholding things. And when I lived in cities I would pay particular attention to what we rather naïvely call weeds. Or I would go out to a small park next to the video shop in Brockley, where there was a rather dejected-looking rowan tree. And I would spend an enormous amount of time just attending to this rowan. There's a lovely line by the French philosopher Gaston Bachelard, where he says something like 'the Earth seeks to be admired by you'.

So if you do nothing else, admire the thing. Learn to give it praise. Learn to speak its 12 secret names. You hear about the Inuit having all these different names for snow. Well, I thought, what are the 12 secret names of those old-growth oaks that I see down near Greenwich docks? My advice really is what the Hindus call the 'joyful participation in the sorrows of the world'. You have to get amongst the cities. You have to glean what you can, praise what you can, raise up what you can. I used to bemoan the fact that I didn't have 400 acres of prime old-growth forest on my back door, until I realised that this was just a surly child in me – one of these mythic characters I was talking about.

So, I told myself: 'you're going to go out and become a praise-maker. You're going to go out and praise and be generous to things.'

You asked a question about chivalry or gallantry earlier on, and when I was a little kid, one of my favourite books was called *The Book of Chivalry*, and I got my mum to make me a little cape. And I would wander around, constantly throwing this cape over puddles – it's very embarrassing...

CDC: Oh, that's sweet!

MS: But I now realise I was right. I wasn't throwing capes over puddles to maintain a patriarchal system of domination over women, I just wanted to behave in a beautiful and good manner to the Earth and its inhabitants. In the face of 1980s Thatcher's Britain that was my response – to get my little cape out. And I realise now in my mid-40s that absolutely nothing has changed in me.

CDC: Your cape is still on the back of the door, Martin?

MS: Yes, it absolutely is. Anybody with a cape gets into the School of Myth!

So, what I'm saying really is: soul doesn't end with a tree or a stream. If you're interested in animism, everything is alive. So how is a city alive? There's a wonderful storyteller and mythologist called Michael Meade, who grew up in New York. And he has a great description of being a kid on the subway. And every time he went up the stairs of the underground, he was in a different district of New York with a radically different ethnicity. So he goes up one set of stairs and it's Little Italy; he goes up another it's China; he goes up another it's Poland. And he said: I realised that the city itself was teeming with its mythologies, that over a couple of decades, those two cultures of the Poles and the Irish would inexorably start to weave parts of their lives together, and this third thing would happen.

My attention has been on the diminishing tracts of wilderness in Great Britain. But it can't stop there for many of us, because that's simply not the environment we are living in.

CDC: I wanted to ask you finally about breaking enchantment, about breaking the spell, which is a predicament in so many fairy stories. Many of the illusions that we've been brought up with are now being cracked open. Do you feel that the myths contain insights that we might reach out for, not as a handrail but as a tiller, so we might steer our way through these choppy waters ahead?

MS: First of all, I would say again that the word enchantment, which ironically is often used about hearing a myth or a story, is the opposite of what's actually taking place. A story like 'The Red Bead Woman' and its effect on a room is not an enchantment, it's a waking up…

CDC: A disenchantment…

MS: Yes, if you've done your job well as a storyteller, your story itself has a magical sensibility to ward off enchantment and to raise up. Secondly, people often prefer to dismiss myths, saying: it's not true. But a way to think about myth is as something that never was and always is. Or as a beautiful lie that tells a much deeper truth. But one way or another when we lose our mythic sensibility, the powers in this world that may not wish us well have a greater purchase on us, a greater hold.

I notice that several times a day I go into what you could call a mild trance state. I'm not talking about ouija boards here! I'm just talking about falling under the influence of advertising, or various politically engineered neuroses that might be floating around. But I recognise I have come into a kind of enchantment. And the way I recognise it is that I feel less than grounded. I feel I'm not in the realm of imagination, I'm in the realm of fantasy. So the imaginal is not present; the Earth as a lived, breathing, thinking being is not present. What's happening is I'm simply fretting – to use my mother's language – I'm spinning my wheels. And so actually I think stories have a capacity to wake us up.

We are living in a time when we need symbolic intelligence, not just sign language. We are being fed signs, and signs that frighten us, and then paralyse us, and then colonise us. And imagination, through myth, wants to give you symbols to raise you up.

A story is not just an allegory, or a metaphorical point. It's a love affair, and one of the most wonderful ways of breaking the trance states being put on us at this point in time, is to figure out what you love. Figure out what you're going to defend. And develop the *metis*, develop the artfulness, to bring it out into the world.

NINA PICK

Crow

Visited my dream last night, wings splayed
like hands, black to my brown, your wings
were words, your words were hills (over which
we flew), your claws were commas, and the cries
of your beak were wings. You carried a message
from the branches. *Peace?* I thought it said. But
I had forgotten, dear trickster, you are crow.
You place words in my mouth, truth in my
lies and in the cumulous space between them,
your wingspan opens over me, black
mother-protector, like night. And when I wake
I wonder why I dream of you, in this land,
here where I see no birds.

STINNE STORM

from *The Handbook of Caves and Obituaries*

an animal: the last monkey to live among us was female. she walked out of
the bush, already a reminiscence back in the 2010s, her lone body seemed
shy of the attention captured on digital media. timid and so you don't hear
her voice.
celebrations were held on her behalf, scientists of the time called her a
praise to her species for coming forth and a joy to work with as she let
them do all kinds of things to her
(unspeakable)
after the disappearing of the last piece of her habitat, she's among
humans. she reads kafka's 'a report to an academy' and weeps. she falls
in love and gets abandoned. she grows older, less tragic. tends to her
garden. she tells stories of her time in the wild and how she still dreams
of this wildness
– this is one of the stories she told: monkey came out of a seedpod of the
tree with the biggest leaves. in the misty woods monkey was small and
alone among the other seeds. all day she'd spend crawling her little body
into the trunk of the tree to reach an even higher branch to see if other
seedpods had friends inside. yet any time monkey opened a seedpod there's
just more seed and no relatives. one day the blue heron or the stork landed
to sit down and ask about her long face and sad little hands that tear all
pods apart instead of eating them.

– i'm looking for family, monkey says. and heron or stork says – well,
we all do. and that is why monkey and heron or stork are now relatives.

when the monkey was very old she stopped telling stories in their full
length. she'd shake her head, having heron or stork over for tea time in the
dim afternoons, they'd sit there in their inverted bestiary, pour each other
the hot liquid, sip and look out at the humans in their many cages.

in her last public appearance she stared right into the camera and saw you.
her gaze had a mist and a vastness that pierced you and you felt how as an
embryo you were the small seed; legs growing out of your kidneys, arms
extending from the top of the lungs and you wanted to touch her. let your
fingers stroke the fur. carry her like you carry a child of your own or a
grandparent that can no longer walk but still loves you more sophisticated
or devoted than any of your present desires. loving wildness.
when the monkey died, all prior monkeys died out with her and you are
one less in the seed pod.

ANNE HAVEN MCDONNELL

Messenger

In the parking lot outside my office,
a roadrunner stood on top of my car –
a real one, not a hood ornament.
I'm not bragging,
but there were other cars,
endless perches.
Maybe she liked my old truck –
the dragonfly-blue of the hood
or the faded circles of worn-away paint
like dried desert puddles, lined in salt.
Before, I had only seen the bird in cartoons,
so when she leaned her neck forward to run,
red eye-streak lit like a little flame,
her body still and pointed like a rudder,
and her legs spun in speed,
I laughed out loud at the wonder of it –
the bird zipping across the silent campus,
a blunt noon sun, all the cars hot and still
and bored in their shining metal.
Trust me, there was no one else
to see this – nothing chased
the bird as she ran like a messenger,
like the world was on fire and
no one was watching.

FRANCESCA SCHMIDT

Losing Home

My story is about two kinds of change: one slow, one very quick. It's about the end of a way of life that is haunting me personally because it is the way of life of my parents, my grandparents, my people in the most basic sense of the word. It is about my village. It's not the story of an indigenous people in a far-away corner of the global south, it is about Germany. Plain old ordinary Germany, wealthy and complacent and world-record holder in exporting cars we shouldn't be building in the first place (here, incidentally, lies the tangent to another story of creative destruction: in order to meet our climate goals, the German car industry will have to go. It is the very basis of our economic stability and prosperity, and it is politically entangled, subsidised, unfairly favoured and currently preventing counter-narratives from taking hold in this country).

'The way we live' is a strange, hard-to-grasp thing. Sometimes, things change dramatically in a very short time. People in the eastern German village I want to tell you about have ample experience of this. In 1988, people here thought that things would never change. That they would always live in a one-party state with a censored press and without the right to travel or to express their opinion. That the only change they were likely to see anytime soon would be the slow, depressing decay of their cities and monuments and the rusting-away of an industrial infrastructure that was out-of-date, polluting, and had nevertheless been their life's work.

My parents were no political activists. They had stayed in the Church and out of the Party, and had compensated for their frustration like most other people did – by telling forbidden jokes to their friends and otherwise keeping their heads down. But in 1989 they joined the demonstrators. They did it, my mother once told me, because the sense of inertia and stagnation had become too oppressive to bear. They were stuck in a system that had become ossified, locked into dogmatism. While the country was falling apart, its leaders proclaimed a myth of progress and success. They had become blind to reality, deaf to facts, and unable to change. My parents had two little children and were terrified, and they were no heroes. Not more heroic, anyway, than any other East German taking to the streets in 1989, knowing full well that every single uprising in Soviet history had ended violently. They did it because the discrepancy between reality as proclaimed by the State and reality as perceived all around them was becoming too much, and their frustration was becoming the worst option available. They also did it – as would become clear with hindsight – because from afar capitalism just looks too good to resist. Either way, the East Germans demonstrated for change, and change they got. More than they had bargained for, and more than most of them could handle.

So this story is first and foremost about radical change. About pivotal events, definite ruptures with the past. Radical change actually builds up over long periods of time, the result of many minor developments that eventually reach a tipping point. Like underground rivers, they can gather strength and momentum out of sight for long stretches of time to then suddenly appear, seemingly from nowhere.

Then there is the second type of change. It is incremental, likewise barely noticeable, but it doesn't lead to cataclysmic events. Instead, you increasingly stumble across a reality that no longer matches your assumptions of it. At some point, you realise that the world is no longer the one that you took for granted. We adapt to change, we adapt to almost anything, and so we barely notice change until we don't feel at home in our homes any more. It no longer resembles the place we call home in our minds. Perhaps each event is so minor that we barely take note of it. Perhaps we don't perceive the connection between these events, don't see the pattern. Perhaps we perceive it, but don't know what it means.

My parents were raised in villages ten kilometres apart from each other, and when they married in 1975 they did the traditional thing: they moved into my father's family home. Much like its neighbours, it's a two-storeyed, rectangular affair with a kitchen garden and one or two sheds thrown in, and my family has been living in it since the 1850s. My grandparents renovated to split the house into two dwellings: they moved into a flat downstairs, while my parents lived upstairs. This was not only extremely common, it was the practical thing to do in a country experiencing chronic shortage of housing. Hence, normality in East German villages consisted of grandparents doing most of the cooking and child-

My family's house in the 1920s

care, while parents went to work. In my case, my grandfather picked me up from kindergarten, and my grandmother cooked lunch for us five days a week. Sometimes, two of her great-grandchildren living in the next village along would join as well, and when my father opened a small shop in our shed she cooked lunch for him, too. There were a few kids who lived with only their parents, and who consequently had to stay in day care after school, but this was rare, and, to be honest, a bit strange to most of us. As far as normal was concerned, grandparents lived in the same house or perhaps down the road. Normal also meant that we grew much of our own fruit and vegetables, kept a few hens and rabbits for meat. People didn't starve in East Germany, but fresh produce was never reliably plentiful or especially tasty. And so people stayed in the habit of keeping a kitchen garden, gathering and preserving what they could.

This way of doing things wasn't unique to East Germany. Village life had been organised around these terms forever, and mainly for practical reasons. It remained viable, even necessary, for longer here because decent flats were scarce, because people never had to move for job

My family's house in the 1920s. My grandfather is the boy wearing braces.

reasons, and because women as well as men were expected to work outside the home. It also worked because people didn't expect to have impressive careers. In fact, having an impressive career wasn't possible without cosying up to the Party, and so insignificance became rather attractive.

That's how their world worked, and for a long time it was how my world worked, too. I was born at the precipice of change and I am the first in my family who does not need to follow tradition, who has other options. Or rather: I am the first in my family who has many options, except for the option to stay here.

Because (you already know this, don't you?) my parents didn't get that better world. They did get foreign holidays, a colour TV and 15 brands of chocolate to choose from, and they got children who took all of this for granted. They also got to choose between different parties every so often, but they didn't get to choose a new narrative. People got all these new things ready-made, and they got a ready-made story with it. Capitalism had proven superior, the story went. People had chosen it, had

My mother and her extended family in the 1950s

chosen freedom and aspiration. In my village, some people believed this new story more strongly than others. Some fared better with it than others. On the whole, though, people soon realised that the new freedom wasn't so free after all. The tyranny of the party had been replaced by the tyranny of the market. Their places of work were outcompeted, sold, divided up and sold again to raise a few digits on a computer screen. They were no longer subject to the Stasi, but to shareholders instead. It was fine for the young, flexible and well-educated. They left. They went to Munich or Cologne and often did well for themselves there. They left behind large, rectangular, two-storeyed farm houses and their extended families. They found affluence and opportunity, and in order to do this,

My mother and her extended family in the 1950s

they had to let their parents grow old alone, and their children grow up without grandparents. It's the new normal.

It's not worth the bother having your own apple tree any more, either. There are plenty of apples to be had at any time of the year, and without the effort. Time is too precious now, more so than money. Nowadays, many of these houses are occupied by only one or two elderly people. It's hard to manage a kitchen garden if there's only two of you, and not worth it either. Eastern Germany is ageing and shrinking fast, and my home region is ageing and shrinking faster than average. Capitalism was all about a bright new future, more choices, better opportunities. And if you choose to leave to where capitalism accumulates, you can have all

New extended families: the Lobelei project near Leipzig. [photo: lobelei.de]

that. Capitalism creates inequality, and it creates losers. That's part of the narrative, but they forgot to mention that during the 1989 sales pitch.

The ones left behind have often grown bitter, disillusioned. The grand new story has proven a lie, and already other stories are filling the void, fast. One of these is about blame and hatred, another about the virtues of the past. Yet another one is about muddling through, about taking the safe option. The people in charge are baffled, mainly. They think that if only we can make the official story come true for more of these people at the rural fringe, things will be fine. We just have to try harder. We were promised the land of milk and honey, and we *will* have it. But by now, our own maltreatment at the hands of capitalism isn't the biggest problem any more. Despite having re-invested some of the exploits of capitalism into cleaning up our rivers and retrofitting our houses and efficiency-rating our devices, it looks as though the story has overlooked a key protagonist. We can correct that, though, people will tell you. In fact, all of this is a great opportunity for German precision-engineering. It will create jobs, market opportunities. Not in the rural fringe, mind, but whoever wants to live *there* anyway?

Voids create opportunities. Land is cheap where I come from, relatively speaking. Houses are very cheap, provided you know how to renovate them yourself. In some places, new kinds of people are moving into almost clear-cut villages, bringing new kinds of ideas, rejuvenation. Most importantly, they bring different narratives. To exist, these narratives need room – or rather, the people trying to live them need room to exist. Room is one of the few things my home has an abundance of.

They do many of the things people in my village used to do when I was young. They consume less, not because there is nothing to buy, but because they don't want to buy it. Instead, they grow some of their own food, raise their own meat. Often, they live together cross-generationally – by choice rather than by default. They can't step outside the system – nobody can. But they try to re-weave some of the frayed threads, give a different ending to this story.

For them, the discrepancy between reality as proclaimed by the powers that be and reality as perceived all around them has become too great, the frustration too acute. This time round, of course, there isn't a ready-made narrative waiting to take over. And so it is like navigating with a very rough map. Some of it shows past landscapes, some of it is even blank. It might be a case of drawing the map while walking the path.

ELIZABETH RIMMER

The Wren in the Ash Tree

The Wren

The birds have come back to the garden,
second brood starlings and sparrows
lined up along hedges, combing the lawn's thatch
for spilt grass seeds, emerging ants. Blue tits
cling to whippy branches, dunnocks pry into cracks
in the bark, goldfinches pick apart seed heads
of nettle and marigold. A willow warbler slips
furtive between the stiff dulling birch leaves
and blackbirds plunder the ripening currants.
The last swifts scythe the hot air, quilted
with sulk and threat of storm. The cormorant's
black crossbow looms above, heavy with hunger
and this year's wren sings on a high branch
claiming in summer his winter territory.
El Niño has exhaled a great hot sigh.
The ice is melting, sliding off Greenland's cliffs
into seas blooming with plankton. There are storms
and flash floods, blight and failure of crops.
There is drought in Africa and famine and war.
But the wren is on his high perch singing.
The druid's bird, the bard's bird, shaman's bird,
Brigid's chicken, the mouse's brother,
sits on his high perch and cries out, so loud
a voice in his small breast, 'Now! Now! Now!'

Canto 1 *The Outcry*

The hanging man says,
'Outcry of grief
goes up and down the world-tree,
grumble of ravens and chattering classes
in tweets and rumours on smartphones.
Her leaves are nibbled by squirrels,
in curtained bedrooms and behind
the facades of abandoned shops,
browsed to the bark by greedy stags,
in city suits and plate-glassed offices,
her roots undermined by serpents
wasting the soil. The hedges are down,
the fenlands drained and the red dust
is washed off suburban car fronts.'

The wren is singing in the bramble bush.

The woman at the ford says,
'On one bank of the river,
there is a lament for the fallen,
on the other, the outcry
of those who have lost everything
and there is never enough
of blood or tears.'

El duende says,
'This is the place of pain.
To sing here you will need
to open the heart,
the lungs and voice,
and meet it square.
You can't sing from hiding,
nor drunk or afraid.
You can't sing this softly

like chocolate in the sun.
You must give yourself
to the fight with all your strength.
It will take all you've got.
It will feel like death.'

The wren slips between the branches
 of the birch tree without a sound.

And the field says,
'You can't write my music.
There ain't no sixteen bars,
no twelve bar phrases here –
field music has to come
straight from the heart.'

The song from the city is sung
behind a proscenium arch,
in other voices, not ours.

The city is silent.
All the roundabouts
are wearing flowers
dressed in cellophane
and there are soft toys
on every doorstep.

The wren is hidden
among the leaves of the ash
and sings without ceasing.

And the *púca* sings
in the depths of the sea,
'The water is poisoned with oil
and the krill is scarce. We are hungry
and choking on plastic.

There are small boats, sinking
beneath the weight of sorrow
and the men with guns who turn
the lost ones away from their coasts.'

And the *völva* is casting the runes.

The leather bag is thick and tough,
gives away no secrets, but the stones
mutter and grind against each other.
The black angular lines – tree, hammer,
wealth, ocean, ice – will come together,
fall in the right configuration,
give their bleak verdict soon enough.

And the rune for harvest is the same
as the rune for the day of reckoning.

And the wren sings on the bare branches,
sings without ceasing.

Canto 2 *Fuga Mundi*

What do you do when the earth is stolen
from under your feet? What do you do when
the landlord says your rent isn't enough
so you can't stay where your grandfathers
lived and died? where your children
were born, under weather you understand?
Where do you go when the sea boils
and the rocks shudder with the weight
of destruction raining from planes
belonging to people you never heard of?

Where do you go when the job is killing you
and you never see your children and your pay
is gone from your bank account before
you have thought how to spend it?
You ask yourself, 'Why pay money
for what is not bread?' And you ask yourself
the price of sleep.

Where do you go when the water is poisoned
with salt or nitrate, or when the mud is inches deep
in your kitchen and the rain has not stopped for a week.

Wrens are hiding from bitter weather
deep in the cracks between stones
huddled together for warmth in a space
smaller than you would think possible.

When the nights are dark and open-eyed you dream
of building the last homely house, an ark,
a treasury for all that is going to be lost.
In the centrally-heated houses the people
are dreaming of a life off-grid, of growing their own,
of communities made over, honest and kindly,
where there is welcome for the stranger,

but nobody comes, because everybody
has a home of their own, and the sick are healed,
but no-one gets sick, because the air is clean
and the life is so healthy. There will be orchards
and bees and chickens, and the laughter
of children in sunlit meadows, and fires
on the hearth, and time for songs.
All you need is the land, you say,
but who owns the land?

Who owns the land? Who owns the seeds?
And where does the water come from?
How did we get so ignorant? And who
will teach us now, how to live
without waste, without breaking the earth,
without so much fear, without despair?

This place is done, broken and worn out.
We need somewhere else, somewhere new,
clean and unspoiled. And there is no such place.

A wren flits over the frost-hard ground,
mouse-brown, mouse-quiet and the eye
of the hawk does not see him.

CONSTANTIN SCHLACHTER
from The Gyrovagi's Trajectory

Nature and its influences on the human psyche are the main topics that Schlachter explores in his project, *The Gyrovagi's Trajectory*. In a free interpretation of the notion of an ascetic quest, his self-interrogations are nurtured through extended solitary retreats in the wild.

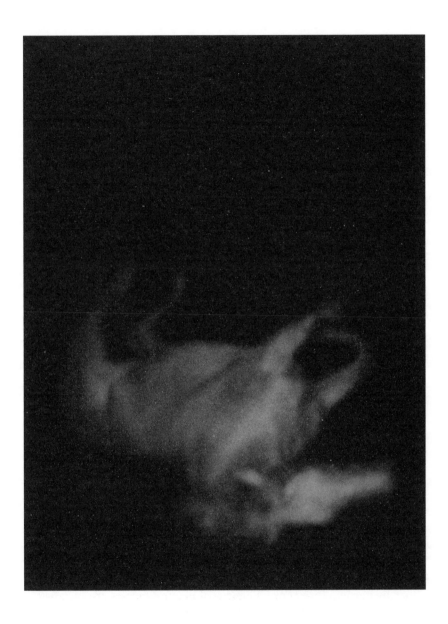

Schlachter shoots with instinct, sometimes manipulating photographs through both analogue and digital means. This process crystallises his thoughts, which focus on the emotion contained within the images. It loosens the images' links with concrete reality, allowing the viewer to roam a mystical realm dominated by nature and our primeval myths.

JOHN REMBER

The Way We Live Now

The metaphors of extinction

I

Life these days in Sawtooth Valley, sheltered by mountains and supported by a bounteous local tourist economy, is unequivocally benign. It's good to wake up in the morning when production and distribution chains are swaying in the wind but still standing, when the world outside my window is still white in the winter and green in the summer, when the air is clear except for fire season, when there's a gassed-up SUV in the driveway for Costco runs, when there's UPS and Amazon for anything we forgot at Costco, when hospitals still believe in Medicare, when the Social Security Administration and TIAA deposit money in my checking account every month, when my physician gives me – thus far – a clean bill of health every January. In summer, good food is in the local restaurants, and good music is played on the lawns of local lodges and hotels. In winter, there are airline tickets to someplace warm with a beach.

Life is good in a 20-year marriage to Julie, with whom I share substantive conversation, hard money, a solid roof over our heads, the privilege of skiing out our door during the parts of winter when we're not on a beach, intelligent books to read, and the education and inclination to enjoy reading and conversing about intelligent books.

We live under a wide and gorgeous sky, which stretches to the ragged horizons of the valley. The sunsets are good, even when they're made gauzy by burning forests or Chinese coal plants. Sunrises are even better, with their promise of another day. Full moons are good, even when they're a ruddy orange. Stars are good, and most cloudless nights the Milky Way looks like bright dust hovering in the sky. The experience is a bit giddy when you realise you're looking down, not up. From our earth-balcony, we look down on meteor showers in August and December, although we don't last long outside in December.

Routine is good. It keeps your feet on the ground when your mind is falling into the sky.

So I lock and load the coffee maker every night, and the one of us who wakes first turns it on in the morning. If it's me, I check three or four doomsday sites on the internet while Julie's still sleeping, just to make sure somebody still has certainty in this uncertain world. Then I check the headlines of the *New York Times* just to make sure that consensus reality has made it through the night. When Julie gets up, she invokes a separate, smaller, and equally iffy consensus reality by logging into her job, which involves editing technical literature for technology companies.

In the summer I cut firewood, build fences, and engage in the 3M's of lawn care: maintaining the gasoline-powered sprinkler system, mowing the grass and weeds, and murdering the occasional ground squirrel or gopher. In the winter I work on skis, repairing their bases, sharpening their edges, and waxing them according to the next day's weather forecast. Depending on the season, we drink gin-and-tonics on the deck and watch the sun go down behind the peaks at nine, or sit by the woodstove with cups of tea and detective novels after the sun has disappeared into dark snow clouds at four-thirty. We play to our domestic strengths, which means that unless I'm making spaghetti, Julie cooks and I do the dishes and clean up the kitchen. On Tuesdays Julie has a yoga class in town and I go with her and sit and talk with a couple of other old guys in the bar next to the yoga studio. We call Tuesday Beer and Yoga Night.

At least four times a year – on the equinoxes and solstices – we invite friends in the valley to our house for a potluck. We gossip and stay up late, but with our crowd that means everybody is home and in bed by midnight, and our kitchen is clean. We have engaged in a small quiet ceremony of thankfulness that we have such good friends and that they have such a good time talking and laughing with each other. Laughing and talking are wonderful sounds to have in your kitchen and living room.

When you're not sure the world that sustains you will last through the week, but you want very much for it to last for a couple more decades, everyday life becomes ritual. My spaghetti sauce has become one of the pillars of the world, or at least of dinner.

And like an Aztec priest, trapped by the axiom that human sacrifice is necessary to bring the sun up every morning, I believe in my heart that switching on the coffee maker is the only thing that will prevent eternal night.

Sympathetic magic is what I perform to keep the world from falling into the black hole at the centre of the Milky Way. It wasn't always so effective.

II

In 1989 the American author William Styron published *Darkness Visible*, an account of his year-long clinical depression. The book is not proof of Styron's eloquence or of his prowess as a metaphorical thinker, but of his complete failure to articulate what he went through. Again and again his description shows depression as a state of fear and pain without words for fear and pain. It also lacks convincing words for past and future, self and other.

I read the book twice, once before I had gone through a clinical depression and once after.

As a yet-to-be-depressed reader, I admired Styron's skill with words and the scope and variety of his metaphors. I thought he had explained what it's like to be depressed. But in the aftermath of depression, all I could see in his book was its failure to give meaning to experience – a failure that was, by then, familiar.

Styron's many metaphors are attempts to communicate something – anything – about what depression feels like. When one metaphor doesn't work, he tries another, which doesn't work either. The book and even its narrator feel made-up, hollow edifices of words erected as flimsy bulwarks against the unspeakable.

In the end, Styron simply says he went mad and then emerged from madness, damaged but alive. There's a blank and impenetrable barrier between the person he was when depressed and the person he was when writing a book about being depressed.

My own experience has been similar. Once I realised I was falling into a depression, I determined that I was going to meet it head-on. I would take whatever it had to give and emerge from it stronger. That was like standing on the tracks, waiting for the bullet train to come along and teach me about life.

My metaphors of depression aren't any more enlightening than Styron's, but here are some:

- The self, that thing you once thought was a brilliant supergiant star, has exhausted its fuel and become a black hole, infinitely small with infinite gravity, the unwelcome centre of the universe.
- Everything in your world is silently and endlessly turning to ashes.
- A demon resides in your skull, whispering a hundred or two hundred times a day that you should kill yourself.
- Reality becomes an all-encompassing intolerable stasis, a stasis marked by a thousand meaningless lifetimes a minute. That doesn't make sense, but little about depression does.

Towards the end of my depression, when a combination of drugs and cognitive therapy had begun to bring me back into a world I could believe was real, I told my psychiatrist that I was well enough to stop taking a tricyclic anti-depressant, hoping that I could avoid its unpleasant side-effects and still live. He was concerned that I was stopping it too soon, and talked me into taking it for another 30 days, which in itself indicated that I was coming out of depression. Thirty days would have seemed an unendurable eternity a few months before.

I also told him that I was beginning to identify the wellsprings of my depression:

- A year before, I had ended a decade-long relationship that had been marked by infidelity and magical thinking (practices that had ended up as somewhat less joyous than they had been at the start of the relationship).
- I had turned 41. I had thought I would stop aging at age 40, and my 41st birthday came as a surprise.
- My parents were showing signs of their eventual deaths. My father had had a series of small strokes, and my mother was showing hoarding behaviours that I feared (correctly, it turned out) were the start of dementia.
- A student advisee had killed herself after having been the driver in a single-car accident that killed her boyfriend.
- A good, much-loved dog, one I had raised on the trail while working as a wilderness ranger, had been killed by a speeding pickup on the highway. I later received a letter from the wife of the driver of that pickup, saying he had aimed for my dog deliberately, and that she knew it meant that she and her husband were going to hell. The letter, in all its cosmological permutations, made it impossible for

me to see myself in any benign universe. After some years of not thinking about this incident, I had begun thinking about it again.

– After attaining tenure at a small liberal arts college, I had begun to see that I had bought into an existential swindle: I was not going to end up as a beloved Mr. Chips wandering around a green campus imparting wisdom, but as a bored and self-loathing Mr. Chips correcting an endless stack of first-year essays in a cramped and stuffy office.

My psychiatrist was impressed with this sad list. He told me he had never had a patient with as much insight into his depression. Most people, he said, didn't want to know what had made them depressed.

Perhaps I was lucky in that the sources of my depression seemed close, and fresh, and undeniable, but I don't think so. Most people, by the time they're 41, have tragedy in their history, or if not tragedy, lost friends, ageing parents, dead pets, dream jobs that turned into nightmares, and an awareness that they're not going to be forever young. Most people refuse to think about these things, if my psychiatrist is to be believed.

What happened to me then is that the 30 days went by, and with them my last 30 capsules of tricyclic antidepressant. I spent an additional 30 days on Prozac, which blessed me with a gently euphoric I-don't-give-a-shit attitude toward school shootings, suicides of friends, nuclear war, nihilistic politicians, dead oceans, and fatal-disease pandemics.

When the Prozac was gone, the euphoria went away, but I remained an impartial witness to catastrophe. It's been almost 25 years since that time. I haven't been depressed again, and haven't had to use antidepressants again. I haven't read *Darkness Visible* again, even as the pile of shit I don't give has grown into something you could put a ski lift on and wait for snow.

I arrived back in sanity – as opposed to consensus reality – with an appreciation of how insignificant I am in the totality of things, how little my decisions can affect the world, and how right that insignificance feels to me. Depression cures narcissism if it lets you live. It also cures consensus reality, or at least an unquestioning faith in it.

I understand depression is something you shouldn't wish upon your worst enemy. I know – too well, even if I can't articulate it – how my student advisee who killed herself must have looked forward to death as the end of her grief and pain and empty horror where a self used to be.

But if and when you get back from depression, you've gained insight into the nature of the self as artifice. You understand that you can't have a life story without first making up a storyteller, the one you call you.

You understand that the stories you once told yourself about your life and place in the world were flimsy and flawed constructions that wouldn't survive five minutes in a therapist's waiting room. Some of those stories came from your cultural heritage, and failed miserably in their job of keeping you an unalienated actor in the cultural theatre. In the case of industrial civilisation, of course, the theatre wasn't that good in the first place, and the moment when you broke character wasn't, in retrospect, that much to grieve about.

Ernest Becker, in his seminal work *The Denial of Death*, says what we know as the world is simply a happy construct that one way or another lets us avoid thinking about our own death. Becker considered this denial to be the motive for all civilisations, the source of all art, and the foundation of human character itself.

That's a bit of a leap from the consensus reality he lived in as an honoured and prolific teacher and writer, but Becker was writing as cancer was killing him. He ended up confronting death the way I attempted to confront depression. Nothing surprising about the way things worked out for him.

Unlike *Darkness Visible,* I continue to read *The Denial of Death* every two or three years, not because I enjoy being told I'm going to die, but because I've become fascinated with the idea that it's what we *refuse to think* that makes us who we are. Character is a kind of inspired lie, and what inspires it is the fear of eventual nonexistence.

But as a formerly depressed person, and as a person who cared for a parent fading into dementia, I know there are at least two things worse than death. Three, if you include caring – in more than one sense of the word – for a person with dementia. So for me, it's a short step from *Denial of Death* to *Denial of Dementia* or *Denial of Depression,* or even *Denial of Care.* Denial of Care is a big part of what's on the Advance Directive card I carry in my wallet. Denial of Dementia is the real reason Julie will smother me with a pillow if I ever forget the date of our wedding anniversary.

III

Depression nearly killed me once, and it's killed a bunch of my friends and neighbours and people I went to school with. The only thing that saved me is the knowledge that at some point my life had ceased to be my property, and had become the property of the people who loved me. It takes time to understand that distinction, and you can't understand it at all if nobody loves you.

Although there's not enough love in the world, chances are that somebody loves you, and for that reason you can't decide to kill yourself without consulting the person or persons doing the loving. Your depression is going to tell you that they don't love you, but you should at least ask.

That said, we live in a world where industrial civilisation has had, for a century at least, excellent reasons to believe that nobody loves it. It's gone and committed suicide. I use past tense because the poison has been swallowed, the gun stuck in the mouth and the trigger pulled, the bridge rail released to the sky, the toy pistol waved at the cop, the car aimed between the headlights of the semi. These are all dubious metaphors, of course, for such things as population growth, ocean acidification, increasing atmospheric levels of CO_2, nuclear waste, nuclear war, genetic modification of pathogens, resource and habitat depletion, or plain old late-stage debt-fuelled capitalism. These and other lethal non-linear feedback loops are in motion, and some combination of them will likely result in the not-so-distant extinction of not just industrial civilisation, but of most life more complex than hot springs bacteria.

But don't take my word for it. Do some simple research. If you stick with peer-reviewed science you'll find that it's time to call in the industrial civilisation grief counsellors.

Industrial civilisation has 15 years in this planet-sized ICU before it flatlines. Then, because so many of us depend on it, we'll also have a massive die-off of humanity. Not many of these deaths will be clean deaths, or as we once said in the caregiver community, good deaths. They will be messy. Zombies have emerged out of the cultural unconscious to give us a metaphor for the people we will become.

Fifteen years. I should know better than to give civilisation a deadline, because I also know that it's impossible to predict the future. Non-DNA lifeforms could suddenly appear on the White House lawn and give us the plans for portable water-fuelled fusion plants and AAA batteries that hold the energy equivalent of 50 gallons of gasoline. Genetic advances could make it possible for us to live on thorns, toadflax, and cheat grass. Sulphur dioxide could transform the atmosphere into giant orange sunscreen. We could switch to a solar and geothermal economy and go to a global one-child policy. We could pass laws prohibiting anyone with a Y chromosome from operating an internal combustion engine.

But none of those things are as likely as the Second Coming of Christ, which I'm not betting on either. I've gotten to the point where my own common sense is taking the place of science in my worldview, with much the same dark results.

I realise that limitless technological advance has become a god for a humanity that no longer puts its faith in confession or grace. Even if humanity were willing to confess its sins, even if it were able to wrap its collective mind around the concept of sin, no deity I've ever heard of would forgive it. Technology certainly wouldn't. It's a savage god, one not inclined to mercy.

Another metaphor: common sense tells me that industrial civilisation is in the tumbril, heading for the guillotine, and any hopeful ideas it comes up with while knocking along the cobblestones, in the middle of a jeering crowd, probably aren't going to work.

I don't blame you if you refuse to think about it.

As you know by now, I don't have the option of not thinking about it. But it's easier to think clearly about the end of industrial civilisation without getting depressed if you're over 60. It's progressively harder if you're younger or if you have children, or if your children have children, or if you've done what you thought was the right thing and had only one child, the one who will die of disease, starvation, or violence about the same time you do.

Fifteen years, a little more or a little less.

IV

One of the great projects of any dying empire is normalcy. What has gone on will always go on, is the official line. Keep moving, nothing to see here, is what the cop says as you drive by, even when he's just retrieved a head in a motorcycle helmet from the crotch of a roadside tree. It's important to keep the traffic moving if you're a cop, just like it's important to keep the exchange of goods and services going if you're an empire. Never mind the blood – it's already factored into the balance sheets.

These days, things look decidedly normal in Sawtooth Valley. On the highway that fronts our driveway, giant diesel pickups go by every 40 seconds or so, towing trailers full of jet-skis or four-wheelers. Quarter-million dollar motorhomes go by in between them, giving new meaning to the real-estate industry's phrase, 'Parade of Homes'. Cars rented at the Boise Airport follow the motorhomes, signalling to get into the passing lane, hoping to move up a place or two before the oncoming traffic makes a head-on collision inevitable. Hordes of roaring motorcycles race by, ridden by armoured riders who look like Imperial Stormtroopers. Also the occasional bicyclist hovering between fog line and barrow pit, hoping his bike helmet will protect his skull from the extended mirror of the F-250 that's closing on him at 85 mph.

It's a carnival of recreation, a decades-long debt-and-pension-fuelled retirement party for the 20th-century middle class. It's a solid line of old people on the move, heading for the glacial lakes that line the east side of the Sawtooths, or for the small town of Stanley, where restaurants and patios are filled with wine drinkers and hors d'oeuvre nibblers, the fly-fishing and hiking equipment shops filled with customers, and the lawn at the local library filled with the intent faces of people staring at pictures of their grandchildren on the screens of tablets and laptops. At night, there's live music in the bars, but the crowd doesn't last long after dinner.

There are young people in Sawtooth Valley in the summer. They're waiting tables in the restaurants. Or driving the powerboat shuttles across Redfish Lake. Or waiting in line at the grocery checkout counter, beer and cheese snacks in their baskets, wearing their firefighting gear.

It's normal this summer for old people to spend money and young people to work for it. It's normal this summer for old people to think they might coast into that great Gas Station in the Sky on the fumes of a dying economy. It's normal for old people to tip generously in our restaurants, because they think that the young people who are serving them won't get any returns on the FICA tax that is taken from their paychecks, and that the ones who are returning to college in the fall will graduate with debt that cannot be repaid in 20 years, if ever, and that if the young people themselves have kids, they won't be able to afford them, that what remains of the great American horn of plenty is located right here in the middle of Idaho, backstopped by an industrial tourism movie set, dribbling out its last few honeyed nectarines and grapes and ribeyes.

It's normal that the young people here don't want to think about any of that at all.

V

Every October, Julie and I put on gloves and carry large orange plastic bags out to the highway, and pick up the trash that a summer's worth of tourists has deposited in the barrow pits. Along the empty road we find beer cans, beach towels, life jackets, long strips of truck tires, junk food wrappers, junk mail, grocery bags, water bottles, car parts, tarps, packing peanuts, used disposable diapers, small boxes full of restaurant leftovers, beach toys and shattered cameras that, when taken home and fitted with new batteries, never seem to work. We do get the pictures off the camera chips to see if we recognise anybody, but we never do, even though a lot of them are close-up selfies.

We imagine ourselves as alien archaeologists on a starship heading back to Tau Ceti, poring over artefacts from a ruined planet, wondering what the creatures in the digital photos talked about as they destroyed their own biosphere before they had the means to live apart from it. 'One thing we know is that they were religious,' Julie says. 'They worshipped plastic.'

VI

Idaho is a desert state getting more so. Our fire seasons are getting longer, and more than half of some of our national forests have already burned. Sawtooth Valley is one of the few places in the state with an abundance of cool water, so when the temperatures in the lower country get above 100 degrees Fahrenheit, as they do quite often from June through September, even young people drive up to enjoy the water. They fish in the Salmon River and float down it and the Middle Fork, both of them wild and scenic rivers, protected because they've been relatively untouched by industrial civilisation.

In July and August we take our camp chairs to Redfish Lake Lodge to listen to Sunday afternoon music on their lawn. We demarcate a square of grass with a small picnic blanket and put our chairs on it. I go to the bar for margaritas and Julie heads for the food kiosk for sweet potato fries. We meet back at the blanket, which is in the middle of a thousand or so humans by the time the music starts. Another thousand are on the nearby beaches.

Then people in tall chairs put them just ahead of us and block our view of the musicians. A half-dozen relatives and a couple of slobbering pit bulls join them on their giant blanket. Two couples crowd in on our left, saying, 'You like babies, don't you?' A single mother with two sullen and sprawling teenagers arrives on our right. Our blanket gets sprawled.

We have to leave, and the bare lawn that was under our little blanket disappears as the people on all sides experience a sudden people-vacuum and rush to fill it. The singer-songwriter is singing an angry song about an old lover who left her, and it's a warm clear afternoon, so we stow chairs and blanket in the car and walk down the beach, away from the music and the crowds.

By the end of September they will all be gone.

By January we will be here on the beach, on skis. The ice will be solid enough to walk on the lake. We'll ski out on the docks and sit for a few minutes above the ice, staring back at the empty, boarded-up lodge.

Powdery spindrifts will dance between the trees where musicians once leaned their instruments. The food kiosk will be empty and cold. The only blanket on the lawn will be thin and cold and made of snow.

In the place of the million tourists of the summer, a hundred surviving locals will live in the middle of an empty hundred square miles. There'll be enough space, finally. It won't matter that the restaurants will be closed and that the produce in the grocery store will smell of decay.

For all we will know, everyone beyond the valley walls could be dead.

The shadows on the lake surface will shift towards darkness, the cold will seep through our parkas, and we will hear the distant, austere music of the wind. We will contemplate death from hypothermia, which is supposed to be pleasant once you get past the initial stages.

We won't want to get past the initial stages, at least not this winter. Not while our solitude is due to the season and not to plague, or war, or non-existent gasoline. Not while the currency is worth anything and not while we can return home to a functional electrical grid and a woodpile, and a well-stocked freezer and web portal. We will turn our skis back down the two-mile track to our car. Fifteen minutes later we'll be warm, and dry, and putting pieces of fresh-chopped wood on the still-warm embers in the wood stove, and maybe ordering something from Amazon.

VII

'As you know, there is no such thing as society. There are individual men and women, and there are families.' Margaret Thatcher, the demented prime minister of the United Kingdom, said that in 1987. She still had three years to go as prime minister, and 18 years before her dementia would be publicly announced by her daughter.

But Thatcher's remark indicates she was already demented in 1987. She was much further along in her dementia in 2004 when she attended, against the advice of her doctors, the funeral of her demented friend Ronald Reagan. Reagan had died that year of Alzheimer's, ten years after he had announced his diagnosis in a farewell speech to the American people. Reagan summed up much of his administration when he said, 'They say the world has become too complex for simple answers. They are wrong.' That was his Alzheimer's speaking.

One of the symptoms of dementia, from what I've seen of it, is an increasing literal-mindedness. Both Reagan and Thatcher, arguably the two most influential leaders of the late 20th century, adopted a muscular literality in the face of complex social and ecological issues. Their life stories indicate that dementia begins decades before it shows up as confusion and memory loss. It's no wonder that they both rejected the idea that humanity might be a complex social organism, seeing it instead as an atomised horde of separate individuals. That they both became avatars of industrial civilisation suggests that late-stage capitalism temporarily favours those who, because of brain damage on the cellular level, must take its metaphors literally. I'm thinking of debt, or the balance of terror, or national borders, or religion, or the individual.

I list the individual as a metaphor because for most of humanity's history, individuality has only been an improbable and abstract idea, a metaphor for embodied loneliness. For the first quarter-million years of our species, the true human unit was the tribe, and for a great many people around the planet it still is. The self exists in relation to the tribe, and is defined by the tribe, and is connected to the past and the future by the tribe. If the tribe goes away, so does the self. It's a state quite similar to depression. For anyone in a tribe, the individual is a whispering demon, even as – the world over – such demons crowd them off their lands and murder them, tribe by tribe by tribe.

During my mother's descent into dementia, it was possible to imagine that the person I knew as my mother was gone, and in her place was a perverse intelligence that took pleasure in asking, again and again, who of her friends and family had died. When she had asked about everyone she could think of, she would declare herself to be the only one left. It was true. Once, her husband, sons, friends and co-workers had been parts of her reality. Now, if you left the room after visiting her for an hour or two, she asked if you were dead, too, sometimes to your face. Then she would ask again if her parents were gone.

It's not a metaphor to say that eight billion humans are a giant collective organism, with a collective intelligence and a collective will, and a collective unconscious, and a collective vulnerability to cultural dementia. That's what I would have told Margaret Thatcher and Ronald Reagan, had I been able to talk to them when they were in power. They would have disagreed with me, and Thatcher would have kept transferring to corporations, at a huge loss, the property of generations of British taxpayers, and Reagan would have kept on funnelling public money to the defence industry.

If I had asked them why they were doing things that were hurting millions of people in their own countries, they would have grinned vacantly and said, in unison, 'Those people are gone. I'm the only one left.'

VIII

Maybe we don't need metaphor here. Medical investigators have discovered that the Zika virus can infect the hippocampus of its adult victims, destroying neuronal stem cells and shrinking the memory-retaining parts of the brain. The discovery gives rise to the suspicion that there are yet more pathogens out there, and that the increase in dementia cases might not be completely cultural – it might be a disease similar to Zika, except that it's been around awhile, feasting on human hippocampi, turning tribal thinkers into isolated and lonely individuals, turning adolescents into social media narcissists, turning idealistic business-school graduates into the sociopathic CEOs of corporations producing cluster bombs or overpriced pharmaceuticals or F-35 parts.

And cultural dementia itself can be depressingly non-metaphoric. Researchers are reporting that chronic traumatic encephalopathy afflicts a substantial majority of ex-football players, ones who never played in the NFL – high school and college players, in other words. CTE doesn't stem from concussions as much as from small repetitive blows to the head, the kind that can be described as business-as-usual in football. Our educational institutions, which purportedly exist to promote better and more sophisticated thinking, are really in the business of destroying higher thought and memory in a substantial portion of our population.

One way of looking at late-stage capitalism is that it's an ethical adaptation to human beings no longer capable of higher thought.

Another way of looking at late-stage capitalism is that in a culture in which an inability to conduct abstract thought is rewarded with promotions and hard cash, it gets harder and harder to detect brain damage.

IX

Population is the Ur-problem, according to people who choose not to have children. They cite the fact that an industrially civilised kid's contribution to atmospheric carbon will dwarf anything the kid's entire family could do to offset it.

Over a lifetime, such kids produce more carbon dioxide than a giant diesel pickup, especially if they decide to buy giant diesel pickups, or have children themselves and those children buy giant diesel pickups, or use electricity, or consume stuff from China.

The false assumption behind this thinking is that industrial civilisation will survive for several more generations.

When industrial civilisation goes down, those children won't be grown up, and it doesn't really matter if you've had them, or how many you've had. It will matter to you, of course, and to the amount of grief you accrue in the short lifetimes of you and your progeny. But on a planetary scale, adding one or two or ten children to eight billion isn't going to change anything. Ten children might sound like a lot, especially when you go to Costco to buy car-sized cartons of disposable diapers for them. But in a colonial organism of eight billion cells, they won't even show up as a trace element.

I'm getting dangerously close to nihilism here. If having kids doesn't matter, anything is permitted. Once you've understood the numbers, it's hard to find any single decision or effort or person that matters – unless you're looking at, say, a Russian submarine commander deciding to launch a nuclear-armed torpedo at an American aircraft carrier. You hope, then, that there are no Russian submarine commanders who are nihilists. (You also hope that there are no Russian submarine commanders who have been bitten by virus-carrying mosquitos. You hope none of them played football in high school.)

You hope against hope that humanity, subliminally aware of its imminent death, isn't scribbling down a bucket list.

Because I predict the first and only item on its bucket list will be nuclear war. Climate change and population growth will pinch countries into starvation, disease, and civil war. World leaders, facing their own unthinkable demise after a lifetime of wishing their enemies dead, will decide to take their enemies with them. That takes care of the other items on the bucket list, and the bucket, as well.

If you think that eight billion humans are too many to go extinct, I refer you to a book called *The Fate of the Earth,* by Jonathan Schell. Schell is a meticulous researcher if a ponderous writer, and he ponderously and meticulously demonstrates that no-one, not even the most well-equipped prepper, can survive even a small nuclear war. There's no such thing as a small nuclear war, for one thing.

He also spends a long chapter mourning the death of human consciousness, which causes a bit of cognitive dissonance. You start thinking that if there's no consciousness to mourn the death of consciousness, what's the problem? And if the only reason you mourn consciousness is by consciously believing in its near-term demise, what's the problem?

For Jonathan Schell, the problem for consciousness was nuclear war, and the solution was avoiding it. But for me, the problem is a culture that has perversely literalised at least one collective metaphor for depression and one metaphor for dementia. That is, we're silently and endlessly turning the world into ashes. And we've become convinced that we're individual human beings, each one of us the only one left.

Cultural depression. Cultural dementia. These things kill consciousness, just as surely as would 10,000 nuclear weapons detonating in the biosphere.

X

Shortly after my 65th birthday, I use the stairs to arrive at my physician's office for my initial Medicare physical.

That's a more remarkable sentence than it looks like at first glance.

It means I've lived through above-ground nuclear testing in the American West, and haven't sucked in one of the particles of plutonium that were dancing around Ketchum Elementary School in the 1950s. It means that whatever data my physician takes from my session will become a baseline from which my decline is more or less guaranteed. It means I'll be eighty by the end of industrial civilisation, too old to demand sympathy for a much-shortened life.

It means I have been able to afford medical insurance for long enough to develop a relationship with a doctor, which implies a functional national insurance industry, a system of stable medical practices, and health maintenance instead of health emergencies. It suggests that I still have my wits about me, at least to the extent I can show up at a clinic at an appointed time.

It means I live in a culture still ethically alive enough to give some of its old people medical care. It means that there still exists a hierarchy of knowledge, and that the people with medical knowledge get to have offices and taxpayer money. It means I have the strength and agility, at age 65, to take the stairs instead of the elevator. And because all of the above *is* remarkable – it also means that there are people for whom none of it is true. I'm a most fortunate human being, a walking metaphor for global inequality.

My physician draws my blood, thumps on my back and belly, tests my reflexes, looks at the whites of my eyes, asks me how I'm sleeping, checks my toenails to see that I can still bend far enough to trim them, and, finally, burns actinic keratoses off my face with liquid nitrogen. He pronounces me good for another year.

Then, as he is about to leave and attend to his next patient, he asks me if there's anything new in my life, and I tell him that Julie and I have a new puppy. He gives me a big smile, which is remarkable because he's normally reserved and precise and not professionally inclined to give his patients reason for long-term optimism.

'That's great,' he says. 'Getting a puppy is one of the best things you can do for your healthspan.'

He says healthspan instead of lifespan because he knows there are worse things than death. At my age, another clinical depression or diagnosis of Alzheimer's would be the end of my healthspan.

'Puppies make you get out and exercise every day,' he says. 'They make you laugh. They make you crawl around on the floor cleaning up puppy messes. They lower your blood pressure. They take your mind off the terrible things you can't do anything about.'

I walk out of the clinic feeling considerably better than when I went in. Because everything he's said is true. Exercise will keep you healthier longer, and when the puppy wants to go outside to run or ski, she lets you know, and you start feeling guilty if you don't take her. And she does stand between me and thoughts of dead oceans and child soldiers being forced, as a hazing ritual, to kill their parents.

It has occurred to me that Juno – that's our puppy's name – and I have about the same 15 years' worth of future, if all goes well and she doesn't get out on the highway in front of a semi, and I, digging a post-hole, don't stir up and breathe in a plutonium particle from a 1962 atomic test over the border in Nevada. Julie has a couple of decades more if the actuarial tables hold true, and industrial civilisation holds together longer than I think it will.

It's also certain that in those 15 years the world is going to be filled with a never-ending grief. Elizabeth Kubler-Ross says that the final stage of grief is acceptance, but in my instance the acceptance has brought a kind of clarity, and that clarity has shown me that when you're looking at the death of humanity, acceptance is only the beginning. Getting a puppy is first of all a defence against grief you can't see the end of.

It's possible that our puppy is a metaphor for a fragile, beautiful, short-lived world, one full of terror and tragedy, but one that is worth nurturing and being kind to. It is possible, in such a world, to have a kind of puppy-scale ethics, where the silhouette of the peaks that surround our valley becomes an ethical horizon. You focus on the small things in front of you, the things you can do something about. It's a matter of turning attention away from the hopeless to the hopeful. In that way you avoid depression and dementia and the strange, alien intelligences that speak through them.

Right now, Juno is growling and shaking her rope, and I'm pretty sure her rope is her metaphor for a squirrel, or would be if she weren't afraid of squirrels.

Also, we are expecting friends for our end-of-summer dinner. The table is set. Wine glasses sit on folded napkins and I've swept the floor and vacuumed the rugs. Soon, people will arrive with bottles of wine and food. Potlucks are happy occasions in Sawtooth Valley, where the lack of open restaurants in the winter makes for well-practised cooks. I'm making spaghetti. With special sympathetic magic sauce.

Juno and her rope and our potluck and its covered dishes may seem trivial in the face of extinction. You might think I should be spending my time looking for solutions to humanity's problems. But looking for solutions where none exist is trivial in itself. It's far more important to remain a careful and conscious witness to the good things that humanity still embodies. Those are love, kindness, empathy, and caring. They don't seem to work well on a planet-wide scale, so if you can embody them as an individual human, so much the better.

No doubt people had the same thoughts in Roman villas above the Mediterranean during the summer of the year 400. Or on the river in Baghdad in the early fall of 1256. Or in sumptuous homes outside of Constantinople in 1450. Or in London, at a pre-theatre fête on a darkening evening in 1914, the war only just begun. Guests must have brought food and wine even then, and the evenings must have been full of talk and laughter, and it must have seemed to those hosts that the summers would always return, and the guests would always be kind and conscious and intelligent people, bearing gifts.

Mountaineers

Darren Allen is a writer, artist and media-botherer who publishes subversive ephemera and revolutionary permanentia on his site – expressiveegg.org. *The Apocalypedia* (Green Books) is available from the usual online retailers and independent bookshops.

Andrew Boyd is a gallows-humorist and long-time veteran of creative campaigns for social change. He co-created the grief-storytelling ritual The Climate Ribbon, and is the author/editor of *Beautiful Trouble* and *Daily Afflictions*. His submissions to *Dark Mountain 11* are excerpts from his current project: *I Want a Better Catastrophe*. andrewboyd.com

Brendan C. Byrne's fiction has appeared in *Flurb* and *Flapperhouse*, his non-fiction in *Rhizome* and *Arc*.

Tina Carlson is a poet and a psychiatric healthcare provider at Albuquerque Healthcare for the Homeless. Her poems have appeared in many journals including *bosque (the magazine)*, *Blue Mesa Review*, *New Mexico Mercury*, *The Best of Kore Press 2012* and *Waving, Not Drowning*, among others. Her book *Ground, Wind, This Body* is forthcoming from UNM Press this winter.

The Confraternity of Neoflagellants (Norman Hogg and Neil Mulholland) are lay peoples dedicated to the ascetic, aesthetic and athletic treatment and application of neomedievalism in the hypereconomy of the Chthulucene. They are absorbed in the world-building ventures of speculative hagiography, avatar bestiaries, mall-rat confessions, technocratic relic translations, liturgical strategising and scholastic conflict management. confraternityofneoflagellants.org.

Katie Craney lives in a small cabin with no running water in Haines, Alaska, a small town adjacent to over 25 million protected acres of ice-carved mountains, rivers, fjords and ocean. Her work reflects on what it means to rely on the land for survival. To learn more, visit www.katieionecraney.com.

Gram Joel Davies lives in Devon. His poetry has appeared elsewhere in *Magma*, *The Moth*, *Envoi* and more. His first collection of poems, *Bolt Down This Earth*, is published by V. Press in the first half of 2017. Find him online at gramjoeldavies.uk.

AJ Dehany wrote 700 haiku in two years (*A Haiku A Day*), 50 art writing pieces in a year (*Fig-2*), 29 plays in a month (*29 Plays Later*), and regularly reviews live jazz and contemporary art. He is the founder and organiser of Blakespeare and Bob Dylan Thomas.

Damian Van Denburgh's work has been published in the *New York Times*, the *San Francisco Chronicle*, *Prairie Schooner*, *Fourth Genre* and *LIT*. He's been a New York Foundation for the Arts recipient, and has had residencies at the MacDowell and the Millay colonies. He's currently working on a novel, *Death and Change*.

Charlotte Du Cann works as an editor and producer for The Dark Mountain Project. She is currently writing a performance about divestment based on Innana's Descent into the Underworld and a book on the mythology of return called *Nostoi*. charlotteducann.blogpost.com

Matt Dubuque is a writer living among the treetops in the wilds south of San Francisco. He is unable to distinguish sanity from the direct experience of deep nature. He enjoys planting redwoods and singing with the finches, warblers and white-crowned sparrows about the changing weather. His occasional "Artist, Engineer, Surgeon" blog is at tinyurl.com/l7qmpqb.

Mairead Dunne is an artist and illustrator with a MA in Authorial Illustration from Falmouth University. She has exhibited throughout Ireland and the UK and completed several international residencies. Her artwork for *the clearing* (Atlantic Press) by Luke Thompson, won the Michael Marks Illustrated Poetry Award 2016 at the British Library. maireaddunne.com

Rachel Economy is a writer, educator and farmer living in Berkeley, California. Rachel serves as fiction editor at Hematopoiesis Press, and was recently nominated for a Pushcart Prize. Her poetry and essays have appeared in *Animal: A Beast of a Literary Magazine*, *Watershed Journal of Environment and Culture*, *Index/Fist* and the *Round*.

Ecological integrity. What does it mean? This question lives at the heart of **Tim Fox**'s writing, which appears in the anthology *Forest Under Story, Dark Mountain Issues 4, 5* and *9*, *Orion* magazine, and on-line in the *Forest Log*, the *Yes!* magazine website and on his blog: wildintegrity.blogspot.com.

Charlotte McGuinn Freeman makes her home in Livingston, Montana. She's a graduate of the University of Utah PhD program, the author of *Place Last Seen*. She's published in several anthologies, including the *Montana Quarterly*, *Big Sky Journal*, *Terrain*, *HTML Giant*, *The Rumpus* and others. She can be reached at charlottemcguinnfreeman.com.

Christos Galanis is a Canadian/Greek artist, researcher and teacher who enjoys migration. Currently a PhD candidate in Human Geography at Edinburgh University, he is researching practices of walking/belonging within the Scottish Highlands. He holds an MFA in Art & Ecology (University of New Mexico), where he practised inter-species research-collaboration with his donkey Fairuz. christosgalanis.com

Will Gill is a Newfoundland-based Canadian artist whose practice spans photography, painting, sculpture and live-action work. He has exhibited nationally and internationally and has work in numerous private and public collections in Canada and abroad. williamgill.ca

Anne Haven McDonnell's poetry has been published or is forthcoming in the *Georgia Review*, *Orion Magazine*, *Terrain.org*, *Tar River* and elsewhere. Anne lives in Santa Fe, NM with her partner and their rescue dog. She teaches as an associate professor at the Institute of American Indian Arts.

Eleanor Hooker's second collection *A Tug of Blue* (Dedalus Press) was published in November 2016. Her poetry's been published in journals including: *Poetry, PN Review* and *Poetry Ireland Review*. She won the Bare Fiction Flash Fiction Prize (UK) 2016.

Eleanor holds an MPhil (Distinction) in Creative Writing from Trinity College, Dublin. She helms Lough Derg RNLI Lifeboat. eleanorhooker.com

Nick Hunt is a writer and storyteller. His first book *Walking the Woods and the Water* is an account of a walk across Europe. His second book *Where the Wild Winds Are* is the story of following Europe's winds. He also writes fiction, and co-edits the Dark Mountain books. nickhuntscrutiny.com

Antony Johae has lived and worked in Ghana, Tunisia and Kuwait. He currently divides his time between Lebanon and the UK. Eco-poems have appeared in *Earth Love* poetry magazine and the anthology, *Earth Love: Poetry for the Environment* (2013); in his collection, *Poems of the East* (2015), and in *Ornith-ology* (2016).

Mat Joiner lives near Birmingham, England, where they haunt edgelands, second-hand bookshops and real-ale pubs. Their fiction and poetry has appeared in the likes of *Strange Horizons*, *Not One Of Us*, *Lackingtons* and *Something Remains*. They also co-edit the poetry webzine *Liminality*.

Lucy Kerr creates illusions, in various forms – images whose ambiguity pull the viewer into a dreamlike experience, inviting a meditative dislocation from the everyday. Kerr's work brings a sense of the unknown to the familiar. lucyrosekerr.com

Albert Vetere Lannon grew up as a blue-collar worker, and later a union official and labour educator. Obtaining his high school diploma at 51 he then earned several degrees. He has published two history books, won poetry prizes, and is now finishing a novel. He has lived on both coasts, retiring to Arizona in 2001.

Matt Leivers lives in the south of England with his girlfriend and cats. He is a writer, an archaeologist, runs the Awkward Formats record label, and plays with psych-folk improvisers United Bible Studies. awkwardformats.co.uk

Tanja Leonhardt is a German artist. Born in 1966, she studied Fine Art at the University of Mainz and for the past 25 years has worked with words and images, as well as in the area of Land art. She teaches writing and literature, develops writing-performances, creates language installations in nature and produces artists' books. For more info see: atelierleonhardt.de

Jane Lovell has had work published in a variety of anthologies and journals including *Agenda*, *Earthlines*, *Poetry Wales*, *Envoi*, the *North*, *Zoomorphic*, *Mslexia* and the *New Welsh Review*. She won the Flambard Prize in 2015 and, in 2016, was shortlisted for the Basil Bunting Prize and named as runner-up for the Wisehouse Award and the Silver Wyvern (Poetry on the Lake).

There is no wisdom. Most of **Daniel Marrone**'s time is spent reading Bukowski or Joyce. His other work appears in *Massacre Magazine*, the *Literary Hatchet* and the *Creepy Campfire Quarterly*. If you liked his story, want some book recommendations, or just want to say hello, shoot him an email: dannymarrone54@gmail.com

Alastair McIntosh wrote *Soil and Soul: People versus Corporate Power* (Aurum 2001). His latest work, *Poacher's Pilgrimage: an Island Journey* (Birlinn 2016), does for the inner life what the earlier work did for outer protest. It has been described by the TV mountaineer Cameron McNeish as 'the book I've been waiting to read all my life'.

Sophie McKeand is an award-winning poet and Young People's Laureate Wales. Her work is widely published with a full-length collection *Rebel Sun* out soon with Parthian Books. Currently selling up to live in a van with her partner and two hounds. sophiemckeand.com

Matt Miles is a writer, poet, permaculturist, maker, rock climber and ambivalent web developer. He lives in the Blue Ridge Mountains of North Carolina where he and Tasha Greer run the reLuxe Ranch, a whole-systems farmstead. They occasionally blog about it and other things at the-way-back.com

Daro Montag's art practice starts from the premise that the natural world is best understood as being constituted of interacting events rather than consisting of discrete objects. This philosophical position foregrounds the significance of process and its residue. Another ongoing project is RANE-CHAR, in which biochar is produced and distributed as a means of raising awareness and mitigating climate change. rane-research.org

Ben Mylius grew up in rural South Australia, and is currently pursuing a doctorate at Columbia University, NYC. Some of the most important places in his life and thinking are the Flinders Ranges, Australia; Pallier, France; and Canyonlands, Utah. He's interested in the idea of 'thinking ecologically', and in the relationships between masculinity and the natural world. benmylius.com

Hal Niedzviecki is a writer, speaker, culture commentator and editor whose work challenges preconceptions and confronts readers with the offences of everyday life. He is the author of 11 books of fiction and non-fiction and the publisher/founder of *Broken Pencil*: the magazine of zine culture and the independent arts. alongcametomorrow.com

Tom Pazderka is an interdisciplinary installation artist, painter, sculptor, teacher and writer. He holds a MFA from the University of California Santa Barbara. Pazderka's paintings and installations (de)construct the use of nationalist and cultural symbols, history and ideology. Melding research and personal experience his work critiques and engages nostalgia, self-exile and obscure aspects of American and European cultures. tompazderka.com

Nina Pick is a project editor and poet who is passionate about working at the intersection of literature, radical ecology and spirituality. The author of two chapbooks, *À Luz* and *Leaving the Lecture on Dance*, she is a founding editor of the *Inverness Almanac* and Mount Vision Press, lead editor of *The New Farmer's Almanac*, and an oral historian with the Yiddish Book Center.

Over the course of 15 years, **Michiel Pijpe** has developed an image-processing procedure that combines optics, light and complex physico-chemical processes, to produce detailed and strange visual configurations. Michiel Pijpe lives and works in The Hague, (NL) where he is part of the teaching staff at the ArtScience Interfaculty, an interdisciplinary department of the Royal Academy of Art. michielpijpe.eu

Leonie van der Plas lives and works in Leiden, the Netherlands and has a background in African studies and visual art. She is slowly exploring the vast (and sometimes hidden) undercurrents of human culture, and searching for ways to communicate about what she is finding. She loves coffee, but she drinks tea. And she tries to discover a bit of the wild.

John Rember lives and works in Idaho's Sawtooth Valley. He is the author of five books: *Coyote in the Mountains*, *Cheerleaders from Gomorrah*, *Traplines*, *MFA in a Box*, and *Sudden Death, Over Time*. His piece in this anthology is taken from a yet-to-be-published manuscript, *A Hundred Little Pieces on the End of the World*. johnrember.com

Elizabeth Rimmer has published two poetry collections with Red Squirrel Press, *Wherever We Live Now* and *The Territory of Rain*. Her third, *Haggards*, includes poems, herbs, wild landscapes and music as a response to personal grief and social upheaval, and will be out in early 2018. She blogs at burnedthumb.co.uk.

Caroline Ross lives on the River Thames where she draws and makes things from natural materials. She also studies and teaches T'ai Chi. greatrivertaichi.blogspot.com

Francesca Schmidt studied Environmental Sociology in Edinburgh and now divides her time between environmental education and research. She writes about the human-environment relationship at francescaschmidt.wordpress.com.

Constantin Schlachter is an artist who works mainly with photography. Nature, the invisible and matter are all dominant entities in his work, through which he creates sensorial fictions that examine the spiritual dimension of being. Schlachter's work is instinctive: a continuous stream of pictures within which named projects serve to punctuate the flow by crystallising his evolving feelings. constantin-schlachter.com

Martin Shaw is a writer, mythologist and teacher. He has recently co-designed (with anthropologist Carla Stang) the upcoming MA in myth and ecology at Schumacher college, as well as being the creator of the oral tradition course at Stanford University and the author of *A Branch from the Lightning Tree*, *Snowy Tower* and *Scatterlings: Getting Claimed in the Age of Amnesia*. schoolofmyth.com

Stinne Storm is a Danish poet and translator who holds three Master's degrees; the University of Utah, Gothenburg University and the Royal Danish Academy. Her third book of poetry, *Jämtska*, will be out this spring. Among her translations are writings of Agnes Martin and letters of Edith Södergran. info: stinne-storm.com

Sarah Thomas is a writer and journeyer currently working on a memoir about a period she spent living in remote northwest Iceland. She is particularly interested in how we engender an active and reciprocal relationship with place. She is doing a PhD in creative writing, on a fell in Cumbria.

Roseanne Watt is a poet and filmmaker from Shetland. She is a third-year PhD student at the University of Stirling, where she makes film-poems and film-portraits concerned with memory, loss and islands. Roseanne is poetry editor for *The Island Review*. You can find more of her work at haegri.tumblr.com.

Between 2002 and 2007, **Steve Wheeler** lived in a major cosmopolis while writing a PhD dissertation on Oswald Spengler and complexity theory. He has since moved to the West, where he practices Daoism, edits *Dark Mountain* books, and occasionally still finds he wants to write something.

Garry Williams lives and works in Oslo, Norway. His work focusses on ideas, places and situations that are in tension or jeopardy. garry-williams.com

SUBSCRIBE TO

DARK MOUNTAIN

Since 2009, we have made Dark Mountain a home for the work of writers, thinkers and artists exploring the unknown territory beyond the Pale of an unravelling civilisation. This project has taken many forms, but at its heart are books like this.

Everything we have published has been made possible through the support and generosity of our readers. At first, this was a case of hundreds of you joining in with our crowdfunding campaigns. Now, we're asking for a more ongoing form of support.

Take out a subscription to Dark Mountain and you will get each issue as soon as it comes out, at a lower price than anywhere else. You will also be giving us the security we need to continue producing these books.

To read more about the different levels of subscription, please visit:

www.dark-mountain.net/subscribe

The new collection of essays by Paul Kingsnorth,
drawn from seven years of Dark Mountain writing.

*'An important and stimulating collection of essays
by a radically original writer'* – Geoff Dyer

Published by Faber and Faber, and on sale now.

www.faber.co.uk

Roll of honour

The publication of this book is made possible by the support of subscribers to the Dark Mountain Project. The following subscribers have provided financial support beyond the call of duty. We are very grateful for their belief in our work, and for that of all our subscribers across the world.

Robin Hine
William Johnson
Matthew Osmond
Gregory Webster
Trayton Davis
Paula Boyle
Christopher Hall
Howard Jones
Jennifer Loewen
Andrew Junius
Peter McDonald
Atlantis Johnson
Matt Leivers
Charles McDougal
Jack Gates-Browne

Simeon Gallu
Wendy Robertson Fyfe
Jasper M. Mispelters
Ed Luschei
Sara Solnick
Andrew Hurley
Richard Pinner
Matt Godwin
Deirdre McAdams
Sumner Nichols
Stephen Nally
Evan Young
Keith Badger
Ric Cheyney
Phillip Lombard